5/92

Whose Life?

Whose Life?

A Balanced, Comprehensive View of Abortion from Its Historical Context to the Current Debate

Catherine Whitney

William Morrow and Company, Inc.
New York

It is the policy of William Morrow and Company, Inc., and its imprints and affiliates, recognizing the importance of preserving what has been written, to print the books we publish on acid-free paper, and we exert our best efforts to that end.

Library of Congress Cataloging-in-Publication Data

Whitney, Catherine.
    Whose life? : A balanced, comprehensive view of abortion from its historical context to the current debate / by Catherine Whitney.
       p.   cm.
    ISBN 0-688-09622-0
    1. Abortion—United States.   2. Abortion—Moral and ethical aspects.   3. Pro-choice movement—United States.   I. Title.
HQ767.5.U5W55   1991
363.4'6—dc20   90-19899
                                                                                  CIP

Printed in the United States of America

First Edition

1   2   3   4   5   6   7   8   9   10

BOOK DESIGN BY MANUELA PAUL

To my son, Paul—
that he might come of age in a society where men
and women feel mutual respect and all people are
equal and free

Acknowledgments

Writing a book on such a vast and complex topic is truly a lesson in humility. My limited range of experience, knowledge, and understanding must by necessity be enhanced by the contributions of others. Far from being a solitary task, writing a book like this is a process that involves an intense engagement with people. I was very fortunate to have so much support.

Most essential has been my friend and agent, Jane Dystel. This book was her idea; she encouraged me to write it and found a wonderful editorial home for it at William Morrow. Jane has consistently been there for me in every way, and she deserves a large amount of the credit for making this book happen.

Early on Lisa Drew, my editor, inspired me with her enthusiasm about this project. Lisa is a wonderful editor, but beyond that she is socially conscientious and committed to making a meaningful contribution to the important issues of the day. Her dedication to the subject matter of this book has been a great encouragement to me.

Of course, I could not have written the book without the help of the dozens of individuals who shared their personal stories and insights about abortion. Many times, in the course of interviews, I saw how painful it was for people to speak openly, yet they did it anyway. There is a tremendous sense of personal commitment surrounding this issue that gives the impetus for involvement, even when there is an emotional cost. I would like to express my deep appreciation to all those people, named and unnamed, who opened themselves up to me. In particular I am grateful to Simma Holt, who performed a remarkably selfless act for a journalist and handed over to me her notes and inside information from the

Bush campaign. Simma's commitment to the abortion issue out-weighed her desire to keep this material for her own use. And I think she can be heartened by the extent to which her selfless act will make a difference.

I am grateful to all my friends who urged me on, sent me clippings, and were always willing to engage in discussion when I was looking for other points of view. In particular, I want to thank Tom and Priscilla Fleischman, who gave me their love, their home, and the benefits of their well-informed insights during the final stages of writing the book.

Directly or indirectly many friends made contributions during the process and formed my network of support: Lillian Fried-man, Lynn Wilson, Paul Krafin, Wayne and Maggie Callaway, Lynne Dumas, Rick and Brenda Tulka, Steve Brazen, Jim Cap-parell, and many others.

Finally, I am thankful to my parents. They are good Catholic people who are opposed to abortion, but they have remained supportive of my efforts as a writer. It is the foundation of ethics and compassion that I learned from my parents that has made the most difference in my life.

NOTE: Some of the identities of the individuals interviewed have been changed to protect their confidentiality.

Contents

Introduction

I stand at the edge of the Reflecting Pool, looking up toward the white columns of the Lincoln Memorial. On either side of me people squeeze in, clutching signs and waving banners. A half million men, women, and children have gathered here in Washington, D.C. for a pro-choice rally. They cover the area with a cheerful roar that turns into a united chant when a speaker strikes an emotional chord. It's a riveting scene. There is movement here—a movement.

I sit on a folding chair in the cramped office of New York Right to Life as middle-aged and elderly keepers of the flame buzz around me, answering phones, stuffing envelopes. The grim art of bloodied fetuses lines the walls. Plastic models, imaginatively, if not scientifically designed, stare down from the shelves. There is determination and perfect clarity in the eyes of the women.

I walk along the fringes of an angry sit-down strike sponsored by Operation Rescue outside a suburban abortion clinic. There are maybe a hundred people sitting on the ground, a hundred more crowded off to the side in strong opposition. There is pushing, shoving, shaking, singing, shouting. Slogans fly like verbal slingshots. The clinic's clients arrive, looking baffled by the huge audience there to witness a private moment. Policemen stand by, looking bored. For them this is routine.

I sit in the homey living room of Ruth, who is eighty-eight, while she recollects with astonishing detail an illegal abortion she had more than sixty years ago. Her daughter sits next to her, nodding. She's heard the story many times, and she also had an illegal abortion. The memory of her alienation clouds Ruth's pale eyes. She is near the end of her life, and she struggles not to linger over her regrets.

I find a pew near the back in the dark cavern of a Catholic cathedral and breathe in the smells still familiar from my childhood. The incense gets in my hair and eyes; it is part of the experience. The bishop speaks of the sacred life of the unborn. Everything said in this holy environment seems sanctified and true, and the world, the gritty world, seems very far away.

I visit the courts and the classrooms and the rallies and the lecture halls until my head is spinning. I read everything I can get my hands on—about women, the church, legal systems, medical facts, global population trends, political maneuvering, philosophy, human ethics, pockets of poverty, wins and losses.

Still, it is not enough. Most often the experience of writing about abortion in 1990 is a dance with a dervish. There is no single focus to hang one's hat on, and those who think there is are either fortunate in their fantasy or doomed to despair. Abortion is an impossibly tangled topic.

So I step back as far as I can away from my own prejudices, which I admit are substantial, and away, too, from the thousands of emotions that simmer inside me whenever I touch the issue. I remember my initial goal in writing this book: to shed light, not to persuade. I wanted to present the issue like a historical tale—

which it surely is, on a grand scale—and take the reader to a place where he or she might also let go for a moment of the firm convictions about what is right or wrong in the current debate and see something more essential about the human story.

What has troubled me most about the abortion debate has been the absence of a historical context, a rooting point that acknowledges the complexity of the human journey: how we came to find our common morality; how the choices we have made over the centuries have risen from the mire of our dilemmas. We must, I believe, begin a dialogue about abortion from these premises:

- Every human action is political, for we all are part of a community that must survive together.
- Every human action is spiritual, for as humans we are lifted by our minds and souls above the simple material of our world.
- Every human action is scientific, for we live in our bodies and on our planet.
- Every human action is economic, for we are conditioned for survival.
- Every human action is historical, for we are linked with immediate and ancient ancestors.

Each domain of our lives touches every other, and we long to simplify; but the truth is that an issue as fundamental to the human community as abortion cannot be categorized in only one domain. It must be observed as a dynamic event that plays a role in every part of the human story.

It has been said that life does not begin at conception; rather, human life is an unbroken chain, stretching back to the origin of the species. From the farthest reaches of our memory and beyond we are born, we die, a new generation rises. In the links of that unbroken chain, life struggles against death in an eternal dance. How is it that some life breaks through and flourishes while other life does not? What natural or supernatural power determines which of the hundreds of millions of sperm cells contained in a single male ejaculation will be the fertile seed? How is it that each person alive on earth crossed the barrier into being?

We observe the mystery of human life with awe and bewilderment. At moments it strikes us as sturdy and enduring; other times we are subdued by the recognition of its fragility. We study its intricate patterns, searching for clues.

We struggle to control our universe: through subservience to faith; through obedience to law; through observance of the scientific code.

Science exposes the essence of matter.

Faith reaches for the higher soul.

Law holds the tension between the two. In the law we find both the solace and the agony of a choice made on our behalf.

But all these—faith, science, and law—collide, mingle, confuse.

We are more than anonymous travelers on the long path of history. We are individuals, each of us unique. We identify less with our ancient ancestors than with our own moment; we have trouble naming ourselves beyond the span of two or three generations. At birth we become the products both of our environment and of the mysterious "natural" gifts of personality and talent.

And though we belong, in a larger sense, to the human race, our actions ultimately spring from the intimacies of our own minds and consciences. The voices of the past speak to us, but they can't *be* us. In moments of critical decision, religion and the law become abstract, and science fails to give answers.

I see the vastness of the abortion issue but am also touched by its uniquely personal nature and by the way each individual defines its parameters. Everyone has an opinion. My sixteen-year-old son, Paul, says to me, "I'm not pro-abortion. I'm pro-choice."

"You think there are people who are pro-abortion?" I ask him.

"Yes, the ones who use it for other reasons."

"Other reasons than what?" I wonder why this is coming up now, then remember a television special he watched the night before.

"Like sex selection," he answers. "And pretty soon they're going to be able to tell what your baby looks like, so people might have abortions because they want better-looking kids."

I resist the temptation to lecture him because I am pleased that he is even considering the matter. In spite of the hue and cry, there is no evidence that women are seeking abortions for sex selection or would do so for cosmetic reasons.

"I think an individual has the right to decide to have an abortion," Paul adds. "I just don't think it's a choice I'll ever make."

I smile at him affectionately. "Well, it's a choice that will never be yours to make," I remind him.

Later I think about how easily Paul accepts the idea that there are pro-abortionists—people who favor abortion. One of the stickiest points of the current debate is this idea that those in favor of choice are actually promoters of abortion and that women make the decision casually. I am a woman and a mother. I cannot fathom how such a choice could be casual.

I am fourteen years old, and my mother is pregnant with her eighth child. My parents are devout Roman Catholics, and they have never used birth control. In truth, they wanted a large family. They are wonderful, happy parents who love their children. But my mother is forty years old, and she is having problems with this pregnancy. In her third month she begins to hemorrhage and is hospitalized. For most of the next three months she lies in the hospital, connected to tubes, wavering between life and death, as her doctor tries to save her life and the life of her child.

At Easter he lets her come home for a weekend. She is a little more than six months pregnant. I remember sitting in the living room, and the mood is light; we all are so glad to see her. Suddenly a dark stain spreads out over the sofa. It's more blood than

I have ever seen. It looks as if her whole body is erupting. My father picks her up and carries her to the car, and they drive off to the hospital. My sister Margy is born hours later, weighing less than three pounds. She lives but remains in the hospital for three months. I later learn that my mother was moments from death that night.

Her doctor tells her she must not have more children; she would be risking her life if she does. Her priest doesn't see it that way. Two years later my mother is pregnant again. Everyone is very worried about this. My mother's face is filled with strain and apology when she announces her pregnancy. My parents try to justify the ways in which this is God's will. We walk on eggshells during what turns out to be a normal pregnancy. I remember my grandmother grabbing my hand and saying tearfully of her daughter, "She could die. . . . She could die."

Two years later my mother has a hysterectomy, and we all breathe sighs of relief.

My younger sisters, Margy and Joanne, have grown into wonderful young women. Margy is in the Peace Corps; Joanne is a warm, empathic teacher. The value of their lives cannot be measured by any objective standards, but I suspect that if my mother had not been Catholic, she might have practiced birth control, and would not have found herself in a position where her ethics were in conflict with her survival. The suffering that choice precipitated is long forgotten, replaced by the pleasure these two young women give.

But twenty-five years later there is still something that haunts me about that episode in my mother's life. At forty-two, against all medical advice, she placed her own life on the line with a ninth pregnancy and risked leaving eight children motherless. Her priest counseled her that it was God's will. It is not for me to decide what might have been right or whether or not my mother's life was "worth" the risk she took. It is dangerous to usurp another person's conscience, and I leave it to the theologians to debate the finer technicalities of human ethics. All I know is that no important life choice is ever simple.

*   *   *

A friend calls me. "What does pro-choice mean?" she asks, explaining that a telephone research company just asked her if she was pro-choice. "I'm not sure if I am."

"Pro-choice means you support each woman's right to control her reproduction—whether that means having an abortion or carrying a baby to term," I say.

"So it's pro-abortion. I'm not pro-abortion."

"No, it's not pro-abortion," I tell her. "You can be pro-choice and antiabortion in the sense that it isn't a choice you would make for yourself."

She sighs. "I'm so confused. There are too many different terms. I don't think it's any of my business what another woman decides, but I'm not for abortion."

I sympathize with her, for abortion is an issue that is played out in a complicated linguistic battlefield. Pro-life, pro-choice, antichoice, pro-abortion—each term sets an emotional tone. My friend thinks that she is at the same time pro-life and pro-choice, but there is little room for shades of gray in this debate. Each side is intractable.

Abortion has become for us an issue, a debate, a war, but I struggle to frame the matter in a different light. Can we really believe that from this war will emerge a single victor, that the debate will force the loser into submission? Do we think that there is an answer that will finally be revealed once we have stripped away the thousands of layers of argument? A friend says tiredly, "I can't bear to listen to the arguments for another ten years." She is wistful. "Wouldn't it be nice if it would just go away? No one can win."

There is perhaps no other issue in current times about which people are so sure of the answer—and so divided about what that answer is. If abortion were a drama, the characters would crowd the stage with a dizzying clamor of voices. But the noisy debate rarely brings enlightenment, nor does it promise resolution. The language of the arguments is usually misleading, and often they clutch at our emotions and seem persuasive even when they are based on blatant falsehood or appalling manipulation of truth.

Ronald Reagan once described the way abortionists coldly assembled and tagged fetal body parts as though it were a real process rather than the clever invention of a zealous speech writer. Posters, films, books, and other literature vividly portray the bloody remains of aborted fetuses stuffed into garbage cans. It is impossible to look at them and not feel gripped by an instinctive horror. The pictures, the words, the accusations—they all make us shudder even when we know they have been carefully contrived to do just that.

Until recently the antiabortionists have effectively controlled the direction of the public debate. Once considered merely a radical fringe of fundamentalist Christians and staunch Roman Catholics who were capable of little impact, they are now treated with utmost seriousness as both their numbers and their levels of sophistication have grown. They are armed with the clarity of missionary zealots; their stance leaves no room for dialogue. As one leader proposed calmly, "It's very simple. You are either *for* murdering innocent unborn children or you're not. There's no middle ground."

Ambiguity is never comfortable, especially when it touches the moral center of who we are as humans and as a community of people. Throughout history human beings have always clung to their faith in the absence of certainty, but faith implies the humility of those who follow their consciences in the face of moral dilemma, not the arrogance of those who claim absolute moral rightness.

The righteousness of the antiabortionists makes a standoff inevitable, and the heat of the debate provides little space for examining the broader issues involved. Abortion is normally viewed through a very narrow window, but in fact, the issue exists in a far greater context than we are accustomed to seeing. It is a full-blown historical drama, filled with many twists and turns and some puzzling contradictions. Abortion is a much larger and more complex story than the parameters of the current debate would suggest.

There is no simple truth to this debate, and abortion is not a clear-cut constitutional issue that can be resolved by the dictate of court or government. We are locked in a historic moment—one of billions such moments humanity has experienced and has yet to experience. But it is not, as some would suggest, a classic confrontation between good and evil—the brilliantly pure angel of light against the dark prince of evil. It is far more than that. It cannot be neatly tied up by the creation of opposing moralities. Indeed, we can fully address abortion in only one way: by telling its human story.

The individual conscience is the highest court.
—HANS KÜNG

PROLOGUE

In the Back Rooms . . .

WASHINGTON, D.C., Spring 1988

Doug Wead was anxious. Since 1981 he had been working his way, step by step, toward the highest power in the United States. Now he was moving, almost unseen, along one of the final ledges toward the pinnacle. As the Bush campaign's liaison to the religious right he had the responsibility to see to it that Vice President George Bush was presented as a man in sympathy with the right's agenda—especially with regard to linchpin issues like abortion. As the primary results came rolling in, Wead was faced with the uphill fight to move the religious right away from Pat Robertson, a strong and famous televangelist with seemingly unlimited resources.

His first task was to convince the candidate himself that there was something to be gained by seriously courting the religious right. Wead labored hard to fine-tune a convincing memo titled "Vice President George Bush and the Evangelical Movement," which he used as the basis for converting Bush to the idea that the Oval Office could not be won without the support of this population.

He used statistics and public opinion polls with simple clarity

23

to persuade Bush. According to his report, an estimated 40 to 42 percent of American voters were religious Christians. He cited a four-year-old Gallup poll that claimed 39 percent of those surveyed admitted to being born-again Christians, with 45 percent of those stating that they actively tried to enlist others in the belief that Jesus was their personal Savior.

Bush acknowledged the value of Wead's contribution by making him liaison for the Coalitions to the George Bush Committee. Thus began Wead's most important link with the seat of power. During the campaign he was to report directly to George Bush, Jr., the Vice President's eldest son and his surrogate in the campaign.

Now as the primaries reached a peak, Wead had reason to feel anxious, for he had to produce tangible evidence that he could bring the religious right into Bush's corner.

This was not a trouble-free task. Bush had spent his career building a reputation as a moderate, and his low profile during the Reagan years had not opened many doors for him on the right. Bush radiated a mainstream American presence—comfortable, not pushy. He lacked Reagan's spontaneous fire of moral indignation. After Michael Dukakis was nominated by the Democrats, there was widespread talk that the differences between the Massachusetts governor and the Vice President wouldn't fill an ideological thimble. Even on the subject of abortion Bush was less than predictable. Although as Reagan's Vice President he had adopted an antiabortion profile consistent with the administration's, he had a history of flip-flopping. In fact, he had even said, shortly after *Roe* v. *Wade*, that he thought it a proper decision. There was no telling where his true convictions lay. As far as the religious right was concerned, it wasn't enough for a President to offer limp-wristed support on abortion. He had to be 100 percent with them—committed to change. And it wasn't clear whether Bush could be trusted.

Now it was up to Wead to prove to the power brokers among the evangelists, the born-agains, and the televangelists (the top ten having audiences ranging from 2.8 million to 970,000) and all the other preachers with large constituencies that Bush would deliver on their most cherished causes. And their highest priority, the goal that would shadow all others, was obtaining an end to legal abortion and a Supreme Court that would sustain it.

During the early primaries Doug Wead accurately predicted the results in Iowa and Michigan. He knew that Pat Robertson was the natural choice of the religious right. He forecasted the outcome as though having twenty-twenty vision and explained to George Bush why it happened and why it would continue to happen unless Bush got serious about winning the support of evangelical leaders. He argued against those at the Bush for President campaign headquarters who snickered that Pat Robertson didn't have a chance. Wead was angered by his detractors, but he had a direct line to the Vice President through George junior and was growing more confident of the vital connection he was building with Bush's campaign manager, Lee Atwater. He considered both George junior and Atwater his personal friends, and he was pleased that they took him seriously when he listed Robertson's impressive credentials: Robertson had been a Southern Baptist clergyman since 1961, had seen combat in the U.S. Marine Corps in Korea, had been graduated from Yale University Law School, had earned his Master of Divinity degree from New York Theological Seminary, and even had a sports credit as a Golden Gloves boxer. Most significant, Robertson was head of the Christian Broadcasting Network, which drew 2,208,900 viewers.

George Bush, Jr., recognized before his father the accuracy of what Wead was saying, and he began to seek Wead out more and more often for advice.

On March 8, Super Tuesday, Doug Wead proved his worth by mobilizing an army of Amway workers to help put his candidate over the top. Bush recognized Wead's contribution, and in his characteristic handwritten note, he thanked his religious liaison for the victory. Now the Vice President was committed to the religious right. It had proved itself a voter bloc worthy of wooing.

Abortion in twentieth-century America is a deal made in the mostly male back rooms of politics. It is a deal made on the backs of women who are sacrificed by the power brokers in pursuit of their own personal goals. In George Bush's case it was the deal he made to win the presidency, and men like Doug Wead helped him do it.

It might be argued that George Bush did not actually win the election because of his stand on abortion. There is ultimately no way to measure the role this single issue might have played. But it cannot be denied that he formed a pact with the religious right. It cannot be denied that Bush made promises to the most extreme and antiwomen constituencies in America—promises they would fight to see kept. There is only one conclusion that can be drawn when a moderate and pragmatic man like George Bush takes a sudden ideological shift to the right. It wasn't a bolt of lightning that inspired his conversion. It was long months of manipulation by Doug Wead and his colleagues in the back rooms.

In every political campaign there are small, hidden cadres of people who work the back rooms and constitute the ever-present and mysterious power behind the throne. They are everywhere, working on behalf of their candidates but more specifically in the interest of their own goals—in great office towers, luxury apartments, rooming houses, and miniature alcoves in the basement of the White House. Although most of the workers are guided by altruism, the leaders of these cadres are more selfishly driven, for their candidate's victory moves them to the top of the winner's ladder, where they are within reach of the ultimate gold ring: power. They hide in the back rooms and cherish the roles that allow them to make decisions, plan, write, and distribute statements and determine policy—at times without the candidate's tacit knowledge or approval. Their impact cannot be known or measured, but as a group they can change the body politic of a nation. Armed with their candidate's power, they cut their way into the political heartland, gaining their own power in the process.

For Doug Wead, the promise was tangible; he could taste victory for Bush, and as he worked, he held fast to his own grand visions of how his contribution might be rewarded. Wead was a good man for the job of liaison to the religious right. He was a committed evangelical Christian and had a magnetic presence with dark, good looks and a bright, winning smile. He had a talent for making people feel important, and he could elicit commitment with a wink of the eye or a touch on the arm.

Doug Wead was the third of four sons of Assembly of God preacher, Roy Wead, and was himself an ordained Assembly of God minister. Moreover, he was a talented "motivational" speaker and writer who was perfect for the task of packaging and merchandising the Bush image. Wead was well known to the religious right, and he counted among his closest friends some of the right's most visible leaders: Jim and Tammy Bakker, whose PTL program ranked higher than Robertson's, with 2,344,000 viewers, and lifelong family friend Oral Roberts, who had 2,500,000 viewers.

Wead's home base was a large and luxurious suite in Crystal City in Arlington, Virginia, which overlooked the Potomac and the Capitol. There took place the back room manipulation of a candidate who seemed ready to do whatever was necessary to win the White House. Telephone bills from the Crystal City apartment ran into the thousands of dollars as Wead, with the help of his older brother Bill, called up preachers across the nation and urged them to tell their congregations about George Bush. Here was a man, they said, who supported a return to old-fashioned family values; who was concerned about the moral decline of the country; who would go to the line with them on abortion, making even a greater commitment than Ronald Reagan had made.

One of the conservatives Doug Wead set out to know and draw into the alliance for Bush was the New Hampshire governor, John Sununu, who had already proved his mettle by delivering his state to Bush at a critical turning point in the primaries. Sununu was a cartoon caricaturist's dream, with a broad face, widely spaced eyes sandwiching a bulbous nose, and a strangely broad smirk that seemed to defy the gravitational pull of his small Cupid's bow mouth. Sununu's friendly gait masked a volcanic temperament and a fiery ideology. He was a complex man, many said brilliant, and he possessed the one characteristic that Doug Wead needed most: an undying commitment to conservative causes.

As the Republican National Convention drew nearer, Wead was frequently on the phone to Sununu, offering special invitations or delivering personal messages from George Bush, Jr. It was not unusual for him to slip into these chats, in an incidental and seemingly nonmalicious way, a mention of some member or other of the Bush White House staff who appeared to be thwarting his efforts. In particular, he complained about the Vice President's chief of staff, Craig Fuller, who was vehemently opposed to Wead's agenda and was constantly trying to turn Bush away from the religious right. Sununu listened, sympathized, and offered his support. By convention time Sununu had become a key insider, whose influence grew more substantial as time went on.

If Doug Wead was the favorite son of the religious right, Simma Holt was one of the least likely people to turn up as an unpaid member of his staff. Holt, a well-respected Canadian journalist who had been a member of Parliament during Pierre Trudeau's Liberal administration, was not exactly representative of the religious right. She was Jewish and a female, a longtime feminist, and determinedly open-minded, with a journalist's curiosity about seeing the inside of a big story.

It was a sunny mid-April day in the Pacific Northwest, and Simma was working at her retreat in Washington State, sixty miles from her home on the west coast of Canada. The phone rang, and it was her friend Bill Wead. Simma and Bill had met when he lived in Vancouver for three years trying to get on the Vancouver Stock Exchange to finance a publishing company he had started. Rostrum Publishing had only one book in its files at the time—Bill Wead's own book, called *Second Opinion*, about the use of lapacho tea in the treatment of cancer. Now Bill was helping his brother Doug in the Bush campaign, and he had called Simma two or three times a week, sometimes oftener, telling her with excitement about the inside machinations and activities in the Bush campaign—all the gossip of politics at the highest level.

But this call was different. Bill Wead knew Simma Holt was between books, recently widowed, and without any family responsibilities. He began immediately by telling her, "We need someone who can write, do research, and field questions from the media, someone who knows politics and can write Bush positions on issues in response to questions, someone who can deal with both the press and the religious community. There is only one person in the world Dougie and I could think of who meets all these requirements. That's you!"

Simma was interested, and not only because she had a journalist's curiosity. Most alluring was the fact that Bill assured her, "You can write whatever you want, use whatever you want on anything and everything that happens here or in the campaign. You'll have a unique view of the inside."

It was a tempting offer, and in any case Simma liked George Bush and believed he had the depth of experience to be a fair and capable leader. She was confident he would care about women and women's rights because of the type of marriage and family he had built.

Many of her friends in the Liberal party and her former associates in the media were dumbfounded. It seemed inconceivable to them that someone so remote from George Bush and his politics could get involved in his campaign. But Simma was fascinated by American politics, and as a Canadian she thought this was a rare chance to see things from an insider's perspective. She figured that as long as she kept her journalistic standards high, she could handle working on a campaign.

Simma was by no means a naive young girl. During her thirty years as an award-winning journalist and best-selling author and her five years in the Trudeau government, she had learned how to survive the toughest experiences. But in Crystal City she was to find that the manipulation of power to control public policy surpassed anything she had seen before. What disturbed her most were the insidious politics that operated around the abortion issue.

"Here were little men with no elected or appointed responsibility in government," she said later, "who could move a moderate and fair-minded man like George Bush into the extreme and intractable right on women's issues and abortion." If Simma was shocked by the level of manipulation, she was even more disappointed that Bush could be persuaded to abandon his ideals for the sake of winning votes in the 1988 election.

On May 3, 1988, within two hours of her arrival at Washington's National Airport, Simma Holt found herself seated at a meeting with eight evangelicals in the boardroom of the downtown campaign headquarters. The meeting was chaired by the Reverend Stan Walksteader, an influential Washington clergyman, and featured as its guest of honor George Bush, Jr. The Vice President's son assured the religious leaders that his father was committed to their goals. George Bush, he said, had deep concerns about the number of abortions being performed in the United States; one of his first acts as President would be to take steps to overturn *Roe* v. *Wade*.

When the meeting ended, Reverend Walksteader invited the Vice President's son to rise with his associates and join hands in prayer for a Bush victory in November. While the laying on of the hands continued, Bush's face flushed, and he looked visibly uncomfortable. Clearly this was not a natural setting for the buttoned-up Episcopalian Ivy Leaguer. But Doug Wead had convinced him that it was good for the election, so he did what he had to do. The prayers continued. Simma Holt stood apart from the others, feeling uneasy about her first look at the world she had entered that day.

"At first it seemed worth it," Simma reflected later. "Not only the effort but also the investment of my time, which is the most precious thing of all for an older person. It was, after all, a reporter's dream—having the single and exclusive inside post on one of the biggest stories of the late twentieth century: the election of a President within a society of polarized and highly organized single-issue blocs. And I was especially interested in the mechanisms of the new religious right."

Simma was intrigued but almost chilled at times by the myriad activities that blossomed out of the Crystal City apartment. For her, it was a new experience to watch the handlers and supermanipulators at work. But this was the big leagues of politics. And as the mid-August Republican National Convention neared, and the pressures intensified with dozens of deadlines and tasks piled high, all the inside politeness and caution that gave a cool and reasoned facade to Doug Wead's operation disappeared. There was no longer time for subtlety. The operation became more blunt, more specific in its promises to any group that could ensure the votes. There were many meetings arranged by Doug Wead or his brother Bill between the Vice President or George Jr. and key people in the conservative Christian leadership. Deals were struck. Promises were made. The goal was to convince the religious right that George Bush was its man.

Simma observed the fast-developing events with horror. "Suddenly," she recalled, "I felt sick as the reality of what I was sharing shook at my consciousness. I searched my soul to rationalize my presence there—and I came up empty. I saw the candidate sliding away from his principles on issues that were important to me. Abortion was forever their fundamental agenda. Everything else—all the major national and international issues crucial in sustaining the greatness of America—was treated as irrelevant in Doug Wead's office or at best as a camouflage pretense that the evangelicals cared about other issues. These men were completely driven in their goal to establish legal control over the women of this country. I heard it said every day.

"What I witnessed, and inadvertently shared, was a massive trade-off among four men—a trade-off I believed was made for their own power and glory. George Bush would do anything to become President of the United States. His eldest son, George, and Doug Wead would do anything to help him get that power—his son out of love, and Doug Wead out of his own insatiable need for personal power and influence. Bill Wead, like George Bush, Jr., was driven most by familial love and the desire to help his brother get what he wanted most."

It was, for Simma, an ugly and frightening conversion. The man destined to become a world leader was prepared to sacrifice his integrity for the huge vote of the intransigent extremists, the new American religious right.

One of Simma's tasks was to write the question-and-answer pieces that went to the religious press, stating Bush's views on family issues. She was always careful to soften the words, to highlight Bush's genuine love of family. She used material from Bush's interviews, speeches, and position papers, and in them she found no indication that Bush was polarized on the abortion issue. He always played it down, and it seemed to Simma that the Vice President was searching his heart and mind for a way to compromise. In particular, he was consistent in making exceptions for victims of rape and incest and for mothers whose lives were in danger.

But as the convention neared, the phone lines were heating up with calls from the leaders of the religious right, demanding a clear and unqualified current statement from Bush about abortion. They wanted more than his vague pro-family rhetoric or the secondhand assurances of his son and the Weads. What was needed, they told the Weads, was a direct statement from George Bush himself expressing his commitment to overturning *Roe* v. *Wade* once he became President.

Bill Wead paced the Crystal City apartment in frustration. "We need a statement. We need a statement," he said over and over again. "The old speeches aren't good enough anymore."

Finally the statement came.

Simma Holt remembered the moment when George Bush finally opened his mouth and gave the commitment on abortion that the religious leaders were waiting for. Bush's brief, sharp, unequivocal antiabortion statement came into the Crystal City apartment a week after the Democratic National Convention. Intended for distribution to the religious community, the statement began:

One of the guiding principles upon which our country was founded was the inalienable right to life. This year, President Reagan reaffirmed that right by proclaiming the inalienable personhood of every American, from the moment of conception until death. What a fitting legacy to his historic presidency. Now, the torch passes to us. Now it is up to us to defend the dignity of human life. Now it is up to us to speak for those innocent unborn children who have no voice of their own.

And then the commitment:

I believe that abortion is wrong. I believe that we should work to change *Roe* v. *Wade*, and I pledge to join you in that struggle. Abortion on demand should not be legal. And it won't be—but only if we persevere. . . . This fall, you've got a very clear choice. Together, we can continue the struggle to protect human life. Or we can turn the Executive Branch over to those for whom this is not a priority.

I intend to persevere. I ask you to join me. And I look forward to joining you as a pro-life president at this time next year.

Bill Wead started shrieking, "Eureka! We've got it! We've got it!" He immediately put in a call to his brother Doug, then was on the phone throughout the day, passing the word to the evangelists, preachers, and conservative leaders across the continent. "We've got it! We've got it!"

"It was raw truth what was happening around me," Simma said, "and at times I was mesmerized. Every day leading into August and the convention, the phone calls and messages came hot and heavy into the Crystal City command post. They came from Bush's son, from campaign chairman Lee Atwater, from John Sununu."

The network was now diverse and powerful. Holt took message after message. She remembered one in particular, a call from a church leader who announced that he had just sent out letters to seventy thousand pastors asking them to urge their parishioners to support George Bush.

Listening to George Bush promise his support to the most extremist antiabortion groups in America, Simma Holt felt herself shudder. "I knew Bush had compromised his principles for votes," she said sadly, "and my little sisters, the young women of America, were going to pay for it. Bush had made his promise, and as an honorable man he would keep that promise. But the debt would be paid for him by women. It was sick."

And so it was that in the August issue of *Focus on Family*, printed in time for the Republican National Convention in New Orleans, the conservative ranks tightened behind George Bush. Writing about the necessity of supporting Bush, Mike Yorkey, a frequent caller on the Wead phone, wrote in his front-page article:

> Where Bush is likely to help the pro-life, pro-family cause is the Supreme Court. Four justices—William Brennan, Thurgood Marshall, Harry Blackmun (who was part of the majority that decided the pro-abortion *Roe* v. *Wade* case in 1973), and Byron White are long past retirement age. If Brennan, Marshall and Blackmun were to retire or die . . . Bush would be in a position to strengthen the emerging conservative majority on the high court. That fact alone makes the presidential election one of critical importance to family advocates.

In the same report Bill Wead was quoted as a "campaign spokesman," saying, "George Bush is aware of the desires and concerns of the evangelical community. His agenda, his personal convictions are the same as the evangelicals. He's listened to them, he understands their priorities and they would always have an ear in the White House if George Bush were to become president."

Bill Wead's statement constituted a promise made on behalf of the Vice President. Yorkey ended his article hinting at the payoff that would result from the religious vote. "Christian voters will be learning a lot in the coming months about George Bush, a pragmatic politician who goes with what works," he wrote. "If Bush sees that it is important to heed the interests of the evangelicals, they may well be surprised by the strength of a Bush administration."

Simma Holt knew she had to get out. The implications of her continued involvement were too clear. It was as though the handlers around George Bush, and Bush himself, had made a pact with the devil, although surely they would be indignant to hear that description. And it was well known that the devil was never satisfied. He required a payoff, and that payoff would haunt George Bush from the moment he took the oath of office as President of the United States.

PART ONE

The Human Story:

A Shifting Landscape of

Law and Morality

ONE

Motherhood and the

Historical Journey

Down how many roads among the stars must
man propel himself in search of the final secret?
The journey is difficult, immense, at times impossible, yet that will not deter some of us from attempting it. . . . We have joined the caravan, you
might say, at a certain point; we will travel as far
as we can, but we cannot in one lifetime see all
that we would like to see or learn all that we hunger to know.
                    —LOREN EISELEY, *The Immense Journey*

In the beginning, before George Bush and the religious right,
before women's emancipation, before issues and marches and
political platforms, before the concept of sin was invented, there
was only the human community, born with an instinct for survival, locked into a life that was brutal and bloody, devoid of
high concepts like "quality of life" or "freedom of choice."

Its vision was defined by the symbol makers and the story-
tellers and later by the priests and philosophers. It was a vision
grounded in a certain moral premise, an understanding that in
order not to perish, some care must be given to provide for the
larger community.

It may shock our modern sensibilities to learn that not only abortion but infanticide has been rampant throughout history, especially in ancient nomadic tribes in which the burden of additional offspring threatened the survival of an entire community. The idea of personal destiny and the value of individual life apart from group culture gained status relatively recently, if one considers the thousands of years of unrecorded human history that preceded written record. Anthropologist George Devereux, who made a study of abortion, found that it was prevalent in hundreds of primitive societies. Even the "advanced" societies of ancient Greece and Rome practiced abortion with the full blessing of both Aristotle and Plato. The philosophers always balanced the value of individual life with that of the larger community. In the fourth century B.C. Aristotle advised "abortion for parents with too many children," warning that "neglect of an effective birth control policy is a never failing source of poverty which in turn is the parent of revolution." Under the common law of the times the fetus was not recognized as a person until birth.

Any examination of human behavior and ideology must be grounded in history, for we did not spring to this century from a black hole. Humanity has context, and sometimes we try to ignore that context when it conflicts with our more idealistic visions of humankind's journey. So, while it may be jarring to contemplate, it cannot be denied that birth control, abortion, and infanticide all were part of the regular practice of human society as far back as studies exist. There has always been a thriving folklore surrounding birth control and abortion; ironically, it began to fade only with the introduction of technology that was designed to make these procedures safer and more accessible.

In an even larger sense, to talk about abortion is to grapple with the ancient secrets, to travel deep into the earth's core, to define the meaning of life and the unique purpose of human life. When we ask, "When does life begin?" we feel pulled backward in time—perhaps millions of years—to the moment when the first being took its breath. When we ask, "What is the value of life?" we recall how valiantly our ancestors struggled to communicate ideas and create rituals. In the terse pragmatism of America's political machinery, there is little room for speculation. It is too important to dictate and resolve. Modern politicians are not philosophers; the imperatives of contemporary society leave little time for musing. Nevertheless, whether we acknowledge it or not, every current human dilemma carries on its back the historical experience. There are no new issues, only new eras in which we grapple with old issues.

Is there a "right to life"—a divinely instituted "natural law" governing abortion? The evidence of history would suggest otherwise, and the Bible contains not a single direct reference to abortion or contraception. Even St. Paul, who had much to say about the family, did not mention birth control or abortion.

So how did the Catholic Church and many segments of society come to view abortion as a shameful act?

While the righteous inflexibility of today's Catholic Church might indicate a dogmatic continuity on critical family issues like contraception and abortion, in fact, teachings on human sexuality and its link with procreation were forged amid much dissension in the early centuries of Christianity. In the solemn corridors of the papacy, where law is said to be formed by divine inspiration, the centuries have witnessed frequent and often bloody battles over the particulars of divine law.

The modern Catholic Church, so single-minded in its certainty about that law, often behaves as though the centuries of discord never existed. It speaks, for instance, of papal infallibility while failing to acknowledge the rocky periods in its history when that infallibility seemed shaky—such as the time when there was such deep division that two men simultaneously claimed to be heir to Peter's throne. It is a convenient amnesia.

Two men—one a monk, the other a scholar—were to be responsible for shaping generations of Christian attitudes toward women, sexuality, and contraception. These attitudes, which over time were elevated to the status of "natural law," were unarguably antifemale, sexually repressive, and blatantly moralistic. In tone, they seemed light-years away from the life-affirming message of the Gospels.

The first of these influential voices was St. Augustine of Hippo, who lived in the declining Roman Empire from A.D. 354 to 430. Augustine's writings became the foundation of early church philosophy, but these writings, particularly his *Confessions*, provide a window to Augustine's own ambivalence and guilt regarding his sexual needs. Modern Catholic women might well question and even resent the fact that much of the church's sexual ideology was formulated with a nod to this gravely troubled man, who, tormented by his past promiscuity and his continued struggle with sexual desire, once described his vision of hell as the "burning of lust."

Augustine sowed wild oats with abandon in his youth, but after his conversion to Christianity he became a spiritual purist who considered his soul at war with the longings of his flesh. He abandoned his mistress and turned to the monastic life, but the woman he had loved became the source of much agonizing. Since it was she whom he desired—and with whom he experienced his greatest pleasure—she was resurrected in his postconversion writing as the source of evil and temptation. Shunning the material, Augustine recommended celibacy as the highest form of love for God. He proclaimed that sex was valid only if it served a procreative purpose (never for pleasure), and he condemned sex during pregnancy and in old age, times when it would obviously have other goals besides procreation.

In a sense, Augustine was merely reflecting the values of his tradition when he alluded to women as temptresses. Countless biblical references noted the irresistible temptation that women presented to men in order to test their faith, beginning, of course, with Eve. The holy women of the Bible—notable among these being Mary, the virgin mother of Jesus—were chaste. Female virgins were the polar opposite of woman as temptress and were sanctified in the mythology of the church. The young female Christian martyrs were slain when they refused to give up their virginity.

By devaluing sex as an act of pleasure and sanctifying it as an act of procreation, the church fathers found a justification that perfectly suited their needs. In its early years the church establishment had pragmatic reasons to encourage the procreative act since the church's survival and growth were dependent upon its ability to control and increase the numbers of its faithful. During that period the church was an aggressively missionary body that sought to place its (supposedly benevolent) stamp upon the state and achieve domination of the globe. The original ragtag band of radicals who established the church was replaced by a powerful bureaucracy that was very much in the mainstream of political and cultural life. Its mission of conversion and expansion dominated virtually all its pronouncements. Perhaps for this reason, its theologians, struggling to buttress the church's mission with a foundational philosophy, invented a family ethic that would embrace the value of abstinence while at the same time blessing procreation as the holy sacrifice couples made for the life of the church. (Lest there be any doubt that sex was not intended for pleasure, St. Jerome wrote definitively during that time that there would be no sex in heaven.)

The first clearly articulated thinking about when human life begins—that is, when it is infused with a soul—came from Thomas Aquinas, the thirteenth-century scholar who was to become the father of accepted Catholic thought. Like other religious thinkers of his time, Aquinas viewed women as appendages to men—"the image of God is found in man and not in woman"—and built his moral premises on that basis. Aquinas wrote that the soul entered the body of a male fetus forty days after conception and that of a female fetus eighty days after conception. The point when the soul entered the body and imbued it with human qualities was the breath of life; Aquinas suggested that prior to this point, abortion could not be considered a mortal sin since life did not begin until one had a soul. (How one was supposed to determine whether the fetus was a male, human at forty days, or a female, human at eighty days, is not known, but it is clear that this standard gave a numerical edge to the male population.) Aquinas's standard was adopted by the church and consequently by secular society for many centuries. Later, the term *quickening* was used to define the point when a fetus became human—when the mother felt it move.

This is not to say that the church after Aquinas did not frown upon efforts to control procreation; it surely did. But it stopped short of calling early abortion murder—the sin that could potentially damn one to hell. For a long time one could "go to hell" for failing to worship on Sunday, but not for having an early abortion. But in the church that claims to represent the never-changing law of God, that was to change yet again during the nineteenth century, when Pope Pius IX made abortion of any kind an excommunicable offense.

The change was sparked by a sudden impassioned coalition that developed between the church and the state.

Abortion was the dirty little secret of the ages, commonly practiced but rarely spoken of. Without the existence of reliable birth control technology, abortion was the only avenue of family limitation. Women sought abortions for reasons unrelated to their personal freedom or the scarcely acknowledged idea of emancipation. More often it was necessitated by health or economy or to prevent the scandalous discovery of unmarried sex. An entire culture grew up around the procurement of abortions. Women of means could easily arrange them through doctors; others went to the underground abortionists. Ironically, medical doctors and unlicensed abortionists often used the same archaic and dangerous methods, such as making women ingest poisons or inserting sharp objects into the uterus. But even with these dangerous techniques, mortality from abortions was lower than it was for childbirth.

Abortion remained legal in the United States until the mid-1800's, but by the early part of the nineteenth century there was growing concern in the medical establishment over the risks women were taking by obtaining abortions from unlicensed abortionists. In the beginning abortion controls were based not on morality or the alleged rights of the unborn but on concern for the health of the mother. A group of doctors who described themselves as the "regulars as opposed to the irregulars" (meaning midwives and pharmacists) spearheaded the effort to make abortion the sole domain of licensed physicians. This concern was somewhat valid in that there were no controls over who could perform abortions; but the medical community also had an interest in exerting firm control over medical procedures, and this control was slipping from its grasp. By mid-century the newly formed American Medical Association (AMA) had forced into being abortion restrictions written for the sake of women's health. It was particularly outspoken in decrying midwifery, which had been practiced for centuries.

In the first years of abortion restriction, most abortionists continued to operate as before, since public sympathy was strongly in their favor. Prosecutors who attempted to bring illegal abortionists to court discovered that it was nearly impossible to find juries that would convict them.

The church came late to its public stand on the sinfulness of abortion and birth control. But in the end it joined the medical community and government in public condemnation of these practices.

By the second half of the nineteenth century the medical establishment, the church, and the state had joined forces and mounted an aggressive campaign against abortion, calling it the "evil of the ages." Underlying the high-minded talk of morality and medical safety was a more urgent fear that was taking hold of the country at that time: the consequences of the emancipation of women—in particular, how the movement toward "voluntary motherhood" might endanger the stability of the family and community. In a statement criticizing abortion on moral grounds, the AMA wrote that a woman who sought an abortion was "unmindful of the course marked out for her by Providence. . . . She overlooks the duties imposed on her by the marriage contract. She yields to the pleasures but shrinks from the pains and responsibilities of maternity." The focus of the moral drive was not fetal rights, a concept that blossomed later in the twentieth century, but female responsibility and the disturbing implications of the new freedom women were seeking.

The patriarchal grip had begun to tighten.

But women were changing, pushing at the limits of their prescribed role in society. At the core of this change was the growing realization that they could achieve no expansion of opportunity, no control of their lives and their environment, and no personhood in their own right until they gained control over their bodies.

By the mid-nineteenth century abortion, even before quickening, was declared illegal in nearly every state, and the early pioneers of the birth control movement had similarly been shut down. In 1873 the United States passed the Comstock Law, named for young Henry Comstock, who, at twenty-eight, headed the New York Society for the Suppression of Vice. The Comstock Law made it a criminal offense to import, mail, or transport any article or medicine for the prevention of conception or for causing an abortion.

Comstock was a fierce and dedicated proponent of what today would be called family values. He opposed all those who would encourage or enable what he considered the moral decline of society. After the law was passed, he set out to enforce its edict personally, targeting one of the most notorious abortionists in the country. Madam Restell ran a thriving abortion clinic on upper Fifth Avenue in New York City. Comstock arrived at her doorstep with a contrived tale of woe, begging her to give him medicine that would cause an abortion. When she agreed, he arrested her and turned a deaf ear to her desperate attempt to bribe him with a sum of forty thousand dollars if he would let her go. When later she was released on bail, Madam Restell went home and slit her throat.

Margaret Sanger, a nurse in New York City's ghettos during the early years of the twentieth century, recognized that much of the human suffering she witnessed daily could be alleviated if contraceptive education was available. Sanger believed that all the other rights women were fighting for, such as the right to vote and the right to own property, would be worthless if they were refused the most fundamental right of all: the right to control their own bodies.

Sanger's style was flamboyant and confrontational. She spoke openly about what had been until then the most private of subjects, including her startlingly progressive views on women's sexuality and right to pleasure. She was immune to the threat of dire consequences—even arrest. She flouted the law against birth control education, creating a publication, *The Woman Rebel*, through which she could air her views and offer advice. In it she penned the statement that became the rallying cry for the prochoice movement: "A woman's body belongs to herself alone." Consequently, her presses were shut down, and she was arrested and prosecuted on the ground that promoting contraception was "obscene." The charge was eventually dropped, but it was not her last arrest.

Two years later, in 1916, she made her boldest move of all. Convinced that waiting for legalization could mean waiting forever, she opened a birth control clinic in the Brownsville section in Brooklyn, then a very poor neighborhood of Jewish and Italian immigrants. To accompany the clinic's opening, Sanger distributed more than five thousand leaflets, printed in English, Yiddish, and Italian, that began: "MOTHERS! Can you afford to have a large family? Do you want any more children? If not, why do you have them?" But the doors to Sanger's clinic had no sooner swung open than she was arrested by an undercover female officer and was imprisoned for thirty days. Nevertheless, when she appealed her conviction, Judge Frederick E. Crane of the New York State Court of Appeals handed her a moral victory, one that was the first crack in the tightly built dam against birth control. Although he upheld Sanger's conviction, Judge Crane also ruled that licensed physicians had the right to supply birth control advice to married women for health reasons.

Sanger went on, in 1921, to found the American Birth Control League which later became the Planned Parenthood Federation of America. But it was not until 1965, a year before her death, that the Supreme Court legalized Sanger's vision and declared that states could not forbid the sale of contraceptives to married couples. The decision came in a case involving the director of the Planned Parenthood League of Connecticut and her medical director. Estelle Griswold and Charles Lee Buxton were arrested for giving information to married couples about contraceptive devices. Under Connecticut law it was a crime punishable by sixty days to one year in jail or a fifty-dollar fine to use "any drug . . . or instrument for the purpose of preventing conception." Griswold and Buxton were arrested as accessories to the crime, and each was fined a hundred dollars. The conviction was upheld by two different appeals courts before it reached the Supreme Court.

In delivering the opinion of the Court in *Griswold* v. *Connecticut*, Justice William Douglas ruled that the law violated the right to privacy of married couples. "Would we allow the police to search the sacred precincts of marital bedrooms for telltale signs of the use of contraceptives?" Douglas asked. "The very idea is repulsive to the notions of a privacy surrounding the marriage relationship."

Not until 1972, only one year before abortion was legalized, was this ruling extended to include individuals who were not married.

In 1930, at the height of debate over birth control, Pope Pius XI issued an encyclical on Christian marriage. The document, published under the aegis of papal infallibility, was to be the cornerstone of church dogma on contraception for the next sixty years. It directly condemned the practice of contraception, in particular withdrawal and the use of condoms. Only the "natural" rhythm method was sanctioned.

The birth control movement spearheaded by Sanger collided head-on with the patriarchal attitudes that dominated society. Once set in motion, it could not be dismissed. Only later would the idea of planned parenthood be expanded to include a woman's right to abortion. But the groundwork had been laid.

ST. LOUIS, MISSOURI, *May 1989*

Even when the efforts to hold women down were at their most fevered, women were going about the business of taking care of their lives and making their choices. The decision to seek an abortion in the early part of this century was a painful and dangerous one, as an elderly woman recalled for this book.

Ruth was eighty-eight, and there were many things she could no longer summon to memory about the hard years she spent trying to get by in the 1920's. But one thing she remembered well—her abortion.

She sat in the living room of her daughter Cynthia's house as she told her story. Cynthia, who was sixty, sat beside her and listened quietly. She had heard her mother's story before, and she had one of her own to tell: two generations of illegal abortions.

"I get mad," Ruth said, "when I hear people say that women are having abortions for frivolous reasons. It's not true. It can't possibly be. My choice was gravely made . . . gravely made. I was married to my first husband at the time; but he was a drunk, and he had left me for another woman. That in itself was shameful, but when I found out I was pregnant, I was desperate. I had to support myself, I was a teacher, and I saw no way out except to get an abortion. They would have fired me if they had known."

"How did you know where to go?" her interviewer asked.

She smiled wryly. "Oh, we all knew where to go. There was quite an underground, if you can call it that, of women talking among themselves. If you were lucky, you found a real doctor, but it wasn't just the doctors who were doing abortions. The woman who performed mine was a nurse, I think. That was my hope at least. I wasn't allowed to ask for credentials, so I never knew. It was painful, I remember that, but reasonably safe, thank God." Her pale blue eyes glistened with the memory. "In any case, it isn't the pain I remember but the shame. I was deeply, deeply ashamed."

"Why? Did you consider what you did immoral? Destructive to the family?"

Ruth frowned. "I'm not sure it was that. You know, those who are opposed to abortion today like to talk about how it represents a collapse in family values that supposedly existed in those days. But I was there, you see. It wasn't such a wonderful time for

families. We were poor; we worked hard; there was abuse.
Maybe we took it for granted that life was a chore. We women
were such grand stoics."

Five years after her abortion Ruth remarried, and three years
after that she and her husband, Hank, had a daughter, Cynthia.
"I was ahead of my time," boasted Ruth, and Cynthia smiled and
nodded in agreement. "I wanted my daughter to have it different
from the way I had it. I felt women of my day had so few options
to be themselves. But it wasn't going to be that way for Cynthia." She paused, slowly raised her teacup with arthritic fingers,
took a sip, and put it down. "Of course, things hadn't changed all
that much, had they? It was wishful thinking. When Cynthia
came to me and told me she was pregnant, she was just a baby
of sixteen. That's when I told her about my abortion."

"I didn't want to hear about it," Cynthia said. "I was angry at
Mother. It's hard to explain why. Maybe I thought she should
have protected me from this. I was one confused kid."

"Yes, indeed, you were," Ruth agreed fervently. "But you
were my baby, and I hurt for you that you had to deal with such
adult things so young. Cynthia's abortion was easy to get. I knew
people by then, and I found a good doctor whom I trusted. Hank
never knew anything about it. Of course, now Cynthia has four
grown children. But abortion is something you don't ever forget.
That is why, over the years, Cynthia and I both have done what
we could to support women's right to choose and receive safe
abortions." Ruth's fingers shook around the stem of her teacup.
"It's not that we're in favor of abortion. Who could possibly be
in favor of it? But it's not so easy to say what's right or wrong,
is it?" she asked. "I'm eighty-eight years old, and I still haven't
figured it out. Let us all hope that in the end God is merciful."

In the same way that every fetus is potentially a human being,
every woman is potentially a mother. And yet the emphasis
must be placed on the potential, not the actuality, for many
women do not become mothers, and even those who do are not
only mothers.

Throughout history motherhood has served as both a source of glorification and a source of subjugation. It was the core of a woman's substance, the embodiment of her womanliness. Even today we struggle with the challenge of separating woman as an individual from woman the life giver and nurturer of others.

Contemplating motherhood as a historical role, Barbara Katz Rothman notes in *Recreating Motherhood*, "The old definition saw motherhood as status. Women were mothers. Mothering was not something women *did*, it was something women *were*. . . . Motherhood was in fact a master status, and everything women did was seen in terms of our motherhood, of our potential for motherhood."

It was necessary that the feminist movement, by its nature, be radical and abrasive. Revolutions are not conducted within the comfort zones of acceptable ideas. But the radicalism also served up a real fear: that women, once emancipated, would turn their backs on the treasured role of motherhood, that society would be left without the support of its natural nurturing force, that women would refuse to be women, that women would refuse to be mothers.

Of course, this has not happened, nor could it, although those who distrust and fear feminism take great pains to associate female emancipation with antifeminine ideals.

But who created the feminine ideals in the first place?

Ideology is man-made. It is not an absolute. Our images of who we are, and our ideals about who we might best become, are defined by ourselves—or rather by the previous generations with whom we choose to agree. It is easy to understand how women became solely identified with their mothering role. Until fairly recent times the propagation of the race was a top priority. Population control did not become a theme until the 1950's. Finding fulfillment and pleasure in one's offspring was quite beside the point. They were the labor force, the workers in the fields, the insurance that communities would survive.

But humans have never been content to define themselves by their material necessities, so motherhood became a culturally revered role that brought with it a lifetime charge to behave a certain way. We have carried this image of the good mother with us down through the centuries. We can see her warm, loving face glowing from the paintings of the masters, and we can hear her speaking quietly from the movie screens. We have witnessed her sacrifices. What contemporary mother, faced with a complex universe that previous generations could not even imagine, has not experienced a pang of guilt whenever she has felt herself slipping from that mold? It seems set in concrete.

But just as concrete is capable of being cracked, so even the most embedded ideals are capable of being changed, transformed to fit the cultural realities of each time. So, too, for women.

The pioneers of the feminist movement were not abdicating motherhood or womanhood. Rather, they were reinventing it with the caveat that only in freedom is responsibility gladly borne.

They argued that the control of one's body is perhaps the most fundamental of freedoms; anything else is slavery. But these daring women pushed even farther, beyond issues of control, and into the secret, murky territory of sexuality. Until that time little was understood about sexuality—especially a woman's sexuality. Women were viewed as procreators and servers of men's needs but rarely as sexual beings in their own right. That most of the female writings of the era seem to reinforce the notion that women barely tolerated sex is not surprising in light of the frequent and inevitable consequence of sexual activity—pregnancy. Forced motherhood took away women's freedom to express their sexuality—and their right to be women independently of their roles as wives and mothers.

In the heady excitement of their new radicalism the women of the early twentieth century might have been discouraged to learn that many decades later, even after women were openly encouraged to reclaim their sexuality, this permission would seem empty of meaning since the absence of effective birth control and the illegality of abortion would rob them of choice when it came to motherhood. Even as freedom was being offered with one hand, the devious mechanisms of the law were making it impossible for that freedom to be experienced without grave consequences.

TWO

Dark Days of Suffering

and Reprisal

We decided it was absolutely necessary for women
to go public about what was really going on. We
were getting abortions anyway. Illegally. And risking our lives and being devastated by this experience. It was just like everybody was ignoring the
reality. We had to speak up for ourselves. . . .
"Speak pains to recall pains."
—AN EARLY PRO-CHOICE ACTIVIST

NEW YORK CITY, Summer 1968

Elizabeth Hanley left her brownstone apartment in Greenwich Village every morning at seven forty-five sharp. She was a
stickler for routine—too much so, her friends said. But the thirty-
six-year-old obstetrician/gynecologist couldn't think of any other
way to keep the pieces of her tightly packed life from flying out
from under her. She had never married, hadn't even had a serious relationship for years, and it didn't bother her too much
except on the rare nights when she allowed herself an extra glass
of wine and sat looking out onto the humming streets below.
Exhaustion is the mother of illusion, and on those nights the
burden of her work, her sheer tiredness, could make her long for
an escape and imagine that out there was a person who would

provide it. It could even make her imagine that everyone else—
all the laughing voices on the streets below—had that someone
close at hand. Of course, she knew this was not true.

If her work taught her anything, it was how fragile were the
bonds of love, how fleeting the moments of attraction, and, finally, how alone each person stands to face the critical moments
of her life.

All the women she had treated became one face to her, and it
was the face of desperation, pain, and isolation. She had seen
that same face more than two thousand times in the past eight
years. And each day she saw it again.

Dr. Elizabeth Hanley began practicing obstetrics and gynecology in New York City in 1960. To be a care giver in the
process of bringing new life into the world had been her lifelong
dream. She cherished her profession, for it was the only medical
specialty that was more about life than about death. Except that
it was becoming more about death.

Elizabeth Hanley was a certified medical doctor who privately,
furtively, performed illegal abortions out of her midtown Man-
hattan office. In doing so, she risked her license, and she risked
prosecution; but she couldn't find it in herself to stop. She could
not always justify her actions, even in her own heart, much less
to a medical board. But she knew one thing, and that was that
her willingness to perform abortions was saving women's lives.
Had she refused, women would only have gone deeper into the
underground, to the places where abortions were not safe medical procedures but butchery. Pregnant women were getting
abortions, whether the medical community and the government
liked it or not. And that, Dr. Hanley saw, was the great tragedy.
She considered the women who made it to the sterile haven of
her office and to other medical doctors the lucky ones—the ones
who survived.

Like many people who take daring stands, Elizabeth Hanley
had come to hers, not through epiphany, but by the ordinary
accident of daily life. The girl's name was Sunny, she still remembered.

Sunny was twenty and thin as a stalk of wheat with hair to

match. She was a student at New York University, a transplant from Kansas or Nebraska or one of those places—Dr. Hanley couldn't remember where—that was always referred to as the heartland of America, the real America, unlike, she supposed, the teeming, clotted city of New York. Sunny showed up at her new office seeking an abortion, and although Dr. Hanley had not planned to get involved in the abortion underground, she could not find it in her heart to turn the young girl away.

Sunny's was not the first abortion she had performed. During her internship she had occasionally been called upon by the hospital underground—the handful of doctors and nurses who were willing to risk performing the procedure. She had always agreed to do it, secure in the knowledge that this wasn't her real calling, that as soon as she opened her own practice, she could get on with the business of life.

But the need for abortions had overwhelmed her and eaten her practice alive.

From her perspective as a care giver, Dr. Hanley witnessed the worst of the abortion underworld. She saw unskilled abortionists who extracted large fees for services that were nothing short of brutality. Many of Dr. Hanley's hospital cases were the victims of botched abortions. She saw economic brutality as well. Brokers sometimes charged as much as five thousand dollars for a referral. Her fee was only three hundred dollars, and she was enraged when patients told her how much they had paid for slips of paper bearing her name. But she was helpless to report the worst of the brokers because according to law, she was as guilty as they were.

All kinds of women found their way to Dr. Hanley's office. Mothers brought their teenage daughters. Young single women came. Married women who had as many children as they could care for. Catholic women came. Jewish women. White women. Black women. Women over forty who had lived honest, good lives and were distraught to find themselves in her office. Desperate women. Lonely women. Women deserted by the system and by those who had promised and then denied their love and support.

Much is known about the suffering and humiliation that women experienced undergoing illegal abortions. But as Dr. Hanley would find, the humiliation could infect everyone involved in abortion. For eight years she was constantly on edge, fearing discovery. Daily she faced the gruesome task of secretly discarding the products of abortions. The process sickened her and sometimes gave her nightmares. She thought it would go on forever—until she stopped practicing or was trapped by the law.

Not all abortion was illegal in the United States during the 1950's and 1960's, although the concept of women's choice did not exist. Abortions were allowed when they were considered "therapeutic," a judgment made by hospital boards that were newly instituted for the purpose of determining when abortions were necessary to protect the life and health of the mother. Under the jurisdiction of hospital boards, very few abortions were performed—no more than a handful per year in any given hospital. Guidelines for therapeutic abortions were vague, and they varied from hospital to hospital. Few recognized the emotional health of a woman to be a sufficient reason for abortion, and there were many examples of abortions that were not allowed even when the fetus was known to be severely deformed or almost certain to die at birth. Such arbitrary standards were unacceptable to a large number of doctors who resented having no voice in the care of their patients. Furthermore, favoritism was not uncommon. Doctors' wives and daughters, hospital patrons, and others with special influence or deep pockets received permissions for abortions with relative ease.

During this period hospitals were strictly policed for signs that doctors might be performing illegal abortions. In California the crackdowns were particularly harsh, and several doctors were brought up on charges for performing abortions in the midst of a severe German measles epidemic. More than 90 percent of pregnant women who contracted German measles delivered babies with severe birth defects. And one woman's terrible trauma became the center of public interest when it clashed with the antiabortion mores of the time.

Sherri Finkbine was the pretty, vivacious host of a popular children's television program, *Romper Room*, and the mother of four children when she became pregnant in 1962. She and her husband were devoted parents, and the prospect of a fifth child was not a disturbing one. Like many women of her time, Sherri occasionally used tranquilizers to settle her nerves; a year earlier her husband had brought home a new tranquilizer called thalidomide from a business trip to London, and it was this tranquilizer that Sherri occasionally took during the early weeks of her pregnancy.

When reports began to be published about the severe deformities suffered by the children of women who had taken thalidomide during pregnancy, Sherri Finkbine and her husband attempted to get permission for a therapeutic abortion. Their case became a public battle as they were refused, in virtually every state, permission to abort. The Finkbines were caught in the middle of a tremendous political struggle that eventually led to their seeking an abortion in Sweden. The fetus was severely deformed.

Only one woman is known to have been prosecuted for undergoing an illegal abortion. Shirley Wheeler, age twenty-three, delivered a stillborn fetus in a Florida hospital, the result of a saline injection. She refused to reveal the name of the doctor who performed the abortion and was herself brought up on charges. She was tried and convicted by the jury on the charge of abortion manslaughter and was sentenced to two years' probation.

ATLANTA, GEORGIA, 1965

At a Catholic home for unwed mothers the common bond was guilt and repentance. Daily Mary Simmons and the six other pregnant teenagers were led to the chapel, where they knelt awkwardly on the benches, their stomachs bulging against the hard, cool wood of the pews. There they prayed for forgiveness and reexperienced their shame. Isolated from family and friends, these young girls were reminded many times a day that they had done wrong. Some of them responded with defiance; others cultivated a casual air. Mary was just plain miserable. She watched her expanding waistline with a sense of deep powerlessness; it seemed that every entitlement had been stripped from her until she was a nonperson. The unformed life she carried inside that was of such great value to others seemed unreal to her. In fact, it would remain so, for she would not be allowed to see the baby when it was born.

At night she sat on her bed and whispered in the dark to Gail, a savvy seventeen-year-old black woman from the inner city of Atlanta.

"Do you think it's a boy or a girl?" Gail wondered.

"I don't know. What difference does it make?"

"They can't force you to give it away, you know," Gail said. "Maybe I'll keep mine. Course, you're a pretty white girl. They'll be lining up to adopt yours. My sister, she got an abortion. I wish I had. I would have, too, if they hadn't sent me to this dumb place. Six months of boring, stupid sitting around."

"I don't think of it as a baby," Mary said. "I didn't want it. It was an accident."

"Did you try to get an abortion?"

"No." Mary sighed. "I didn't know where to go. And once I told my parents, everything was decided for me. They think this is the most embarrassing thing that ever happened to them. Nobody cares about what's happening to me."

Many years later, when the experience was far behind her, Mary still suffered from the memories of her confusion and humiliation. "My family was so deeply ashamed of my pregnancy," she recalled. "As far as the outside world was concerned, we were the perfect family, and my brother and I were the perfect children. Always said please and thank you. We said 'tomaato' instead of 'tomaito.' We were so good. So when I got pregnant, it was a terrible blow. My parents were scared to death that someone would find out, so they sent me away and fabricated this story about my going to a very high-class girls' academy. The whole time I was in that awful home for unwed mothers, my parents made me write phony letters supposedly from the girls' academy, and they would show these letters to their friends and talk about what a wonderful experience I was having. It was a terrible charade at my expense.

"For most of my life I continued to live that lie," Mary said emotionally. "It became second nature to me to say I had been to this girls' academy. But every single time I said it, it gave me a pain. The first person I ever told the truth was my husband, and it wasn't until we were married for six years. Slowly I began to heal and to let go of my own shame and guilt. I see now that my experience was akin to child abuse. It *was* abuse. A young girl of sixteen forced to endure a pregnancy in such an oppressive environment, her child swept away from her as though there were no connection. What was the purpose of that? What was the purpose of my suffering? I wasn't allowed to be a child, and I wasn't allowed to be a mother. I was no one—just a receptacle. Nothing belonged to me, not even my own body."

By the end of the 1960's public opinion polls were publishing evidence that more than 50 percent of the population backed liberalization of the abortion laws. During that period up to 1.2 million illegal abortions were being performed each year, and it was estimated that at least 5,000 women were dying annually as a result. It was growing apparent that the women of America were determined to have abortions, legal or not.

The politicians, however, continued to waffle, and the church continued to retreat deeper into its doctrinaire policies.

Two California women, Pat Maginnis and Rowena Gurner, were early catalysts of the radical abortion movement that gained momentum during the 1960's. The authors of *The Abortion Handbook for Responsible Women* later said that they wrote the book in a tongue-in-cheek manner but with tears in their eyes. Their goal was to provide practical information that would enable women to get around the abortion laws. The clever manual included a section on faking a hemorrhage that could pass muster in a hospital and lead to a D & C (dilation and curettage). The "recipe" called for the use of raw beef liver, whose blood would be used to simulate human blood. The authors wrote:

We are going to make the best blood and guts hemorrhage
we know how to put together and present them with it at
the county hospital. Unlike the woman who begs for an
abortion on grounds of insanity or rape/incest laws, and
must face morality delays, the hemorrhaging woman and
her physician know her condition will not wait for the legal
moralists to carry on long discussions. Thus, if you appear
on the hospital scene with a roaring hemorrhage, you stand
a fair chance of getting abortion care without investigation,
degradations, and rejections presently meted out by medi-
ocre hospital committees and smirking district attorneys.

The first thing you need to know is where and how to
borrow blood for your hemorrhage. So, as all women must,
we turn to our kitchen for the ingredients. . . .

The authors went on to describe a simple method by which
women might deceive medical personnel. If Maginnis and Gurner's tone sounded bitter, that was surely what they intended, for
they themselves had suffered and had seen countless other
women suffer from the restrictive and arbitrary laws.

"The womb is in your body, not his," they wrote, speaking of
the woman's doctor. ". . . You know what is best for you and
yours. It's your body, your life, and your decision as to whether
your pregnancy shall continue and you eventually bear an infant.
Take charge of it now. Then and only then will you receive
decent abortion care. . . ."

SEATTLE, WASHINGTON, 1968

It was a new generation, a new era. And it was so thrilling
because for the first time in recorded history women were being
given permission to be sexual. Of course, this was by no means
an open permission. Although the sexual revolution had irrevo-
cably occurred for a generation of young people, their parents
doggedly kept alive the illusion that nothing had changed. In
their homes sex was still a forbidden topic; mothers did not

dispense birth control advice or even care to acknowledge that their daughters were sexually active. What was known about sex was learned on the streets and in the basements and in the parked cars. So it was an exhilarating time, but also a dangerous one— mere children dabbling in life-threatening, life-shaking areas. There were bound to be consequences, but the young people were protected from fear by idealism and ignorance.

Barbara Allen stood on a street corner, shaking with cold and apprehension as the darkness gathered around her. She had been told only to wait there for a car that would take her to the location of her abortion. It arrived shortly; a young black man was driving. He pulled up alongside Barbara, and she whispered a code word before he motioned her to get into the back seat. Then he reached over and tied a blindfold around her eyes as she choked back hysteria. Nothing in her life had prepared Barbara for an experience so terrifying. She lived in a middle-class sub-urb. She played on the volleyball team at school. She was only sixteen.

Barbara was new to her sexual awakening; she had never been a precocious girl, sexually or otherwise. Her family had effec-tively sheltered her from the early rumblings of the sixties, and for a long time, even though evidence of change was all around her, she didn't see it. She knew little about the women's move-ment, or the bitter battles being waged over racial equality, or the radicalization of the campuses. And then one day she woke up. Walking across the campus near her home, she noticed the groups of people sitting on the grass, arguing vigorously, and she started to listen. The students were nice to her. They didn't treat her like a stupid high school girl. She let her hair grow long and tangled. She started wearing jeans and ragged sweat shirts or madras skirts and sandals. She saw her parents out of different eyes and was shocked by how rigid and unenlightened they seemed. They in turn watched the overnight transformation of their little girl with alarm. In whispered, tense conversations they pored over the reasons, wondered where they had gone wrong and what they could do. They learned from their friends that Barbara was not unique. Something ominous was happening to the youth of this generation.

"It's mind control," they said.

"It's drugs."

And hopefully: "It's just a phase. It will pass."

Barbara got pregnant the first time she ever had sex. She thought she was in love, and in reality she was, if not with her partner, Henry, an intense college boy, then with the whole idea that she could perform an act that was so adult, so intimate. Everything about her former life seemed shallow. She dreamed about marrying Henry and running away from home. Oh, what a life they could lead! That was part of the attraction. To be different, to live differently from the way her parents did. Henry, with his high, ragged Afro and his blazing eyes, was her means of escape.

Getting pregnant wasn't something she considered. She planned to find out about birth control once she and Henry started having sex regularly. She believed that you couldn't get pregnant the first time you had sex. But she missed one period, then another, and her breasts were swollen and sore, and her face grew round, and then she knew.

Henry was gone by then. They had never had sex a second time. He had left with a caravan of students traveling to California. "What about us?" she had asked him.

"Baby, I gotta be free," he said. "There is no us."

She spent long hours locked in her room, lying on her bed, the music battering her eardrums, the tears streaming from her eyes. Her parents were glad to have her safe at home, but they were uneasy and couldn't approach her. They didn't understand her despair.

"I just want to be alone," she mumbled, refusing dinner.

She confided finally in her friend Ellen, a college girl who was three years older. Ellen knew where she could get an abortion.

"But it's Henry's baby," Barbara cried, her heart breaking.

"Honey, Henry's gone. This isn't a love child. This is the end of your freedom. You have no choice."

* * *

The drive lasted about twenty minutes, and there was silence in the car until they arrived. Then the young man removed Barbara's blindfold, and she saw that they were parked in front of an old tenement building on a very busy street. Barbara was so scared that she almost bolted. *My life could end here*, she thought, struggling with tears. But she went with the man into the building and walked up the sticky, filthy stairs that smelled of urine.

He knocked twice on the door, a signal. It opened, and a large black woman filled the doorway. She didn't smile. "Have you brought the money?" she asked. Barbara handed her the envelope that contained five hundred dollars; it had taken her a month to collect it. The woman pocketed the money and led her inside. "Sit here," she said, pointing to a stained sofa. Barbara sat and stared numbly at a huge crack in the wall while the woman made preparations.

Finally the woman came into the room and motioned for Barbara to follow her into the kitchen, where the table was draped with a white sheet. She told Barbara to get up on the table and spread her legs. "Don't scream," she warned. "If you scream, I'll have to gag you." So Barbara bit down on her lip as the woman stuck something sharp into her vagina. She left it in there a couple of minutes, moving it around. The pain was violent, dizzying. Barbara longed to pass out, but then it was over. "I'm going to throw up," she said, and the woman laid a kitchen pan over her stomach, as Barbara retched.

"My son will take you back," the woman said, and that was the first time Barbara knew that the man who had brought her was the woman's son. A real family business.

"What's going to happen to me?"

"You'll start getting contractions, and there will be some blood," the woman said abruptly. "It'll be over by tonight."

Barbara stumbled back downstairs and into the car and was blindfolded again. She felt feverish and nauseated and now more scared than ever because there had been set in motion something that she didn't understand but instinctively realized was going to be terrible.

After the car drove off, she called Ellen from a pay phone. "I can't go home," she sobbed. "It hasn't happened yet. My mother can't see—"

"You can't come here," Ellen said. "There's no room."

"Please . . . just your sofa. Just for a few hours."

Ellen finally agreed, but she sounded scared, too, and it flashed across Barbara's mind that her worldly, sophisticated friend wasn't as self-confident as she liked to appear. She considered for a moment going to a hospital or going home but decided against it. Instead she rode the bus to Ellen's and noticed that people were staring at her strangely. She heard a woman whisper, "Drugs," and she almost laughed. They thought she was stoned, but the truth was that she might be dying.

Ellen wasn't glad to see her. "I don't know anything about this," she said. "What's supposed to happen?"

"I don't know. Just let me sleep." Barbara fell onto the sofa and slept. The first thing she remembered was waking up in terrible pain; cramps were breaking apart her insides. Ellen was screaming, "Blood! Blood!" Then Barbara started screaming, too. There was so much blood; she hadn't realized there would be so much blood. And then she looked down and saw a shape in the blood, and she started screaming in earnest now. Screaming and screaming. Ellen ran to the phone. "I'm calling an ambulance. This is too heavy." And it was a wise move because the doctors later told Barbara that she might have died.

"Who did this?" they demanded.

"I don't know."

"You have to tell us. This person nearly killed you. Do you want him to kill other girls?"

"It was a woman. I don't know who she was. They blind-folded me."

"Where did you hear about her?"

She shook her head.

"Young lady, she butchered you. You'll never have children. Do you understand that? She has to be stopped."

Barbara stared back at the doctor. "I want to go home," she

said. Just then her mother ran into the room, and Barbara had never been so happy to see anyone in her life.

Standing on the front lines of the abortion liberalization movement were men and women who dedicated vast amounts of time and resources to the cause. One of these who rose to the forefront in the late 1960's was a New York doctor named Bernard Nathanson.

As a young obstetrician/gynecologist in New York City Bernard Nathanson had witnessed firsthand the terrible consequences of abortion's illegality. He believed passionately that abortion should be made available to all women who desired it—not just those who were approved by the hospital abortion committees. It enraged him that women were unable to take advantage of safe medical procedures and that desperate women were being refused abortions by hospital committees, even though committee members knew that these women would seek abortions in the dangerous back alleys of the abortion underground.

Nathanson knew from his own experience how agonizing the prospect of illegal abortion was. While he was in medical school, his girl friend had become pregnant, and he would never forget the desperate search, the cloak of secrecy, the fear of discovery. The trauma of the experience tore their relationship apart.

Nathanson organized a movement to change the abortion laws. As cofounder of the National Association for Repeal of Abortion Laws (now the National Abortion Rights Action League or NARAL), Nathanson was to play a pivotal role in legalizing abortion in New York State and in educating the nation about what was happening to the women of America in the back alleys of illegal abortion.

By 1970 several states had repealed the abortion laws and legalized abortion, although there were many restrictions, such as residency, to prevent those states from being flooded by women from all over the country seeking abortions. In many other states abortion laws were under review. Each state action involved a long and bitter battle.

New York was one of the states that repealed their abortion laws. Soon after, Bernard Nathanson, along with several of his colleagues, established the New York Center for Reproductive and Sexual Health, the largest abortion clinic in the world. As director Nathanson earned the title, among antiabortionists, as the Abortion King. Others referred to him as the Scraper.

But it wasn't only the doctors and the feminists who were taking a stand for the liberalization of abortion. Certain clergy were reaching a new point of enlightenment, influenced by the tragic human drama that they saw all around them. Foremost among these was the Reverend Howard Moody, pastor of the Judson Memorial Church in New York's Greenwich Village. Touched by the emotional alienation and physical danger that women were encountering in the abortion underground, Moody searched for a way to bring his ethical understanding into alignment with his mission of pastoral care. Later he explained his position this way: "God is with the human woman who is wrestling with the question of bearing a child. I think God would be offended by mandatory childbearing, and that's what that law was, mandatory childbearing. That's to make chattel out of women. I don't believe in a God that practices that."

Approximately fifteen hundred ministers and rabbis across the country joined Moody in an underground referral service, designed to help women find doctors to give them abortions. The role of pastors and religious in the movement is an often forgotten story since the religious viewpoint seemed fully aligned with the antiabortion movement, as it still does today. The loosely knit organization was called the Clergy Consultation Service on Abortion.

"We knew the risk," Moody recalled. "We had to tell the ministers and rabbis that came aboard, 'This is what we're facing.' " What they were facing was prison sentences and the condemnation of their congregations—not to mention the ongoing personal struggle with their own consciences about their role in the cessation of life.

During the years the Clergy Consultation Service operated,

only two men were charged with a violation of the law. One was an Illinois rabbi accused of conspiracy to commit abortion; the other, a Protestant minister from Ohio who was indicted for aiding and abetting an illegal abortion. Neither prosecution was pursued.

Like a house of cards tumbling in slow motion, individual states began to liberalize and repeal abortion laws. Hawaii and Alaska were the first to liberalize their laws, and in 1970 New York became the first state to make abortion legal without exception. New York Catholic bishops issued an outraged pastoral letter decrying the "death dealing trade" and announced that immediate excommunication would be the penalty for any woman procuring an abortion.

Other protesters used more creative and disruptive means to halt legal abortions. Robert Byrn, Ph.D., was a New York professor of criminal law who in 1971 appointed himself the guardian of all human fetuses between the fourth and twenty-fourth week who were scheduled to be aborted in New York municipal hospitals. Byrn was only the first of many "fetal saviors" who were to emerge during the coming years. His approach, however, was certainly unique. He forced the city's Health and Hospitals Corporation to answer a show cause order in Queens Supreme Court as to why city hospitals had a right to perform abortions. The courtroom scene was high drama, with the attorney for the city demanding that Byrn, as "guardian" of the fetuses, post a forty-thousand-dollar bond for each child that would be born if abortions were not allowed, which was the estimated cost of rearing a child to the age of eighteen. This motion was denied, and after an emotional court hearing, the judge in the case ruled in favor of Byrn, in effect appointing this private citizen the legal guardian of fetuses of women seeking abortions in New York hospitals. Although the ruling was later overturned, the fact that it was granted in the first place indicated how confused the state courts were about the legal premises for liberalizing abortions.

*   *   *

The usual levity of a spring day in New York City was disrupted by a huge march against abortion liberalization whose theme was abortion as genocide. On April 16, 1972, ten thousand antiabortion demonstrators (the largest march recorded to that date for this issue) stormed down Fifth Avenue, screaming slogans and waving placards bearing the evil face of Adolf Hitler, along with a record of deaths from wars and holocausts, placing New York State in the center for its legalization of abortion:

> 4th place: Korean War—34,000
> 3rd place: Vietnam—45,000
> 2nd place: NEW YORK STATE—300,000
> 1st place: Holocaust—6 million

It was a charge that outraged the Jewish community, but was heartily supported by the Catholic Church. Terence Cardinal Cook decreed it Right to Life Day and asked priests to use their Sunday pulpits to remind their congregations of the genocide being committed against the unborn.

The law held no sway over the 1.2 million women who sought out and received abortions each year. The government, with its elaborate systems and its stacked volumes of legal reasoning, was an abstract and distant reality for the women who suffered the intimate personal trauma of unwanted pregnancies. In what might have sounded an alarm for a future generation of legislators (had they the ears to hear), women were ignoring the law. They believed it had deserted them, that the mostly male establishment was passing judgment from a lofty height that could not touch what they were experiencing. The consequences were severe. Thousands died each year from butcheries committed by ill-equipped underground abortionists. But even those who survived and those who had been lucky enough to find legitimate doctors paid the price in other ways: the guilt, the fear, the agonizing responsibility of carrying a heavy burden alone, the dirty feeling that didn't go away long after the shameful appointments in the back alleys of the abortion underworld were past.

Countless women have reported that no matter what else happened in their lives, no matter how successfully they went on to live, no matter how happily they went on to marry, no matter how much joy they found in the children they bore, the experience of abortion was a dark smudge on their psyches that never disappeared. No absolution was given, there was no community of support. More than a million women every year, and each one felt absolutely alone.

THREE

Winning Back the

Womb

I got to thinking, "Is it true what people are saying,
that abortion is killing babies? Is it true?" Then I
thought about all these poor children who I've seen
parked in front of just dives—hungry, dirty, ne-
glected and abused, their families inside boozing it
up. And I thought I did the right thing.
—NORMA MCCORVEY ("JANE ROE")

The Texas lawyers who filed the suit that later became the
basis for the legalization of abortion throughout the United States
never intended it to have such a grandiose outcome. Sarah Weddington and Linda Coffee were young lawyers with practically
no courtroom experience. But both were dedicated feminists,
and they believed that if they could make a dent in the 1857
Texas law forbidding abortion, they would have accomplished
something meaningful. In the early 1970's the fight for abortion
rights was almost entirely concentrated at the state level, and
many states had already initiated reforms (though rarely as broad
as was later ruled in *Roe* v. *Wade*). Now it was time to go to the
ropes in Texas.

But in order to change a law, one must first have a case, for law
in the United States is highly personal before it becomes uni-

70

versal. One woman who was willing to be a plaintiff on behalf of all women in the state would have to be found.

They found her in Norma McCorvey, a twenty-one-year-old pregnant woman who was intent on getting an abortion. McCorvey was tough and fiercely independent but already drained by life. Single and the mother of a five-year-old daughter, she was sinking deeper into the hopelessness of her survival. Hearing her story, Weddington and Coffee recognized that she might be the perfect subject for a test case: a truly needy woman whose options were cut off by poverty, youth, and a history of instability. Though they believed that every woman, regardless of her circumstances, had the right to choose abortion, it was clearly women like McCorvey who made the most poignant case. Furthermore, they needed a woman who was willing to perform a selfless act, for it was unlikely that with the long and tangled legal process Norma McCorvey would personally realize any benefits. The young woman was disappointed to learn that the suit would not settle her pressing personal dilemma, but she was willing to participate in the fight. With McCorvey as their plaintiff, the lawyers set out to present a class action suit against the state on behalf of their client and "others similarly situated."

Their opponent would be formidable. District Attorney Henry Wade was a strict, no-nonsense Calvinist with a sharp legal mind and old-fashioned Texas chauvinism coursing through his veins. When the suit landed on his desk, it never occurred to him that it would be anything but an irritation, leading to an easy victory for the prosecutor's office. Two of his best lawyers were to argue the case: John Tolle, an earthy man with notable legal talent, and Jay Floyd, a meticulous attorney who worked in the enforcement division. The attorney general's office chose to build its argument around the concept of fetal rights, while the plaintiffs based their appeal on the constitutional right to privacy.

Following an emotional and often convoluted courtroom debate, with the two young women pitted against Wade's strongest male representatives, the court found the plaintiff's arguments the more compelling, and they were persuaded to rule in favor of Jane Roe.

There was good news and bad news for Weddington and Coffee in the federal court ruling. The good news was that it declared the Texas abortion law unconstitutional. On that point the judges wrote: "On the merits, plaintiffs argue as their principal contention that the Texas abortion laws must be declared unconstitutional because they deprive single women and married couples of their right, secured by the Ninth Amendment, to choose whether to have children. We agree."

But mostly the news was bad. Even while the court was affirming a constitutional right with one hand, it was denying it with the other. In a frustrating twist the court did not agree to issue an injunction that would force Texas to revise its abortion law. In the end the lawyers felt they had won a shallow victory that would not substantively change the plight of women in their state. In effect, the court had said that although women had a constitutional right to abortions, they would not legally be able to procure them in the state of Texas.

Weddington and Coffee decided to appeal, and the most important case to affect women since they had won the right to vote found its way to the Supreme Court.

A second case, *Doe* v. *Bolton*, was scheduled for review by the Supreme Court at the same time as *Roe* v. *Wade*. Mary Doe was a twenty-two-year-old pregnant married woman from Georgia who already had three children. Because of poverty and mental instability (she had spent time in mental hospitals), two of her children were in foster homes and one had been placed for adoption. Doctors had advised that having another baby would endanger her health more than having an abortion would. Mary Doe initiated a class action suit against the state of Georgia, with results similar to Texas. While the federal court affirmed her right to have an abortion, it failed to establish the legal means for her to receive one. Mary Doe, who was also forced to bear her child, agreed to remain the plaintiff as the case went to the Supreme Court. The major rulings on the two cases would be decided as one.

*   *   *

Preparing to argue a case before the U.S. Supreme Court is especially difficult because speakers are given very little time to make oral arguments and must be prepared for virtually any question a justice may ask, no matter how obscure. In preparing her argument, Sarah Weddington knew that she would have to take a dauntingly complex issue and simplify it into a brief and cogent argument. She concentrated her efforts on uncovering precedents that supported the constitutionality of her case—in particular, cases based upon the Fourteenth Amendment that guaranteed the right to privacy. She also knew she must address the question of fetal rights since it was the basis of her opponents' argument. This was more difficult since there was no precedent. Weddington, however, put together an argument that showed that only those who were born had ever been given rights under the Constitution.

The highest court in the land was packed the day *Roe* v. *Wade* was scheduled to be heard. Interested parties on both sides of the issue filled the room with tense energy, as if in acknowledgment that something gravely historical was about to take place. Weddington was nervous. For a lawyer of her youth and inexperience, it was almost unheard of to have an opportunity to argue a case in the awesome presence of the nine justices on the Supreme Court. But her nervousness was tightly contained by the sober realization that her performance that day would make a difference—good or bad—for millions of women. She elaborated her points clearly and responded evenly to questions posed by the justices, who sat above her on the intimidating perch of their lofty bench. Little of the apprehension she must surely have felt showed. In a flash, it seemed, her turn was over and she was sitting down.

Jay Floyd, who had the experiential edge, nevertheless blundered from the start, attempting to lighten the mood with a joke. "Mr. Chief Justice, and may it please the Court, it's an old joke, but when a man argues against two beautiful ladies like these, they're going to have the last word." His attempt at levity was met with stony silence by the spectators and pained expressions by the justices, and some observers later said that Floyd never quite recovered from the moment. Nevertheless, when the session adjourned, the Texas assistant attorney general remained confident that the Supreme Court would uphold Texas law.

During the following months the justices faced the formidable task of wading through the complex mire of human rights and privacy issues. Chief Justice Burger assigned Justice Harry Blackmun to write the 7 to 2 majority opinion, and Blackmun began his long struggle to articulate the substance of the issue: Was it a medical issue, a personal conscience issue, a legal issue? What were the limits of privacy? Did the state have an interest in protecting fetal life? It was the first time the Court had attempted to tackle abortion in all its facets.

Even though the majority of the justices were in favor of the argument against the state of Texas, that didn't necessarily mean that the final ruling would be broad enough to guarantee the rights that Sarah Weddington asked for. The ruling could have been very narrow, allowing states a great deal of freedom to monitor abortions. Blackmun was far from the most liberal member of the Court, and other justices, in particular William Douglas, feared that his opinion would fall short of the extensive rights they wanted to grant or would be ambiguous enough to open the decision to repeated challenges.

On a cold winter morning, only two days after Richard Nixon was sworn in for his second term as President of the United States, the nine justices released their decision in the case of *Roe* v. *Wade*. There was excitement in the air that Monday morning, for the press had already received leaks that the justices might rule that day. Spectators and reporters jammed the courthouse area. They buzzed with rumors until finally the press was handed copies of the lengthy written opinion—eighty pages of majority opinion and thirty pages of dissent—while inside the courthouse Justice Blackmun began to read a summary of the opinion.

Blackmun's decision was centered on the right to privacy that had been established by the Court in earlier cases. He based his thinking on the concept of personal liberty set forth in the Fourteenth Amendment, which forbids the state to "deprive any person of life, liberty or property without due process of law. . . ." Blackmun wrote that this right of privacy "is broad enough to encompass a woman's decision whether or not to terminate her pregnancy." The right to abortion was recognized as a "fundamental" right (much as freedom of speech is a fundamental right) that could be curtailed only when a state had a "compelling interest" in doing so.

The issue of the state's interest became the grand loophole in the *Roe* decision. It rested primarily on fetal viability, with the suggestion that the state might have a compelling interest once the fetus was viable—normally during the third trimester. Thus, while abortion was declared legal during all nine months of a pregnancy, the states were given the power to intervene late in pregnancy to protect a viable fetus.

This was established through the trimester ruling, which was so arbitrary and constitutionally shaky that it became a constant target in the years to come. The trimester rule established individual versus state rights on the basis of the three marking points of a typical pregnancy:

- In the first trimester of a pregnancy the government could not interfere with abortion in any way except to insist that it be performed by a licensed physician.
- In the second trimester the government could regulate abortion, but only in ways designed to protect a woman's health and welfare.
- In the third trimester, at the point at which there was a potential for viability outside the womb, the government could act to preserve fetal life only if its primary concern was protection of the health and life of the mother.

While the constitutional basis for the Court's decision relied heavily on the rights to privacy that had been established in prior cases, portions of the ruling seemed to have no precedents at all. One of these was the trimester breakdown, in particular the ruling that the state might have an interest prior to the point of viability. The other was the notion of "state's interest" itself, which was vaguely defined.

But the fundamental problem in writing such a sweeping decision on abortion was the need to make some judgment—stated or unstated—about what kind of life a fetus represented. Here, too, the Court's opinion was vague: The fetus was defined as "potential life" as opposed to "actual life," thus avoiding a legal clarification of a matter that had been debated for centuries. Rather than settle the issue within the secure framework of constitutional certainty, the Court's decision opened up even more questions and made the decision vulnerable to one challenge after another in the years ahead.

The Supreme Court's decision was a bittersweet victory for Norma McCorvey, who had given up her baby daughter for adoption in June 1970. The woman who put herself on the line to secure the right to choose for millions of other women never even had an abortion herself.

SEATTLE, WASHINGTON, *January 1973*

In Barbara Allen's college dormitory at the University of Washington, the Supreme Court's decision swept through the building like a brush fire, eliciting hoots of joy. Her friends broke open champagne to celebrate their new emancipation. But Barbara, who carried the physical and emotional scars of the traumatic illegal abortion she had undergone five years earlier, didn't feel much like celebrating. She found that the recent uproar over abortion only served to bring troubling emotions to the surface. Her abortion still haunted her, would always haunt her. Her now-sterile womb served as a constant reminder. Rather than feel happy that her friends would not have to face the butcher's knife if they sought abortions, she felt bitter that they could casually walk into a clinic and have an abortion without thinking about it, then go on to have children later when it was more convenient. The flexibility of their choices seemed brutally unfair to Barbara.

If she had felt confused at sixteen, now all ambivalence had drained out of her. "You can't know what it's like," she confided to the therapist she had been seeing for two years. "You think it's easy, but after it's over, the guilt sneaks up on you. I dream about my child at night, and sometimes I wake up crying because I gave away my one chance to be a mother."

"Why do you blame yourself for someone else's cruelty?" the therapist asked.

"Because it wasn't someone else's," she cried. "It was *mine*. I made the decision. The abortionist just carried out what I wanted."

"You have to get beyond your guilt. Let it go."

Barbara slumped in her chair and shook her head sadly. "I don't think I'll ever get over it."

The therapist countered, "Then use it. Find a way to turn it into a positive."

When her therapist said that, Barbara felt something open up inside her. Yes, use it. But how? She began to look for a way.

The antiabortion cry was loud and angry. Initially caught off guard by the Supreme Court decision, antiabortionists soon let their voices be heard. The National Right to Life Committee quickly announced its plan for a constitutional amendment that would forbid abortion from the point of fertilization. The amendment declared: "With respect to the right to life, the word 'person' as used in this article and in the Fifth and Fourteenth Articles of Amendment to the Constitution of the United States applies to all human beings irrespective of age, health, function, or condition of dependency, including their unborn offspring at every stage of their biologic development."

Senators James Buckley and Jesse Helms also introduced constitutional amendments to ban all abortions. Although none of the amendments passed, Helms was successful in creating legislation that forbade the use of American foreign aid money for abortions and abortifacients (birth control devices, including the pill and the intrauterine device, IUD).

The most immediate and extreme reaction to *Roe* came from

the Catholic Church, whose hierarchy set in motion an oppressive era when even the mildest support for the right to choose abortion could land a practitioner in trouble. San Diego's bishop, Leo T. Maher, who remained a rigid and controversial figure for the next seventeen years, announced that no member of an organization that supported abortion rights (such as the National Organization for Women) could receive the eucharist in any of his churches. In 1973 alone the Catholic Church spent four million dollars lobbying Congress on abortion-related issues.

The legal challenges to abortion rights came hot and heavy—from the states and on the national level. In the years following *Roe* v. *Wade* there was a certain cachet to being opposed to abortion. For politicians, being "pro-life" set them in the moral position of representing America at its best while at the same time offering no serious challenge on the political playing field. Only in one case were they forced to put their money where their mouths were: the challenge presented in 1976 by Henry Hyde, a representative from Illinois, on the use of public funds for abortions. Since *Roe*, more than three hundred thousand abortions a year were being funded by Medicaid. By the time Hyde came on the scene, some states had already banned the use of public money for this purpose, but Hyde sought to impose the ban on a national level. The bill's language was couched in reasonableness: By funding abortions, the state was really *encouraging* them, and taxpayers who opposed abortions should not have to pay for them. The arguments were specious. After all, America was not a democracy in which citizens supported only those specific programs they personally agreed with. It was a representative government. Were not taxpayers often required to pay for programs they did not support, a classic example being the war in Vietnam? The bill was nothing more than antiabortion politics cloaked in the bland language of budgetary considerations.

Members of Congress who opposed the Hyde Amendment focused on the ultimate ramifications of cutting poor women off from abortions. For it was clear that if the Hyde Amendment passed, hundreds of thousands of the poorest of the poor would every year be forced to bear children that they did not want and were least able, of all citizens, to sustain and nurture. The bill reestablished the class distinction that had existed for centuries prior to *Roe* v. *Wade*. There was a historical double standard: Even during the illegal years, women with money could always find the means to obtain abortions, while the poor were left with traumatic back alley options or no options at all. Senators Birch Bayh and Bob Packwood, who argued passionately against the cutoffs on the Senate floor, were angered that the government would perform such an act of irresponsibility, tying the hands of women who, it could be argued, were most in need of the services.

But the Hyde Amendment passed in a strict form that allowed an exception only in cases when the mother's life was endangered. With the law's passage many women in America were effectively cut off from the right to abortion they had won under *Roe*. The act was supported by the new President, Jimmy Carter, a man known for his compassion but also for his religious fundamentalism and his personal opposition to abortion. "There are many things in life that are not fair, that wealthy people can afford and poor people can't," Carter said. "But I don't believe that the Federal Government should take action to try to make these opportunities exactly equal, particularly when there is a moral factor involved."

Immediately after the Hyde Amendment passed, it was challenged by Cora McRae, a young pregnant woman from Brooklyn. The federal court ruled for McRae and ordered the abortion to be funded. The ruling set the stage for a Supreme Court challenge—*Patricia R. Harris, Secretary of Health and Human Services* v. *Cora McRae*.

But before the Supreme Court heard *Harris* v. *McRae*, it was to hear another case based on a state's denial of public funds for the purpose of abortion. In *Maher* v. *Roe* a young woman had sued Connecticut's commissioner of social services because the agency restricted the use of state money for abortions. The district court had ruled in favor of the plaintiff, arguing that since the state funded normal childbirth, it was also required to provide funds if the decision was to abort. The freedom given by *Roe*, the lower federal court ruled, could not be infringed upon by financial pressure from the state.

The Supreme Court disagreed. "An indigent woman desiring an abortion does not come within the limited category of disadvantaged classes," wrote Justice Lewis Powell, adding, "We think the District Court misconceived the nature and scope of the fundamental right recognized in *Roe*."

Coming on the heels of *Maher* v. *Roe*, the plaintiffs in *Harris* v. *McRae* realized that success was unlikely. And once again the Supreme Court ruled that the denial of public funding did not interfere with a woman's right to abortion. In his opinion Justice Potter Stewart wrote that "it simply does not follow that a woman's freedom of choice carries with it a constitutional entitlement to the financial resources to avail herself of the full range of protected choices."

But Stewart went a step farther, suggesting that the state might have a legitimate interest in encouraging childbirth over abortion:

> By subsidizing the medical expenses of indigent women who carry their pregnancies to term while not subsidizing the comparable expenses of women who undergo abortions (except those whose lives are threatened) Congress has established incentives that make childbirth a more attractive alternative than abortion for persons eligible for Medicaid. These incentives bear a direct relationship to the legitimate congressional interest in protecting potential life.

With these two rulings the Supreme Court, in collusion with state and federal legislatures, set in motion the practical means to prevent abortions on a massive scale. The rulings created a precedent for action in the years to come. *Roe* v. *Wade* was to remain intact, even as access to abortions would diminish. The Hyde Amendment was a meanspirited attack on those women who could least protect themselves and an action that ignored pressing economic realities. But it was also a back door victory for antiabortionists who happily tallied the number of "innocent unborn" who would be saved in the ghettos of America.

NEW YORK CITY, 1975

By 1975 it was becoming increasingly clear that Bernard Nathanson, who had led the drive to liberalize abortion laws in New York State, was entertaining serious doubts about abortion. By this time he had supervised more than seventy-five thousand abortions in his clinic and had personally performed fifteen hundred. But now he announced to his colleagues at the New York Center for Sexual and Reproductive Health: "I regret this loss of life. I thought abortions were right at the time, but I am compelled to report that the revolution we undertook was a seductive and ultimately poisonous dream."

Nathanson resigned from the National Abortion Rights Action League but continued for another year to perform abortions on a selective basis. His position was evolving. And then, on an autumn day in 1976, the doctor experienced an unquestionable moment of conversion. "One day, I cannot now recall the patient or the circumstances, I decided that I would perform no more of the grotesque 'second trimester' abortions except on strict medical grounds—even for longtime patients in my private practice," Nathanson remembered later. "Around the same time I also began refusing to do elective abortions at *any* stage for new patients who came to me. And so quietly, without fanfare or notice, I was out of the elective abortion business."

Nathanson's seemingly sincere and "quiet" conversion did not stay under wraps for long. Such a prominent advocate was too valuable to the antiabortion movement. Slowly the doctor became drawn deeper and deeper into the center of political action. Where once he had been on the cutting edge of abortion rights, Nathanson became one of the most strident voices against abortion in the years to come. Among his contributions to his new cause were a best-selling book, *Aborting America*, and a rallying film, *The Silent Scream*.

Nathanson's "conversion" gave new impetus for the antiabortion groups that were gearing up for action in the aftermath of the Supreme Court decision. The following years witnessed a tremendous growth in the movement that led to repeated challenges against *Roe*.

The so-called right-to-life movement believed that it needed to reach the humane instincts and "family values" of Americans in making its appeal. Part of this strategy was to build that appeal around catchphrases that would tug at the heart of the population. Thus was the rhetoric of the debate formed, and thus were invented such terms as "abortion on demand" and "abortion as birth control" to describe what the movement regarded as a rampant disregard for life.

Violence against abortion clinics began almost as soon as these new facilities were opened, and although it was never sanctioned by any antiabortion organization or church body, there was a tacit endorsement of the need to take extreme measures to save the lives of the unborn. (In the seventeen years after *Roe* v. *Wade* more than thirty-five abortion clinics were bombed, and forty destroyed by arson. It is not uncommon for clinic personnel to receive death threats, and bomb threats are a regular occurrence.)

While it is unlikely that the violence was ever mandated by antiabortion organizations, their incendiary rhetoric might have left their position in doubt. This was war, and those who did violence to the clinics were playing by the rules of war.

FOUR

A Revolution in Reverse

We cannot survive as a free nation when some men
decide that others are not fit to live and should be
abandoned to abortion or infanticide.

—RONALD REAGAN

Then, like a flame set to the oil of debate, Ronald Reagan
arrived at the center of the American stage. Reagan was an
enigma to many. His simple, almost childlike demeanor masked
a deep cunning and political savvy. Those who would not give
this former B movie actor a second glance later found him to be
one of the most influential men of the decade, whose impact
reverberated long after he was out of office.

In spite of the appearance of simplicity, Reagan was a man of
deep contradictions. A passionate spokesman for the return to
old-fashioned family values, he himself was a failure as a father—
something his children repeatedly attested to in speech and print.
An avowed born-again Christian, he was rarely found inside a
church, preferring the elite circles of the wealthy and famous
televangelists and preachers. A man who could bring tears to the
eyes of listeners when he described the plight of individuals
among the poor and indigent, he seemed incapable of compassion for those he could not personally see or touch.

In 1980 Reagan caught hold of the wave of moral fervor that
was sweeping the country, and he rode it into the White House.
Unlike George Bush, who would require great coaxing and

83

coaching to be brought around to the religious right's point of view, Reagan took to it immediately. The role of the inflamed ideologue suited him well. He was a good actor and a brilliant public speaker, but when he spoke the words, he believed them from his heart. *Roe* v. *Wade* was at the top of his hit list. Although President Carter had been strongly opposed to abortion, he had never made it a primary theme. Ronald Reagan became the first antiabortion activist to occupy the White House.

In 1983 an essay titled "Abortion and the Conscience of a Nation" appeared in the *Human Life Review*. The essay was assumed to be written by Reagan but was actually prepared for him by those in the White House whose job it was to articulate the President's vision. It was nearly unprecedented for a sitting President to publish an ideological essay, but Reagan was deeply committed to making his voice heard on this issue. He wrote:

> I have often said that when we talk about abortion, we are talking about two lives—the life of the mother and the life of the unborn child. Why else do we call a pregnant woman a mother? . . . The real question today is not when human life begins, but, *What is the value of human life?* The abortionist who reassembles the arms and legs of a tiny baby to make sure all its parts have been torn from its mother's body can hardly doubt whether it is a human being.

The document was classic Reagan as father figure, a role he successfully played throughout his term. Abandoning a hard look at the constitutional issues in favor of a grave moral appeal, Reagan had no trouble inventing the right images (calling pregnant women mothers), defining the "real question" in a manner the courts never thought to define it, and supplying anecdotes that were not necessarily culled from reality.

Later the essay was published in a slim volume that included afterwords by Surgeon General C. Everett Koop and Malcolm Muggeridge. It was widely distributed to religious groups and individuals throughout the nation, constituting a call to arms from the highest office in the land.

Ronald Reagan's vision was culled in the atmosphere of sentimentality that masked a manipulative hard line against women's rights. Being an activist, Reagan was not content to limit himself to rhetoric, although it was his rhetoric more than his actions that touched the heart of the nation. Reagan invented the abortion litmus test for the members of his administration and Cabinet and went about establishing a forceful presence against abortion behind the pillars of the White House.

The most visible antichoice appointment was Surgeon General Koop, who was known for his controversial involvement in a number of arenas, abortion being no exception. Koop, a pediatric surgeon and an outspoken opponent of abortion, had issued a scathing critique of the *Roe* v. *Wade* ruling in 1973. Ten years later, from his position within the Reagan administration, Koop became a more public spokesman against abortion rights, articulating grim predictions of a new holocaust that would become the inevitable outcome of selective birth rights.

In many ways Koop's approach to the issue was far more subtle and more disturbing than that of his more direct colleagues in the movement. In a paper titled "The Slide to Auschwitz," Koop compared the right of women to choose which babies would be born and which would not with the decisions made in Hitler's Germany about which humans were worthy of life and which were not. In Koop's view, abortion was merely a convenient way to eliminate defective or undesirable humans from society—a new twist on Hitler's "master race."

Following Koop's lead, the antiabortion movement began to use similar comparisons, suggesting the vast racist conspiracy behind abortion. In one of the boldest analogies, the 1857 *Dred Scott* decision that black people were not legal "persons" according to the U.S. Constitution was compared with the 1973 Supreme Court decision on abortion. "A slave was the property of the owner and could be bought and sold, or even killed by the owner at the owner's discretion," read one piece of literature.

"An unborn baby is the property of the owner (mother) and she can have the child killed at her request."

During his eight years as President Reagan was responsible for appointing more than half the members of the federal bench, those lower court judges who are responsible for interpreting the rulings of the Supreme Court. And he was to reshape the makeup of the High Court with three conservative appointments, including the first woman ever to serve on the Supreme Court.

Sandra Day O'Connor, who was appointed after Justice Potter Stewart retired in1981, offered little in the way of comfort to pro-choice advocates who might have expected a woman to be more sensitive to their position. Although O'Connor kept a determinedly low profile on the abortion issue, she was known to be a vocal supporter of "family values," code terminology for a conservative position on issues such as abortion. While keeping her own counsel about how she would vote in an actual case, O'Connor did once remark that she had a personal "abhorrence" for abortion, noting, "It is a practice in which I would not have engaged." But she had sent ambiguous signals about how she would actually vote. As a legislator in Arizona O'Connor once voted to decriminalize abortion. As the mother of three sons O'Connor was the only justice in the history of the Court to have experienced motherhood and the only justice to understand on a personal level the conflict between motherhood and career.

In 1986 Chief Justice Warren Burger retired, clearing the way for Reagan to raise William Rehnquist, the most conservative justice, to the position of chief justice. He also appointed Antonin Scalia to the vacant seat. Scalia became the loudest voice on the Court against abortion rights.

When Lewis Powell announced in 1987 that he was retiring from the Supreme Court, pro-choice advocates heaved a massive groan of dismay. It seemed the worst luck that Ronald Reagan would have yet another crack at selecting a Supreme Court justice. But when Reagan announced his nominee, Robert Bork, it was as if a sledgehammer had been aimed at their dreams. Bork, a federal appeals judge for the District of Columbia, was a controversial and abrasive jurist whose writings were widely cited as being examples of a strict interpretation of the Constitution. Essentially Bork opposed everything that was not specifically stated in the Constitution, including homosexual rights and the right to abortion. During hearings on a human life bill in 1981 Bork had said plainly, "*Roe* versus *Wade* is, itself, an unconstitutional decision, a serious and wholly unjustifiable judicial usurpation of state legislative authority." Bork believed that issues like abortion were best settled legislatively, not judicially, and there was little doubt among his detractors that as a member of the High Court, he could do grave damage to the right to abortion. He had even suggested that the *Griswold* decision, which opened the way to legalizing birth control, might be unconstitutional if one adhered to the rigid standards that he promoted.

Bork, who cut an intimidating and somewhat bizarre figure, with his bulging eyes and unmanageably scraggly hair and beard, was a classic Reagan man, who believed that individual rights had gone too far, leading to a permissive society on the verge of moral decline.

The nomination of such an imposing threat to abortion and privacy rights set into motion the most well-organized movement that had ever been activated against a presidential nominee. Hundreds of organizations joined a call to action sent out by Ted Kennedy and Joseph Biden, leaders on the Senate Judiciary Committee. In the wake of the greatest campaign ever waged against a Supreme Court appointee, Bork was defeated. A second nominee, Judge Douglas Ginsburg, was quickly withdrawn from consideration when it was discovered that he had used marijuana while a law professor.

Judge Anthony Kennedy, the third nominee, seemed more moderate than Bork, and he was confirmed by the Senate with little outcry. But later pro-choice advocates, who were elated by Bork's defeat, asked themselves if they had really won at all. Kennedy became one of the most doctrinaire justices on the Supreme Court—not much better and possibly worse than Bork might have been for their cause.

* * *

While Ronald Reagan was fulfilling his mandate to reform the Court, organizations were taking root in the mainstream of American politics, setting out to defeat pro-choice political candidates with a new vigor. Their goal was not only to tip the balance in the House and Senate but also to send a message to the American people that political candidates who supported the right to abortion would be stamped out in the voting booths.

In New Jersey abortion took center stage in a heated congressional race between antiabortion Republican Christopher H. Smith and pro-choice Democrat Jeffrey Laurenti. Antiabortionists, who said this was the most important race of the 1986 election year, were elated when Smith won a resounding victory.

Next door, in Pennsylvania, another heated contest provided a victory for antiabortionists with Democrat Robert Casey's win over pro-choice Republican William Scranton. Before the election a statewide poll conducted by the Pittsburgh *Post-Gazette* and the Philadelphia *Daily News* showed that 26 percent of Pennsylvania voters were more likely to vote for Casey because he was endorsed by the Pro-Life Federation.

Across the country ten new antiabortion governors were elected in 1986, but the movement suffered net losses in the Senate and House. Nevertheless, studies conducted by National Right to Life polling organizations demonstrated that abortion was gaining in influence as a single issue that made a difference in close elections. And they vowed to continue organizing at the grass-roots level to turn the critical 1 or 2 percent of uncommitted voters to their side. The energy of their endeavors was vividly demonstrated in the 1988 elections, when George Bush and his antiabortion platform took the country by storm.

ATLANTA, GEORGIA, August 1988

John Sununu was chairman of the platform committee at the Republican National Convention, and he held a tight rein on committee meetings. Nevertheless, he could not completely avoid a small skirmish that broke out around abortion. The proposed wording of the Republican platform on abortion read:

"The unborn child has a fundamental individual right to life which cannot be infringed." It was a fairly standard antiabortion position, and Sununu didn't expect any discord. But one hesitant voice challenged the wording.

Marjorie Bell Chambers, a committee member from New Mexico, moved to amend the language of the platform by removing the last four words. Chambers argued that the words "which cannot be infringed" sounded antiwomen and indicated that "men and fetuses have a right to life at all times, but women lose that right when they become pregnant."

According to Tanya Melich, executive director of the New York State Republican Family Committee, who was at the platform meetings, "Those opposing Ms. Chambers's amendment unequivocally argued that a fetus took precedence over a woman's life. Their intent was summarized in the words of Gregory Millspauch, a Nevada platform committee member: 'We must never defeat the right of the fetus.'

"There was no ambiguity in the full-blown debate. A vote for the Chambers amendment meant that the platform committee recognized a woman's right to life over the fetus. A vote against it meant the primacy of the fetus in all cases. The committee defeated the amendment 55 to 33, with 11 abstentions." Not surprisingly most of the advocates of the amendment were women.

Later that day Connecticut Senator Lowell Weicker attempted to amend the platform to include a provision for federal funding of abortions for poor women who were the victims of rape and incest. When that amendment was defeated, Connecticut Representative Nancy Johnson cried out in frustration, "Where is your compassion?"

Frank Graves, a delegate from Minnesota, replied without hesitation, "We do not execute a murderer's child, so why should we execute a rapist's?"

The final platform was consistent with the goals of the religious right, as promoted by back room power brokers like Doug Wead and John Sununu. There had been a time when George Bush might have felt the statement was too strong since it allowed no exceptions for rape, incest, or the life of the mother. But by the time of the convention Bush was too far committed to the agenda of the religious right to suggest that the language be softened.

Abortion never turned into a core issue during the campaign, although there were some tense moments for Bush. During a televised debate with Michael Dukakis, he seemed unprepared to field a question on the subject, and scrambling around for a way to explain his position, he indicated that if abortion became illegal (a position he favored), women who sought abortions could be prosecuted and jailed. Almost immediately his staff issued a clarification that Bush would never support the jailing of women—only doctors. His handlers rightly judged that no matter how the American people felt about abortion, they would not sit by and watch their women being carted off to jail.

But even though abortion itself was not a rallying issue in the campaign, Bush's pact with the religious right was apparent throughout it. With the committed backing of evangelical leaders, Bush won 80 percent of the evangelical Christian vote in the election. And religious broadcasters took credit for delivering some thirty-five million of their listeners into the Vice President's camp.

Only forty-eight hours after the polls had closed, and George Bush had been elected President of the United States, the Justice Department filed a brief for a Missouri abortion appeal scheduled to be heard by the Supreme Court. In the brief the administration urged the Court to consider reversing *Roe* v. *Wade*. Some observers noted that the timing of the filing after the election was indicative of the administration's fear that its position on abortion did not reflect the view of the majority. Had the brief been filed prior to the election, it might have created a wave of protest. At the last minute the Bush campaign decided not to take any chances.

After the election the payoffs began, and those who had helped Bush get elected, including Doug and Bill Wead, got their rewards. Watching from her home in Vancouver, Simma Holt noted that Doug Wead did not receive the post he had most coveted—an overseas job as top executive officer of the Agency for International Development. He was to remain in the White House as Bush's liaison to the religious right but with a new venue as one of three advisers on policy in the White House. "This was the payoff," Holt said. "Both Doug and his brother Bill talked about it all the time in the Crystal City apartment. It was always understood that if they delivered the religious right to George Bush, they would be personally rewarded."

Bill Wead was to become speech writer for Dr. Louis Sullivan, director of the Department of Health and Human Services. And John Sununu was to reap the greatest reward of all. Many insiders had thought that Bush would keep on Craig Fuller, his chief of staff as Vice President, when he became president. Fuller was a smart, no-nonsense man and a savvy administrator who had been loyal to the Vice President. But Fuller was not in sympathy with Wead's evangelical program, and Wead had been working hard behind the scenes to sully Fuller's reputation while singing the praises of his new friend John Sununu. During the transition Fuller was fired, and Sununu was appointed to be the President's chief of staff, arguably the most influential position in the White House next to the President himself.

The task of recommending people for Cabinet jobs and filling sub-Cabinet positions fell to Sununu and his tightly knit network of right-wing transition workers. These recommendations and appointments were indirectly vetted through the Washington-based Right to Life Committee, which routinely checked backgrounds to ensure "pro-life purity."

On his first day in office George Bush addressed sixty-five thousand right-to-lifers marching in Washington by telephone, calling abortion "an American tragedy." Abortion rights supporters were sobered by the realization that the phone call was one of Bush's first official acts as President. It was going to be a long four years.

SEATTLE, WASHINGTON, *March 1990*

Pregnant?
Need Help?
Call Birth Hotline

No matter how difficult your problem is, it won't seem so bad when you talk it over with a friend. Let us direct you to sources for pregnancy tests, medical aid, emotional support and practical help now, during and after the birth of your baby.

Abortion Is Not the Answer

Don't act hastily out of fear. Pressures may make it seem that abortion is the only solution. It isn't. Our trained volunteers can talk with you about alternatives to abortion. You have a friend at the other end of the phone, waiting to help you in strictest confidence.

Please Call . . . We Care

"Hello . . . I want to talk to someone about my pregnancy." The voice on the phone was young, hesitant.

"Yes, that's what we're here for." Barbara Allen leaned into the phone, concentrating her attention on the woman's words.

"I need to figure out what to do. I just found out—"

"I can help you. How far along are you?"

"About two months." The woman sighed deeply. "I've thought about an abortion, but I don't know. I'm Catholic, at least I was raised Catholic. I guess I just wanted to see if there was any other way. I'm not married, so it's hard."

"Yes." The sympathy in Barbara's voice was authentic. Traumatized by her own abortion, early in life, which stole her motherhood and sent her into deep despair, Barbara now devoted her life to helping other women avoid a similar fate. Over the years she had reached the simple belief that abortion was wrong and that what she had suffered was a just punishment for her action. This was her calling now: to save the unborn and in the process to save the sanity and souls of women in distress.

"Abortion would be an immediate solution, but it's not necessarily a good solution for the long term," she said carefully. "You're lucky you called now. We see many women who have strong feelings like I think you do. You instinctively know that abortion would be wrong, but you're not sure what to do. Sometimes women panic and go ahead and have abortions, and it's very hard for them after the fact. It can be overwhelming to realize what you've done."

"The thing is, finances are a problem. I'm a waitress in a nice place. I'm afraid I might lose my job. I couldn't make it if I lost my job."

"How old are you?"

"Twenty-nine."

"Does the father know about the pregnancy?"

"Yeah, he knows."

"Is he willing to be involved?"

"No."

"Do you want advice about getting support from him?"

"No."

"How about your parents?"

"My mother isn't alive," the young woman told her. "And I'm not that close to my father. I know he wouldn't help me. I couldn't ask him. I'm pretty much on my own, which is why I'm so worried about losing my job. I couldn't even pay my rent if I lost my job."

Barbara gripped the phone with intensity. "I can understand why you're feeling afraid. It isn't easy to face this alone—what's your name?"

"Roberta."

"Okay, Roberta, I'm going to give you a couple of numbers you can call to find out about the help that's available. Have you thought about whether you will keep the baby or give it up for adoption?"

"Oh, Jesus," Roberta said, flustered. "I haven't thought about it. I just found out, and you know, I'm not even sure whether I'm going to have it."

Barbara kept her voice level, soothing. "I know. That's why we're exploring all of the options. Tell me, Roberta, how much do you know about what happens during an abortion?"

"Some, I guess. Not a lot."

"It's amazing what people don't know. Basically there are two methods. The first is suction-aspiration. A hollow plastic tube with a sharp edge is placed into the uterus. The suction tears the baby apart, and the sharp edge is used to scrape the placenta from the wall of the uterus. Everything is sucked out into a bottle. The second most common method is dilation and curettage, known as a D and C. A curette, which is a loop-shaped steel knife, is inserted into the uterus, and the baby and placenta are cut to pieces and scraped out. Both procedures are usually done under general anesthesia, so they're not painful for the mother. Of course, we know that the child feels pain."

"What do you mean?" Roberta sounded startled.

"I mean the child you're carrying, at eight weeks, has all the organs required to support life. He feels what's going on because his brain is already formed. The remaining months of his development are simply a time for refinement."

"It's just been two months—"

"I know. It's hard to face that you're carrying a real, live human being who would suffer and die in a horrible way with an abortion. But I can tell that deep down, you don't feel right about having an abortion because you already kind of know the fetus you're carrying is a human being."

"It's confusing," Roberta admitted. "I just found out I was pregnant. To tell you the truth, I don't know what to believe. Even if I had the baby and gave him up, he might end up in some orphan home, and that seems wrong, too."

Barbara took a deep breath. This was always the hardest part of the conversation, talking about adoption. She thought of the child that might now be alive if only she had made that choice.

She felt urgently that she must communicate this to the young woman at the other end of the phone line.

"Let me tell you something that might help you," she said. "For many years I have counseled unwed mothers. Some keep their babies, but most do not. I work closely with them and I care deeply. From my own personal experience, almost all the babies are placed in loving homes, with people who really want them and who are extremely grateful. I know you may think, *What kind of mother am I to give up my child?* But in my work I have never seen such great love as that of a mother who gives up her child. Having the baby is the right decision. I promise you, it is a gift that you will never forget. When you think about it, it's so wrong to deprive your baby of life—to kill it now rather than give it up for adoption to a loving and kind family. I can't tell you how happy and relieved women are when they choose to let their babies live. A great burden is lifted." Barbara took a breath and felt her heart pounding.

"I never thought about it that way," Roberta said.

"That's why I'm glad you called. You're obviously a young woman who cares very much about human life. . . . I'll bet you miss your mother."

"Oh, yes. She died five years ago. I guess she'd be upset about this because she was very religious. She never even used birth control. I know she felt bad because she wanted more children than just one."

Barbara was nodding into the phone, feeling new confidence in her words. "You know what I think? I think your dead mother is taking care of you now; she's with you now. It's her voice that is telling you not to be afraid, to have this baby. I'm going to give you the number of a Catholic referral service. I want you to call them and tell them about your concerns. If they can't help you, I want you to call me back. My name is Barbara Allen. Will you do that?"

"Yes."

"Okay, Roberta, I want you to call me and let me know how you're doing. I care very much about you, and I know beyond the shadow of a doubt that having your baby is the right thing to do. Will you call me?"

"Yes . . ."

"Good. I'm so glad you called today, Roberta. I'll wait to hear from you, and I'll pray for you."

Barbara Allen found herself thinking about Roberta later that day as she prepared to go off duty. She felt satisfied that she had reached the young woman, but one could never be sure. Nearly ten years of hot line service had taught her the discouraging truth: Abortion was a potent enemy, a quick and easy way out for a generation that valued the simple solution. She could only hope that Roberta listened to her and would opt for life. It was out of her hands now. On the way home she planned to stop by the church and light a candle for Roberta, hoping that God would take over where she left off.

Tired, she gathered up her bag and coat and walked slowly to her car. Nearing forty, Barbara sometimes felt a lot older; her work on the hot line took its toll. Every day she listened to the painful, tragic stories. They echoed in her brain; she heard them even in her sleep. She wished that she could stay with each woman until the end, soothe her worries, ease her financial burdens, show her someone cared. But the truth was that there was very little she could do but talk—and pray.

She turned her car into the parking lot of a nearby Catholic church. She would light one candle for Roberta and one candle for the soul of the unborn child she had aborted when she was sixteen—the child for whom she had never stopped grieving.

FIVE

Baby Choice and the

Zealots

One of the protesters outside had started playing a tape of a baby crying. I signed my name over and over. Yes, I understand the risks involved; yes, I understand that the alternatives to abortion are birth and adoption. I wanted to do more; I wanted to fill out a page or so explaining why I had chosen to do this. I wanted to explain to someone that I was a responsible person; you see, ladies and gentlemen, I never had sex without condoms unless I was having my period; I got pregnant during my period; isn't there something I could sign swearing to that? I had a three-day affair with a friend; I'm broke and unemployed; I can't give up a baby for adoption; I can't afford to be pregnant while I look for a job.

—DEBORAH SALAZAR, inside an abortion clinic

An aunt of Randall Terry's tells the story of his religious conversion: "He came home claiming he was Jesus Christ, locked himself in the bedroom for two days. Finally he came out and said he had misinterpreted the message: He was a *messenger* of Jesus Christ."

97

Those who knew Terry well would say he was a man who tended to live a little close to the edge. Sometimes, it appears, he slipped all the way over. But nevertheless, he became in the 1980's the most powerful antichoice prophet-activist in America. Terry compared himself by turns with Moses, who rescued the innocents from slaughter, and Martin Luther King, Jr., who led his followers in nonviolent, illegal sit-down demonstrations. He easily equated the extreme measures taken by these two men with his own determination to stop abortion at any cost.

Randall Terry came late to his "higher calling." As a young man growing up in Rochester, New York, he was restless and misdirected, dropping out of school at sixteen to roam the country and pursue his dream of becoming a rock singer. His harsh experiences on the road convinced him to return after a year. Back home in Rochester, he was working in an ice-cream parlor when a customer to whom he had just sold a cone introduced him to Jesus Christ and changed his life forever. He studied for and received his high school equivalency diploma, and in 1978 he entered the Elm Bible Institute in Lima, New York. There his eyes were opened to the "murders" being committed daily in the abortion clinics of America. Thus was his mission begun: "saving babies from the death chamber." He later said that the urgency of his mission was heightened by the fact that he himself was adopted. Had his mother chosen abortion, he would not be alive to carry on God's task.

Charisma is an elusive quality, unrelated, it seems, to physical appearance, personal charm, or intelligence. Terry seemed oddly suited to wear the mantle. Thin, with a tight helmet of curly hair, small, fierce eyes, and a forehead permanently creased by the strain of his intensity, Terry, at only thirty, was nevertheless able to hold thousands under his spell when he spoke and was able to persuade ordinary middle-class Americans to stand on the front lines of a battle that often led to their arrests.

Operation Rescue was Terry's brainchild. By 1988 it was nearly a hundred thousand strong, the guerrilla arm of the antiabortion movement, which sent thousands of people to block the entrances of abortion clinics across the continent, in both the

United States and Canada, and to offer "sidewalk counseling" to women as they arrived for abortions. (This "counseling" often involved their waving pictures of aborted fetuses and shouting, "Don't kill your baby! Don't kill your baby!") Even court orders were not able to prevent the Operation Rescue clinic actions. The sit-downs normally ended with hundreds of Operation Rescue members being physically removed by police and arrested. But in contempt for any decision but their own, they returned again and again, more determined than before. No law seemed capable of dimming the zealotry of Terry's forces. Some critics accused them of being terrorists. But Terry's troops preferred to be called rescuers.

LOS ANGELES, CALIFORNIA, Spring 1989

Bernard Nathanson stood in front of the packed church and squinted at the crowd of one thousand people through thick, black-rimmed glasses that gave his face an owlish look. He was not an attractive man. His jet black hair didn't fit his aging, heavy face; his suit was out of date and ill-fitting. His eyes behind the thick glasses were without charm or light. He looked grim, even angry. But when Nathanson began to speak, his voice was firm and clear. The room was hushed as the crowd hung on every word of the movement's most famous convert. Dr. Nathanson, once called the Abortion King, now sounded the battle cry for the Operation Rescue squads that were preparing to descend on abortion clinics the following day.

"You are the shock troops of the Lord," he told the crowd. "The soldiers of Spartacus, the colonial freedom fighters, the Underground Railroad." The crowd was on its feet now, stamping and cheering.

Nathanson stepped aside, and a younger, intense-looking man with curly hair stood center stage. He smiled widely as the crowd erupted in cheering and waving. There was fire in his eyes. His thin frame trembled with emotion. When he spoke, his voice had a strength and maturity that belied his age and stature. He was Randall Terry.

"We live in a child-hating culture," he cried. "We send our children off to school as soon as possible. . . . We don't bring them to worship with us. I know there are some women, even here tonight, who are saying, 'But I have four children already. I can't afford more.' But I tell you"—his voice resonated, bouncing off the walls of the room—"my God will provide!" Some of the women in the room were crying; many had their eyes tightly shut as though they were praying.

Terry stopped speaking, and the room grew silent again. His next words were delivered softly, reverently. "Tonight we are going to have a memorial service for Baby Choice." He stood aside as two women descended to the stage; one held a tiny coffin in her hands. Terry told the crowds to follow the ushers, one row at a time, to view the body. The lines began to form, and the men and women in the room, some holding small children by the hands, filed past the white coffin, each person looking down. Some gasped and shut their eyes. Others exclaimed in horror. The fetus in the coffin had been preserved in formaldehyde. It was a terrible sight, curled into itself, its body a strangely marbled black and white, the effects of having been burned in the womb of its mother during abortion. The viewing lasted more than an hour. Many people were crying now. There was a renewed fervor in the air, a revived determination. Baby Choice was the murdered outcome of abortion. The hundreds of people gathered here, these shock troops of the Lord, were preparing now to stage several days of rescue efforts at abortion clinics throughout the area. They were to start early the following morning. A minister stepped forward to deliver a final prayer. He closed his eyes. "Lord, bless your enemies, they know not what they are doing," he crooned, swaying against the microphone. "Stand beside us, your humble servants. Give us strength and courage against the evil forces who would murder your most beloved of creatures, your children. Stand beside us so your light might shine in the darkness of this evil age. In your name we pray . . . amen."

"Amen!" A thousand voices responded in unison.

*   *   *

It was nearly midnight, but Kathy L. was still on the phone. She had been calling people all night, organizing supporters around the area, pro-choicers willing to show up at her women's health clinic the following day and escort clients past the Operation Rescue mobs. This was not the first time Operation Rescue had paid a visit to her clinic. She knew the scene would be ugly.

The clinic had just reopened after an arson attack earlier in the year had caused nearly eighty thousand dollars in damage, and already Operation Rescue had targeted it for a sit-in. This week the "big guns" were in town: Randall Terry himself and Bernard Nathanson, the famous antiabortion doctor. Kathy expected a bitter fight.

Out of fairness she warned all the women scheduled for appointments the next day to expect trouble. Some of them had chosen to stay away. Those who tried to keep their appointments would be in for a shock; it was impossible to prepare anyone for the trauma of several hundred voices raised against her, the shouts of "Don't murder your baby!," or the signs bearing bloody pictures of aborted fetuses. The men and women she had organized to try to escort patients past the protesters wouldn't be able to shield women from the impact.

The media would be there, too, and this presented another dilemma. The women were rightfully concerned about appearing on the evening news for all the world to see.

Sometimes Kathy L. believed it was her rage that kept her going in the face of this impossible uphill battle. She had never been so furious in her life as the day after the arson, when she stood in the burned-out clinic. The equipment was a melted mess; the furniture was charred and molten. The carpets were soaked with water. Her first reaction was a deep feeling of grief and hopelessness. How could anyone do this? But the initial reaction was followed quickly by anger. She could not let this stop her. She called her staff and instructed them to come to work. They would do counseling and give pregnancy tests out of their cars if they had to. She found a friend who lent her a van. The arson slowed down business; but it did not stop the operation, and she was proud of that.

It was long after midnight when Kathy L. finally put down the phone. She had to get some sleep. She needed every last ounce of strength available for the next day's battle.

The sun was just coming up when the cars and buses began to arrive. Kathy L. and her staff were already at the clinic, preparing for the day's work. The twelve staff members would remain inside to treat the women who made it through the army of protesters. Kathy was to station herself in the parking lot and help the escorts get the women inside.

The clinic had two entrances, one in front and one in back near the parking lot. The Operation Rescue troops poured from their vehicles and began to sit on the porch and on the ground surrounding the doorways. They were strangely quiet, not talking or shouting, just peacefully singing Christian songs. Their voices—"Ama-zing grace . . . how sweet the sound"—formed an eerie backdrop to the promise of violence. Several policemen were leaning against their cars across the street, yawning and drinking coffee.

By the time the clinic opened at nine, the front and back yards were covered with hundreds of bodies, tightly squeezed together to form a human barrier. Behind them were hundreds more pro-choice activists, who above the strains of "Amazing Grace," shouted "Operation Rescue, your name's a lie! You don't care if women die!" A police bullhorn blared over the din, "Please remove yourselves. This is private property." The demand was ignored. The demonstrators kept singing. The bullhorn blasted again: "Please remove yourselves immediately or you will be arrested."

Of course, the protesters knew this. It was part of the plan. When the police finally moved in to begin the arrests, they would lie on the ground and become dead weight. It would take three or four officers to carry each protester to the van, with lengthy delays while each group of protesters was transported to the police station. It would be late in the day before enough protesters were removed to allow clear passage into the clinic.

A car drove up and paused hesitantly near the parking lot,

which was crowded with protesters from both sides. Immediately a group from Operation Rescue rushed over to plaster pictures of bloody fetuses against the windshield. The young man and woman inside looked frightened. They quickly rolled up their windows. The Operation Rescue "counselors" shouted through the windows, "Don't murder your baby! Please don't kill your baby!"

The woman inside the car was crying. The man shook his head helplessly and finally drove away.

A woman from Operation Rescue screamed with joy, "A baby has been saved!"

The crowd of protesters cried, "Praise the Lord, praise the Lord . . . a baby saved!"

The policemen were carrying out the dead-weight bodies of protesters. As each person was removed, the others scooted together to tighten their ranks.

A young girl arrived with her friend, and Kathy and her aides took their arms and tried to push through the crowds. "It's murder! It's murder!" screamed the rescuers, shoving pictures into the girls' faces.

Pro-choicers surrounded the girls and there was pushing and shoving as the two sides collided. The girls were young, and they looked scared. "Let us through," sobbed one.

"Have your baby!" cried the rescuers.

It was impossible to get through.

One girl tugged at Kathy's sleeve. "I'm sorry, I can't," she said, tears streaming down her cheeks. She and her friend broke away and ran down the street.

"Another life saved!" shouted one of the rescuers, and the protesters on the ground cheered.

It went on and on. The protesters began to sing "The Battle Hymn of the Republic." By noon at least two hundred of them had been carried away by police, but those remaining were like the shifting sands of a sieve. They held together. No one had yet entered the clinic. The police were sweating and looked exhausted from their heavy labors.

Randall Terry perched on a van across the street, calling to the protesters through a bullhorn. "Squeeze together, hold your ranks. Have courage! Be strong! You are doing the Lord's work; you are saving innocent lives." Whenever the singing died down, his voice boomed out, picking up the tune—"Holy, Holy, Holy, Lord God Almighty"—and other voices rose once again.

By midafternoon tempers were flaring. "You have blood on your hands," shouted an Operation Rescue woman to the pro-choice group that was chanting, "Women's bodies, women's choice."

"I pity you!" screamed a young man as he was carried off by police. Reporters and cameramen scrambled on hands and knees to interview protesters and film the action. A line of policemen had secured the back door, and Kathy and her helpers were escorting women along a tightly formed police line. Operation Rescue protesters sobbed and screamed at them as they headed toward the door of the clinic. "Don't murder your baby! Please don't murder your baby!" One of the protesters, an elderly woman, fainted and was carried away by police. Only about fifty protesters remained in front of the clinic. They seemed to be uncertain of what to do.

"Hold your ground . . . be strong," Randall Terry shouted from the safety of his perch across the street.

It was 8:00 P.M. before the action was over. Coffee cups and food wrappers cluttered the grass in front of the clinic. Brochures showing gruesome color photographs of bloody fetuses fluttered in the wind. Wearily Kathy and her staff and supporters began the cleanup. The frustration was thick in the air.

"How long can this go on?" pleaded one of the workers, looking to Kathy for words of hope.

Kathy shook her head. "Seems like forever," she replied.

"I listen to feminists and all these radical gals—most of them are failures. They've blown it. Some of them have been married, but they married some Casper Milquetoast who asked permission to go to the bathroom. These women just need a man in the house. That's all they need. Most of these feminists need a man to tell them what time of day it is and to lead them home. And they blew it and they're mad at all men. Feminists hate men. They're sexist. They hate men—that's their problem."

The abortion debate was complicated by the hostility that men like the Reverend Jerry Falwell, who made that statement, felt toward women who didn't fit a traditional mode. It had jokingly been said—but was it really such a joke?—that if men could get pregnant, abortion would be a sacrament. Instead it was hard not to notice that the voices shouting most loudly from the front lines of the antiabortion movement were male voices:

- Randall Terry, the young born-again Christian leader of Operation Rescue, wasn't universally popular among antiabortionists; some believed his tactics were too confrontational. But he clearly stood on the visible edge of the movement.
- Bernard Nathanson, who was the most influential "convert" in the medical community, devoted his life to overturning the very laws he had once worked so hard to see passed.
- John Wilke, president of the National Right to Life Committee and author of a number of books and tracts on fetal rights, was considered more mainstream than Terry but no less committed to the cause. His goal was to educate people to the miracle of life in the womb. "The fetus is discriminated against," he said, "because of its place of residence." He was fond of comparing abortion with slavery, saying, "There's no difference between the right to end a pregnancy and the right to own slaves—it's all control over the life of another human."
- Joseph Scheidler, head of the Chicago-based Pro-Life Action League and a former Benedictine monk, believed in confrontational tactics, as outlined in his book *Closed: 99 Ways to Stop Abortion.* Scheidler once said, "I think contraception is disgusting—people using each other for pleasure."
- Reverend Donald E. Wildmon, head of the American Family Association, who waged an aggressive campaign

to return America to good old-fashioned family values, was on the far right edge of the debate. His *AFA Journal* was designed to offer tabloid-style shock appeal, with headlines such as WRONG BABY ABORTED and LIBERATED WOMEN DON'T FIND UTOPIA.

- Father Paul Marx, president of Human Life International, a Catholic antiabortion organization, once shrugged off the struggle of women in this century by saying, "Inequality is the natural condition."
- Charles Rice, professor of law at Notre Dame University, was a frequent spokesman against abortion, even in cases of rape and incest. In particular, he believed the incest exception was faulty. "Incest," he once said, "is a voluntary act on the woman's part."
- Reverend Jimmy Swaggart, himself a dubious judge of sexual morality, was staunchly opposed not only to abortion but to contraceptive education and services— especially for the young and unmarried. With baffling logic, Swaggart once declared: "Sex education classes in our public schools are promoting incest."
- Representative Christopher H. Smith, elected to Congress from a leadership position in New Jersey's Right to Life Committee, was a congressional activist against every bill touched by the issue, including foreign aid bills. Smith was one of the right's "test" cases to demonstrate that right-to-life candidates could defeat opponents on the basis of the single issue of abortion.

Men like these often used abortion and family planning issues as an excuse for espousing general antifeminist sentiments. Women were blamed not only for taking innocent life but also for upsetting the fabric of family culture and values in this country. Suddenly women were once again on the receiving end of the full force of white patriarchal wrath.

Antifeminists spoke of the collapse of family values as though such a thing as family values had once existed in a tangible form, only to be discarded. They referred as well to a family norm, which likewise had been abandoned in this century. But in fact, no consistent family norm had ever existed, at least not in the idealized sense that they described. So-called norms were not static realities but merely markers that moved societies from one point to another along the historical landscape. Human society was an ever-changing dynamic, and there were many reasons why the family form had changed in this century—among them the move from an agricultural to an industrial society, the shifting roles of women, a communications technology that provided personal access to the globe, the impossible economics of the one-paycheck family, medical advances, and so on. While it may have been convenient to blame the "man-hating feminists," it was only a smoke screen.

The rhetoric of the antifeminists gave permission for misogynist attitudes to flourish. Were opposition to abortion and a genuine compassion for the unborn really the issue, or did they reflect a much broader concern with the threatening dimensions of women's empowerment, the foremost manifestation being their desire for control over their lives and bodies?

This was not an easy question to answer because the lines separating personal and family issues were smudged by emotional fervor. But the ultimate goals of some antiabortionists became suspect when they declined support for more effective and accessible birth control—in practice, the most meaningful way to eliminate abortion.

Furthermore, misogynist attitudes could be cannon fodder in the hands of the unstable, as was graphically illustrated by the December 1989 massacre of women students at the University of Montreal. Shouting, "You're women, you're going to be engineers. You're all a bunch of feminists, and I hate feminists," twenty-five-year-old Marc Lepine opened fire on the students, striking twenty-seven women before he turned the gun on himself. Fourteen women died. The unemployed killer, who blamed feminists for ruining his life, presented the tip of an iceberg that had long been rising. In the aftermath of the tragedy many people voiced concern that Lepine's actions were not isolated but rather reflected a deep-seated societal hostility against women.

And when a team of Montreal psychologists opened their phone lines to the public to offer free counseling after the tragedy, several men who called admitted feeling good about the incident. "I am very happy Lepine did it," one man said. "You psychologists are just like those women, and I am coming to your office to kill you all." Even though no further violence occurred, the incident exacerbated the already uneasy tensions between women and those men who could not accept their changing role.

The politics of reproductive rights spoke to the core issues of how we identified ourselves as men and women in the modern world—a world that was changing with dizzying speed. Yet it helped to stop the clock, to step back and remember that in this very century there was a time when women could not vote, could not own property, and could not seek custody of their children. They had no more rights under the Constitution than did slaves. They had no voice. And if their voice was now a storm on the waters of social order, it surely made some sense—especially in light of the organized force that was determined to take back their rights and reclaim control over their bodies.

It's not that men were irrelevant to the abortion question or that their concerns were not worthy of a hearing. Society had stereotyped men as well, presenting them as self-absorbed and controlling, likely to abandon their women and children when things got too hard. This view was not entirely surprising considering the social abandonment that was dictated daily by the male-dominated hierarchies of church and state. But it failed to consider that stereotypes of any kind—be they directed toward men or women—weakened the foundations of the human community. In the abortion issue men needed to be heard. That was not the question. The question was, Who had the final choice?

MONTREAL, CANADA, July 1989

Chantal Daigle, twenty-one, and Jean-Guy Tremblay, twenty-five, had known each other less than a year, but they were in love when they decided to have a baby together, and they were overjoyed when Daigle conceived. But eighteen weeks later the bloom was off the rose. Daigle left Tremblay because she said the former nightclub bouncer and car dealer service representative had become physically abusive once she was pregnant. After she moved out, she informed Tremblay that she was going to get an abortion. It was her right.

Tremblay disagreed. Angered by the breakup and now by the prospect of losing their child, he begged Daigle to reconsider. It was probable that Tremblay's interest was in winning back Daigle more than it was concern for the life of their child. He was not even committed to raise the child himself but told Daigle that after its birth he would turn it over to his parents (the very people who had abused him as a child) to be raised. Daigle resisted this plan and firmly stated her intention to have an abortion. Finally, in frustration over his inability to control Daigle and halt the abortion, Tremblay went to court to seek an injunction against it.

He told the court he sought the injunction as much for Daigle's sake as for his own. "The only thing I want to say to her is that I love her, and what I did right now is not just for me, it's for her too," Tremblay said emotionally. Justice Jean Richard issued an injunction and set a hearing date for the following week.

Tremblay was jubilant. "You don't kill a human being like that," he said. But Daigle was suspicious of his motivations, especially after he had admitted to receiving money from the Quebec chapter of the Campaign Life Coalition, an antiabortion organization. It was apparent that her private choice was becoming the focal point of a public abortion battle, and whether Tremblay was sincere in his pursuit or merely a pawn in Quebec politics, the end result was the same: She was being prevented, at least temporarily, from seeking an abortion.

While she waited for her hearing, a woman offered Daigle twenty-five thousand dollars to go through with the pregnancy and turn over the infant for adoption. Daigle responded wearily, "I've made a decision and I'm going to go through with it."

The case was only one in a series of precedent-setting cases in Canada. In Toronto Barbara Dodd's fetus was made a ward of the court after her boyfriend, Gregory Murphy, legally challenged her right to have an abortion—though there was convincing evidence that Murphy might not be the father of the child.

In Winnipeg the ex-boyfriend of a pregnant single mother attempted a court challenge to stop her from getting an abortion. The court challenge failed, and the woman (not identified in the press) went ahead with the abortion. She remarked bitterly, "He's not trying to save the life of a human being. It's revenge to get back at me because I left him."

Three weeks of testimony preceded the court's final decision, and Chantal Daigle was nervous. Already twenty-one weeks pregnant, she would no longer be able to have an abortion in a Quebec clinic and would have to fly to the United States to obtain it. Even there it would be impossible to find a doctor to perform the procedure after twenty-four weeks. On July 27, in a controversial decision, the court ruled, 3–2, against Daigle's right to seek an abortion, stating that the fetus was "a living human entity distinct from the mother . . . and has the right to life and protection from those who conceived it." It was to be the first ruling in Canada supporting fetal rights.

Daigle was dismayed by the decision and vowed to appeal to the Supreme Court. The issue had become a larger one for the young woman—one of rights. "It's shocking," she told a news conference after the decision, "to drag a woman in front of a court because she doesn't have the right to do what she thinks is right for her body. What's important to me is that we recognize the rights of the person and the rights of the woman."

Aware of the time urgency, the five justices of Canada's Supreme Court agreed to meet in a special session on August 1 to decide whether to hear Daigle's appeal. While they deliberated, noisy demonstrators gathered outside the courthouse. A plane flew overhead, trailing a banner that read *"Garde ton enfant—*Keep your baby."

It took the justices less than twenty minutes to decide they would hear Daigle's case immediately, interrupting their summer recess to do so. The hearing was set for August 8, the twenty-third week of Daigle's pregnancy.

Daigle's circumstances brought to the surface many levels of complexity—particularly as her fetus reached the point of viability. Less than half of 1 percent of all abortions conducted in Canada were performed after twenty weeks, and some clinics would not perform them after the first trimester. Even some who had supported Daigle's right to abortion earlier in the pregnancy were uneasy as the weeks passed and the fetus developed. But Daigle argued that she would have had an abortion earlier if she had been permitted to do so, and now her resolve was unshaken. "My rights are my rights," she said, "and they are the rights of all women."

On August 8 the Supreme Court ruled unanimously to reject the lower court injunction against Daigle. It was an important decision, but it made little practical difference to Daigle. The week before, she had flown to the United States and obtained her abortion there.

Across the border Chantal Daigle was able to obtain an abortion, but abortion rights faced emotional challenges throughout the United States. What they had not won by law, antiabortionists sought to take by force.

In Georgia five men arrived first thing in the morning at the Atlanta Surgicenter, a facility where abortions were performed. They pushed Beth Petzelt, executive director of the clinic, to the floor and shoved a lab technician against the wall. Then they chained themselves together with bicycle locks.

The men, members of Operation Rescue, were acting in defiance of a court order that required protesters to remain at least fifty feet from an abortion clinic and at least five feet from patients and clinic workers.

The men were taken to jail and, refusing to post bail, remained there. Ironically, and surely to their dismay, their attack on the clinic did not halt the normal operation of business.

But the incident was only one of hundreds that occurred every month, contributing to the already charged atmosphere around the issue. Abortion was legal in all fifty states, but it was becoming less easily accessible. If in order to exercise her rights, a woman had to walk a gauntlet of jeering protesters and be subject to verbal and physical abuse, they were not rights at all.

The 1989 meeting of the National Right to Life Committee was attended by fifteen hundred supporters from across the nation. They arrived, lugging leaflets, buttons, and T-shirts. They were a smiling, buoyant crowd, composed almost entirely of white Christians. A large contingent of Catholic priests and nuns from the church-sponsored group Birthright was present. Representatives of chapters of the Knights of Columbus, Lutherans for Life, and other groups were on hand to distribute materials on sexuality, family life, and the sanctity of love and marriage. A videotaped welcome from President Bush received thunderous applause. They were there to take the high road, the "moral" ground. And their target was the "great muddled middle"— those Americans who were neither solidly for nor against the right to abortion.

Addressing the attendees, organization president John Wilke urged them to speak plainly about the real story of abortion. Deriding Norma McCorvey, Wilke cried, "Imagine your mother not wanting you so much she went to the Supreme Court to have you aborted!" He wagged his head in disgust, and the crowd howled in protest.

PART TWO

The Current Crisis:

A Battle Inside

America's Soul

SIX

Courting Disaster

To take Vietnam as an analogy: if this country found itself bewildered by trying to invade the home territory of a proud and motivated adversary, can you imagine how bewildered our establishment would be if it seriously tried to invade the reproductive territory of millions of proud and motivated women?

—GLORIA STEINEM

While across the country countless women faced impossible choices, reaching through their numbing ambivalence to decide what was right, the political machinery continued to grind, constructing the foundation for a full-scale fight against abortion across the land.

The state of Missouri had long been interested in tightening its abortion statutes, and in 1988 Attorney General William L. Webster had his chance when two large health concerns filed suit to test a new law that declared "life begins at conception." The suit, *William L. Webster* v. *Reproductive Health Concerns*, became known simply as *Webster* as it made its way to the highest court. Missouri's law, which would virtually eliminate abortion in the state, was declared unconstitutional by both the federal district court and the U.S. court of appeals. But its backers hoped it would find a more sympathetic ear at the Supreme Court.

The Missouri law sought to restrict abortion in the following ways:

1. It declared, in its preamble, that life begins at conception.
2. Hospitals or other taxpayer-supported facilities could not be used for performing abortions that were not necessary to save life, even if public funds were not used.
3. Public employees, including doctors, nurses, and other health care professionals, could not perform or assist in performing abortions, unless they were necessary to save the mothers' lives.
4. Medical tests must be performed on any fetus thought to be at least twenty weeks to determine viability.

U.S. Attorney General Richard Thornburgh agreed that the case presented a good opportunity to take a swipe at *Roe*. Thornburgh, who had been appointed attorney general by Ronald Reagan after the resignation of Edwin Meese (and remained in the post after Bush became President), met the Reagan administration's criteria on abortion. As governor of Pennsylvania Thornburgh had been behind one of the strongest challenges against *Roe* v. *Wade* ever presented. *Thornburgh* v. *American College of Obstetricians and Gynecologists*, which was turned down by the Supreme Court in a narrow 5–4 ruling, was based on a Pennsylvania law that required physicians to warn women about the potential risks of abortions and to provide pregnancy and child care counseling. The studious-looking, mild-mannered Thornburgh could get downright fired up about the subject. "I think there is a societal interest in the preservation of life," he said soon after becoming attorney general. "*Roe* v. *Wade* seems to be an obstacle to that."

Once the *Webster* case had been accepted for review by the Supreme Court, the Justice Department was quick to intervene, filing a friend of the court brief that concluded, "If the Supreme Court is prepared to reconsider *Roe* v. *Wade*, this case presents an appropriate opportunity for doing so." It was this amicus brief that was filed two days after George Bush's election.

WASHINGTON, D.C., April 9, 1989

The Supreme Court justices sit apart from the world of polls and elections. They aren't influenced by the grimy business of American political action. Nor do they hear the voices of the people, or at least that is what they often say. But they are, after all, only human, and being so, they surely could not ignore the storm of events outside their enclosed chambers.

On April 9, 1989, an army of protesters (anywhere from three to six hundred thousand, depending on which count was to be believed) marched on the U.S. Capitol, demanding the preservation of the rights won through the 1973 Supreme Court decision. It was the largest demonstration in Washington's history, and it sent a clear signal that legal abortion was no longer being taken for granted. Many of those who marched were too young to remember a time when abortion had not been legal. But their mothers and grandmothers remembered. The march was an impressive show of force from Middle America, what organizers called the silent majority in support of abortion rights.

Ruth, the eighty-eight-year-old woman from St. Louis, would have given anything to attend the march, but she was ill and could not make the trip. Her daughter, Cynthia, came, however, arriving by train at the cavernous Union Station. Cynthia had seldom been outside Missouri, and she gazed around the historic setting with awe. The first-time visitor perceives a drama about this city that escapes the notice of those who must daily contend with its deadlocked traffic, burgeoning homeless population, and rising crime. Even the buildings have power—or maybe especially the buildings: the Capitol's sturdy dome; the White House, stately behind its fence; the Washington Monument, pointed like a white rocket toward the heavens; the strong pillars of the Lincoln Memorial. As frustrated as Cynthia had grown with the stodgy, slow-moving bureaucracies, she felt respect for the site of America's vision—and close to it. "For the first time I had a sense that this government wasn't abstract," she said later. "It was *me* and all those other people. We, the people."

There was every kind of person represented at the march. Indeed, it seemed that the full spectrum of American life was there—all races, classes, religions, political convictions, and many, many children. Parents walked along pushing baby carriages displaying the sign WANTED BABY. Grandmothers held hands with teenagers. Fathers boosted toddlers onto their shoulders. Family values were in residence in the nation's capital this day. These were people who cared about freedom, who loved their children, who wanted what everyone wants for himself or herself and for loved ones. These were true family values—not the kind found in speeches but the kind found in life.

The army of citizens marched from the Washington Monument, up Constitution Avenue, past the cool pillared silence of the Supreme Court, to the Capitol.

It won't make a difference, said the stone wall of the court. But of course, it would make a difference. It was a wake-up call.

As Cynthia said, shaking her head with the amazement of it, "I am part of something. I have brothers and sisters. It's not just me alone. If only Mother could have been here to see this."

On vacation in Kennebunkport, Maine, President Bush ducked reporters' questions about the march. "No comment," he said from his fishing boat. "We're recreating."

While both sides waited for the Supreme Court hearing, Nancy Klein, a young pregnant woman, lay in a coma in a New York hospital, the victim of an automobile accident. Klein might never know that she had become the subject of one of the most bitter scenarios in the history of abortion rights. Klein's chances of recovery seemed slight, and it was doubtful that she would ever regain consciousness. Nevertheless, her doctors, pulling out all stops to save the young woman, advised her husband that it might improve her chances if the fetus she was carrying were aborted. Martin Klein agreed. North Shore University Hospital required that he receive the court's permission to act as his wife's guardian and approve the abortion, and it might have been a simple matter had it not been for the interference of two anti-abortion activists. John Short and John Broderick appeared before the court to assume guardianship of the fetus and attempt to block the abortion. When the court approved Klein's guardianship, the two men appealed and took the case all the way to the U.S. Supreme Court. While the nation watched in horror, the embattled husband was subjected to numerous stalling tactics from the plaintiffs, even though every moment his wife remained in a coma made the decision more critical. It seemed to many people that this was going too far, and it was not a proud moment for antiabortionists. Eventually Klein won the case, and the abortion took place; but the privacy of the family was severely violated. It would never be known whether the delay made a difference in Nancy Klein's condition, but several months later she emerged from her coma to begin the slow process of recovery. Martin Klein filed a ten-million-dollar suit against the hospital (still pending as of this writing) and the two antiabortionists, charging "intentional or negligent infliction of emotional distress" and violation of his wife's right to an abortion under *Roe* v. *Wade*.

A crowd of noisy demonstrators gathered early on the courtroom steps in the morning of April 26, 1989. It was to be the day of arguments for the *Webster* case, the beginning of a process that could demolish the rights established in 1973.

Inside the courthouse the heavy hand of the Bush administration was apparent in the choice of speakers. The administration had called former Solicitor General Charles Fried to argue the case. He no doubt felt confident that morning since his case was bolstered by substantial authority. In addition to the forty-four amicus curiae briefs from various religious and other friendly groups, Fried had in his possession the Bush administration's brief, which would carry more weight than any of the others.

Fried was the essence of civility and reasonableness as he tried to convince the Court that a favorable decision on *Webster* did not necessarily mean an abandonment of all rights to abortion. As he spoke, his words and demeanor seemed to contradict the intentions of the administration or at least to put a less extreme face on what he was urging the Court to decide.

"We are not asking the Court to unravel the fabric of privacy rights which this court has woven," said Fried. "Rather, we are asking the Court to pull one thread."

Responded Frank Susman, the lawyer representing the Missouri abortion clinics: "It has always been my personal experience that when I pull a thread, my sleeve falls off. It is not a thread he is after. It is the full range of procreational rights and choices."

Susman also had a powerful amicus brief in his hands, submitted by 167 scientists and physicians, including 11 Nobel laureates. The brief disputed the argument that the trimester framework of *Roe* v. *Wade* was on a collision course with medical and technological advancement, stating, "There is no scientific consensus that a human life begins at conception, at a given stage of fetal development, or at birth. The question of 'when a human life begins' cannot be answered by reference to scientific principles. . . . The answer to that question will depend on each individual's social, religious, philosophical, ethical and moral beliefs and values." The brief also noted: "The earliest point of viability remained virtually unchanged at 24 weeks of gestation since 1973, and there is no reason to believe that a change is either imminent or inevitable. . . . Furthermore . . . the capacity for the human thought process as we know it cannot exist until sometime after 28 weeks of gestation."

Fried admitted that the Court could overturn *Roe* if it accepted the premise that life begins at conception. Justices O'Connor and Kennedy seemed uncomfortable with that. They pushed Fried to explain how *Roe* could be overturned (on the basis of his argument) without also overturning the 1965 decision in *Griswold* v. *Connecticut* that recognized the right of privacy and legalized the use of contraceptives.

"Abortion is different," argued Fried. "It involves the purposeful termination, as the Court said, of potential life."

Frank Susman disagreed. "For better or for worse, there no

longer exists any bright line between the fundamental right [to contraception] and the fundamental right of abortion," he said. "These two rights, because of advances in medicine and science, now overlap."

There was no hint of which way the justices would rule on *Webster*, but Charles Fried had reason for confidence as he left the Court that day. Analyzing other cases reviewed that term by the Court, he could cite an unprecedented number that had been decided 5–4, leaving the new Reagan majority victorious over the liberal minority. It was evident to everyone that the Court had taken a sharp conservative turn.

Speculators didn't have to stretch much to surmise that the pro-*Webster* votes in the Court would come from Rehnquist, Kennedy, Scalia, and White, and the anti-*Webster* votes from Blackmun, Brennan, Marshall, and Stevens. But no one was sure how Sandra Day O'Connor would vote.

Two days after the arguments for *Webster* v. *Reproductive Health Services*, the justices gathered in the conference room, beginning their session, by time-honored custom, with a handshake. It was perhaps the last gesture of courtesy if one can judge by the bitterness in their later public statements. But no one would ever know for sure what went on behind those closed doors. Their deliberations were conducted in secrecy, and the final ruling was not to be announced for several months.

It was another noisy scene outside the courthouse on July 3, 1989. Everyone was ready for a decision on *Webster* since it was the last day of the Court session. It turned out to be a morning marred by chaos and confusion, with tempers heightened by the extremely humid midmorning heat. Many had waited all night, hoping to get prized seats inside the courthouse, but most were left standing outside. They chanted, waved coat hangers and placards ("Bush: Get Out of Mine" read one), and displayed the familiar gory pictures of mutilated fetuses. At 10:00 A.M. the nine justices were to file out from behind a red velvet curtain and take their places on the bench.

When the courtroom doors opened and those who had been

inside for the ruling began streaming out, there was no immediate ringing shout of "We won!" or "We lost." No one seemed
sure what the long and convoluted ruling meant. Television reporters flipped through pages, looking for a summary sound
bite. It wasn't until John Wilke, of the National Right to Life
Committee, emerged from the courthouse and gave a thumbs-
up sign that the crowd understood it was a victory for antiabortionists.

But what kind of victory was it?

The first question on everyone's lips was whether or not *Roe*
had been overturned. It hadn't been. In fact, it had remained
intact. But the Court left no doubt that the battle for the right to
abortion was starting all over again. It was plainly dissatisfied
with its own ruling and with the inadequacies of *Webster* as a case
that provided for any precedent-setting decision.

In a narrow decision written by Chief Justice Rehnquist, the
Court upheld the constitutionality of the Missouri law that restricted the availability of publicly funded abortion services, required doctors to test for viability at twenty weeks, and declared
that life begins at the moment of conception. The ruling stopped
short of overturning *Roe* v. *Wade*, but the justices invited states to
present more cases for consideration.

"The goal of constitutional adjudication," said Rehnquist, "is
surely not to remove inexorably 'politically divisive' issues from
the gambit of the legislative process, whereby the people through
their elected representatives deal with matters of concern to
them." He added, in a broad hint regarding the direction he
wanted elected representatives to take, "We do not see why the
state's interest in protecting potential human life should come
into existence only at the point of viability."

Seldom in the Court's history had there been such evidence of
personal bitterness and dissent. The justices, in their elegant
chambers, had always positioned themselves above the fray of
political drama, outside the influence of personal emotion. But
the *Webster* case hit a nerve, and the public caught a glimpse of
what must have been a raging battle inside the hallowed halls and
behind closed doors. The decision was read as 5–4, but in reality

only two justices, White and Kennedy, concurred fully with Rehnquist. O'Connor and Scalia wrote major concerns into the provisions.

The core of the written battle among the judges focused on their avoidance of a reconsideration of *Roe*. Justice O'Connor wrote that there was "no necessity to accept the State's invitation to re-examine the constitutional validity of *Roe* v. *Wade*. Where there is no need to decide a constitutional question, it is a venerable principle of this Court's adjudiciary process not to do so." However, she added ominously, "When the constitutional invalidity of a state's abortion statute actually turns on the constitutional validity of *Roe* v. *Wade*, there will be time enough to re-examine *Roe*. And to do so carefully."

Justice Scalia sounded furious with O'Connor's statement and disgusted with the Court's refusal to reconsider *Roe*. "Justice O'Connor's assertion that a 'fundamental rule of judicial restraint' requires us to avoid reconsidering *Roe* cannot be taken seriously," he wrote. ". . . Of the four courses we might have chosen today—to reaffirm *Roe*, to overrule it explicitly, to overrule it *sub silentio*, or to avoid the question—the last is the least responsible." Leaving his preference no secret, he went on to say, "It thus appears that the mansion of constitutionalized abortion law, constructed overnight in *Roe* v. *Wade*, must be disassembled doorjamb by doorjamb, and never entirely brought down, no matter how wrong it might be." Although several justices seemed inclined to narrow the law established in *Roe*, Scalia remained the only one who was openly in favor of overturning it on the basis of the *Webster* case.

What frustrated Justice Stevens, who wrote a partial dissent, was the portion of the Missouri law that stated life begins at conception. In Stevens's view, the state made an unconstitutional distinction, for such a viewpoint could be substantiated only with religious and moral bases; it did not exist in the secular realm, which, Judge Stevens pointed out, was the place it *must* exist to be declared constitutional. "Indeed," he wrote, "I am persuaded that the absence of any secular purpose for the legislative declarations that life begins at conception and that conception begins at fertilization makes the relevant portion of the preamble invalid . . . the preamble, an unequivocal endorsement of a religious tenet of some but by no means all Christian faiths, serves no identifiable secular purpose."

The strongest dissent came from Justice Blackmun, the author of the Court's decision in *Roe* v. *Wade*. He could barely contain his outrage, writing, "Thus, not with a bang, but a whimper, the plurality discards a landmark case of the last generation and casts into darkness the hopes and visions of every woman in this country who had come to believe that the Constitution guaranteed her the right to exercise some control over her unique ability to bear children." Blackmun seemed to be feeling the shattering impact of the foundations that defined his contribution on the Court and protected millions of women crumbling when he concluded his statement with grave urgency. "For today, at least, the law of abortion stands undisturbed," he wrote. "For today, the women of this nation still retain the liberty to control their destinies. But the signs are evident and very ominous, and a chill wind blows. I dissent."

What observers immediately realized was that the decision represented far more than the support of a law in Missouri. It represented the first real crack in the framework of *Roe* and a clear invitation to state legislators to set in motion new laws to limit the availability of abortions in their states. The Supreme Court seemed ready to roll back *Roe*. It just needed the right opportunity.

The mood outside the courthouse grew confrontational in the aftermath of the decision. Those favoring the *Webster* law were by turns smug, giddy, and elated. The pro-choice advocates, defiant and angry, shouted threats.

But nobody listened to the words anymore or paid much mind to the bobbing coat hangers and brutal photographs. There was too much of the same old anger. The battle was too personal. And all the shouting in the world couldn't even begin to answer the question of what would happen next. But one thing seemed immediately clear: The law as it was ambiguously set forth by the nine justices served only to pit one faction against another in a manner that promised to nurture lawlessness. The *Webster* decision seemed to crystallize a problem in the American judicial system. Rather than settle debates, it set in motion a structure that would lead to an endless series of appeals. Far from being a guiding principle or even a set standard, the law could be tested over and over again—in theory, until it suited each of the 250 million Americans. In the meantime, chaos would prevail.

At the White House Chief of Staff John Sununu read President Bush's statement with satisfaction in his voice: "We welcome this decision. By upholding the Missouri statute, the Court appears to have begun to restore to the people the ability to protect the unborn. We continue to believe that *Roe* v. *Wade* was incorrectly decided and should now be reversed." An observer listening to Sununu's words remarked sardonically, "It's Sisyphus time"—a reference to the mythical character who was doomed to spend eternity pushing a boulder up a hill, only to have it teeter at the top and roll back down.

Later, when the medical community was asked to respond to the twenty-week viability test, it expressed bewilderment. While the Court's ruling clearly indicated its belief that viability was possible at twenty weeks, no experts could be found who had ever heard of a viable twenty-week fetus. In fact, several medical experts pointed out, even in the best medical facilities only about 10 percent of babies born at twenty-three weeks survived.

At issue was the maturity of the lungs. Before twenty-three or twenty-four weeks a fetus's lungs were so underdeveloped that they would have no possibility of functioning properly outside the womb. Furthermore, doctors insisted that the standard lung test given to more mature fetuses would be virtually useless at twenty weeks. In other words, tests for viability at twenty weeks were not only irrelevant but impossible to perform.

ST. LOUIS, MISSOURI, July 4, 1989

The telephone rang in Ruth's house at seven forty-five in the morning.

"Mother, have you seen the news?"

"No. The paper is on the porch, but I just got up."

"Read the paper and call me back." Cynthia's voice sounded unusually tense.

Ruth hung up the phone and walked slowly to the front door. She was using a walker now. Arthritis made the nights unbearable, and the steamy days of the Missouri summer were oppressive.

The newspaper was rolled and placed just inside the screen door, and she bent slowly to pick it up. The entire process of getting the paper and carrying it into the kitchen took five minutes. She poured tea and opened the paper to the front page.

"Oh . . ." she said weakly. She wanted to cry.

Ruth later described the way she felt at that moment: "I was almost ninety years old, and I wanted to leave the world a different place from what it was when I entered it. Just a little better, you know, not anything major. And now, this slippage.

"I felt powerless. Here was this one small change I had participated in, one little thing I was proud of being a part of. And it was wiped out.

"I remember that I felt so old on that day, and God help me, I just wanted to crawl into my grave and pull the dirt over my head. I didn't call my daughter back, and I didn't answer the phone when she called. I just sat there for a good hour until she came and got me. And then we went out for breakfast. It was a very bad day for me. If only it hadn't happened in Missouri."

After *Webster*, a new fervor gripped the pro-choice side. It admitted to having been lazy, complacent, and, because of that, caught off guard. Something else was happening, too, on both sides: an awakening. No single issue since the Vietnam War had managed to capture the public's imagination and will the way abortion seemed to be doing. Activism was back.

The fireworks exploding in local communities across the nation on July 4 were not in all cases related to the celebration of the nation's independence. Some were warning shots lobbed at a government edging ever closer to denying a woman's right to choose abortion.

- In Boston three hundred abortion rights activists clashed with police as they tried to broadcast a message to tens of thousands of people gathered along the Charles River for the July 4 Boston Pops concert.
- In Atlanta five hundred people marched on the Capitol to deliver a stack of coat hangers—the symbol of the back alley abortion era.
- In Minneapolis there was a flamboyant display of outrage and mixed metaphors as abortion rights supporters burned a flag in a topless bar.

There was fury everywhere. A resounding "No!"

And feminism was in vogue again. The feminist movement, characterized by the discomfiting stridency of its early leaders, was due for a revival, and it looked as though abortion might be the issue that would rally the masses and bring women back to a state of urgent consciousness. Finally, here was a real, tangible right that might be in jeopardy—not just the vague refrain of attitudinal inequality. Older women were jolted into a memory of the old days that weren't so good. Younger women grew suddenly aware that something they had always taken for granted was being threatened. "Reproductive freedom *is* a fundamental human right," said Gloria Steinem. "If Patrick Henry, Frederick Douglass and Thomas Jefferson had ever been pregnant against their will, they would have been right there rebelling—and so will we."

In the wake of *Webster*, abortion seemed to push every other issue off the news programs and talk shows. Media stars were born on both sides of the issue, and as often happens in our television-driven society, the messengers became more prominent than their message. The feminist movement, perhaps aware of the need to harness negative energies and appear more mainstream, allowed two women to emerge from the pack to articulate the message in a cool, intelligent way. They were Kate

Michelman, director of the National Abortion Rights Action League (NARAL), and Faye Wattleton, president of Planned Parenthood. The influence of more strident voices, like that of Molly Yard, president of the National Organization for Women, was downplayed.

Kate Michelman was strong and tireless, but her voice remained soft and even, no matter how tense the public debate. The forty-nine-year-old activist and mother maintained a remarkably unflappable air, even when she sat across the table from those who accused her of being a baby murderer. Her style and poise negated the stereotype of the firebrand family-hating feminist. Michelman's appeal was that she was so mainstream; her very presence was a reminder that hard choices are faced by ordinary people. In 1970, when she was thirty years old, Michelman had had an abortion. At the time she had three children and her husband had just left her for another woman. Under those circumstances she chose abortion—not casually, not for "convenience," but, as she saw it then, for the survival of her family. Now, almost twenty years later, Michelman radiated empathy for women like herself as she stared into the hot lights of the camera. And there was a hard edge to her voice as she echoed the imagery of the most famous abortion rights foe George Bush: "To politicians who oppose choice, we say, 'Read our lips. Take our rights. Lose your jobs.' "

Elegant and tightly controlled, Faye Wattleton, forty-five, had movie star good looks, a warm, appealing temperament, and a savvy grasp of the workings of back rooms and high courts. She was perhaps the most effective media presence in the movement; on camera Wattleton never made a mistake. Furthermore, as a black woman she could credibly argue the importance of contraceptive and abortion services in the black community. "The stakes are higher for us as African-American women," she once said. "It will be African-American women who will die first. We suffer disproportionately from poverty. We suffer disproportionately from despair."

Wattleton had deep sympathy for the difficult choices women

had to make, but she had no sympathy for the government's policies. "We must start by telling Mr. Bush that it is not kind and it is not gentle to force a woman to remain pregnant against her will," she said. "Mr. Bush, women are not instruments of the state."

Pro-choice activists let it be known that they were targeting selected 1989 elections in the hopes of demonstrating that any political figure who was opposed to a woman's right to choose— or who was even in the middle on the issue—would be defeated. More than half the states in the country still had long-dormant abortion statutes on the books, and fifteen states had enacted laws (currently unenforceable) since 1973 that were hostile to *Roe*. Abortion rights supporters wanted to make it clear that if these and other states began to revive those laws, legislators would face ouster at the polls. But it remained to be seen whether or not the threat could be backed up with results.

What did people really believe about abortion?

Would they vote a single issue, *this* single issue?

Could the organized activism of the antiabortionists be matched and exceeded?

They were about to find out.

The ink was barely dry on the *Webster* decision when the opinion polls, the mainstay of American politics, began cranking out the results.

- In Virginia the Mason-Dixon poll found that 40 percent of voters would cross party lines to vote for a pro-choice candidate.
- In Florida the Mason-Dixon poll revealed a 71 percent support for current or relaxed laws, and 65 percent opposed a legislative session on abortion.
- In California the Field poll indicated that abortion would be "pivotal" in the 1990 elections, with the San Francisco *Chronicle* reporting "the greatest detriment to candidates who take an anti-abortion position."
- In Massachusetts the KRC Communications poll showed

that 62 percent of registered voters would not support a
candidate for governor whose position on abortion was
substantially different from their own.
- In New Jersey the Bergen *Record* reported that 57 percent
of the population supported legal abortion without restriction.
- A national poll conducted by *Time* magazine and CNN
found that 32 percent of respondents said they would
"never vote for any candidate who would restrict wom-
en's rights to have an abortion."

It appeared that the public was more ambivalent about abortion than either of the two sides would like to admit. Even so,
polls reflected a national discomfort with government interference in the private matters of individuals, and in this sense there
was a pro-choice edge.

But the antiabortion forces were not standing still. They continued to organize and, where necessary, to put a brave spin on
the sudden power of their opponents. An editorial in the *National
Right to Life News* insisted defensively:

We are being tested right now, and I believe for a very good
reason. Paradoxically, we *needed* to have everything but the
kitchen sink thrown at us now—now before the Court over-
turns *Roe*. We *needed* to be toughened. We *needed* to fully
grasp the lengths to which the media will go to protect
abortion on demand. We *needed* to have candidates learn—
admittedly the hard way—that what works is not to hide
their pro-life views under a bushel, but to let them shine.
We *needed* to have the significance of every pro-abortion step
"forward" wildly exaggerated if, for nothing else, than to
teach us how to handle the distortion and the hype. Finally
we *needed* to learn yet again not to take our cues from the
media, but rather to trust in our own instincts and the
innate decency of the American people, properly educated.
We've done well, post-*Webster*, learning invaluable lessons,

which will serve us well in the years to come. Personally, I can't wait for 1990.

While the nation was still reacting to the broader implications of the *Webster* decision, in Missouri things had grown more specific. The immediate impact was to make abortions more expensive for most women and all but impossible to obtain in hospitals. The first post-*Webster* case involved a twenty-four-year-old woman who was refused an abortion at the Truman Medical Center in Kansas City, Missouri, and had to go to the state of Kansas to obtain it. Her circumstances were particularly heartbreaking. The fetus she carried could never have been born alive since its heart was outside the chest wall and its abdominal organs were outside the abdominal wall. Nevertheless, by Missouri law she might have been forced to carry a dead baby to term.

KANSAS CITY, MISSOURI, August 1989

Loretta Farrar, thirty, was pregnant when she was convicted of forgery and sentenced to prison. She was not scheduled for release until 1991. To pro-choice lawyer Michael Box, her case represented the perfect opportunity to test the Missouri law in an unconventional way. Box, who called himself "your basic long-haired liberal strict constructionist," was accustomed to employing guerrilla tactics to jam up the machinery of rigid, inhumane laws. And that was his opinion of the preamble to the Missouri law. Box figured that if they wanted to pass into law that life began at conception, he'd hold them to it.

Box brought Farrar's case before the federal district court in Kansas City, where he argued that by jailing Farrar, the state was unlawfully holding her fetus hostage. The fetus, he pointed out, had not been charged with a crime, received counsel, been granted a trial (by a jury of its peers), or been sentenced. "The state of Missouri says that fetuses are persons," Box said. "You've got somebody in prison for the crime of another person. The 13th Amendment says you can't do that. The fetuses should be treated as persons and should not be put in prison without a trial. The fetus should not serve a sentence for the mother." Box called for the state either to release Farrar or to provide a site where she could receive special prenatal care. The suit was filed on behalf of twenty-five pregnant women currently residing in Missouri prisons.

Box was taking a chance with this approach that worried some pro-choice advocates since it forced the court to address fetal personhood in a direct way that could backfire. But Box was adamant that the courts should be asked to deal with the practical consequences of their broad decisions.

Antiabortion attorneys scoffed at Box's approach. "It's silly . . . the fetus has no 'liberty interest.' It doesn't matter where the womb is," said one attorney with disgust. But Box disagreed. If the fetus was a person, it had a liberty interest.

Box and other Missouri attorneys, intent upon challenging the law, had other cases in the works as well, centered on age and rights. When does life begin? they asked rhetorically. If at conception, did that mean every citizen must add nine months to his or her life? Did it mean that fetuses should be registered in the census? What entitlements did fetuses have? If the attorneys' arguments were valid, it was clear that the introduction of fetal rights could wreak havoc on a whole host of laws.

Box knew that few, if any, of his cases would ever be successful, but he looked ahead to the total picture. Maybe he could drive them crazy. Maybe he could make the life-begins-at-conception premise so absurd, so unwieldly, that it could not possibly be enforced.

Symbolic victories have their place in the lore of political action. And they force a level of consciousness that is not available on the traditional fronts, so in that respect Box's work was not in vain. But there was no doubt that the real battle would be waged in the legislatures, as state by state, the move was on to demolish *Roe* v. *Wade*.

SEVEN

A Bang and a Whimper

Pro-lifers are practically alone in opposing the culture of annihilation. It is an awesome responsibility. We are fighting not only most of the powerful
institutions in this nation . . . but the Spirit of the
Age. There is adrift in the land almost a compul-
sion to kill, fed by a sense that nothing and nobody
will ever be allowed to get in our way. To turn that
around is an overwhelming challenge, one so daunting that only the most hardy will even try to take
up, much less persevere until victory is won."
—DAVE ANDRUSKO, *Right to Life News*

"Pregnant women are too confused to make a rational decision
about whether or not to have an abortion." That was the opinion
of Florida Republican Craig T. James, and it seemed to be a view
that was shared by at least one man, Florida Governor Bob
Martinez. Two days after the Supreme Court delivered the *Webster* decision, Martinez announced that he would call a special
session of the legislature to enact new abortion restrictions.

With the momentum seeming to be in the antiabortion camp,
Martinez perhaps believed he had nothing to lose and everything
to gain from taking an aggressive stand. It wasn't irrelevant that
he would be up for reelection the following year. He was ex-
pecting a tough fight, and he needed a rallying issue.

Bob Martinez was a smart politician who had changed his

party affiliation from Democrat to Republican in 1983, when he decided to run for governor. He judged his conservatism to be out of line with the Democratic party and saw little likelihood that he would be nominated under its banner. However, this made him an attractive candidate for the Republicans. He won their nomination and was elected governor. But his tenure had been an embattled one, and his once-strong image had developed many cracks. So when the Supreme Court handed down its decision on *Webster*, Martinez saw a chance to enhance his stature as a courageous leader and tough administrator.

Eager to cooperate with the apparent trend toward limiting abortion rights, Governor Martinez quickly called a special three-and-a-half-day session of the legislature to consider a series of proposals, partially based on a model developed by the National Right to Life Committee. These included banning public financing and use of public resources for abortions, expanding regulations for abortion clinics, requiring tests for fetal viability at twenty weeks, and requiring physicians to educate women about fetal development when they sought abortions.

The special session was to convene in October 1989.

People started arriving the day before the session, clogging the highways and bus and train stations, their signs and banners fighting for notice in the frenzy:

STOP KILLING BABIES
ABORT MARTINEZ IN THE SECOND TERM!
A FEW CELLS DO NOT A PERSON MAKE
WANTED KIDS ARE HAPPY KIDS
ABORTION IS PREMEDITATED MURDER
THANKS, MOM—I LOVE LIFE!

On the morning of October 10 there were some ten thousand people gathered in front of the Capitol, their noisy chants sometimes drowned out by the buzz of a plane overhead which trailed a banner, "Proud to be Pro-Choice."

It was the opening day of Martinez's special session. He had reason to be nervous; by now he realized that he might have underestimated the passion and size of the opposition. In the weeks preceding the session, pro-choice advocates had descended upon Florida en masse, bombarding the airwaves with advertising designed to counter the accusation that they were "pro-abortion," reframing the question to "Who has the right to make this choice?"

Nevertheless, all the signs were there that the state senate might take kindly to the Martinez plan. Florida legislators had never been shy about establishing abortion restrictions. The previous year they had passed a bill (later struck down by the Florida Supreme Court) requiring minor girls to have parental consent before undergoing abortions.

But by the end of the first day of the special session it was all over but the shouting. Concerned about the political consequences as well as the constitutionality of the proposed abortion restrictions, the senate killed four of Martinez's proposals and appeared ready to turn down the fifth.

A funereal mood gripped the crowd of Martinez supporters waiting outside when they heard the decision. They sang "Onward Christian Soldiers." They cried. Martinez walked out onto the steps of the Capitol, his face haggard and filled with disappointment. But his voice was strong. It rose up amid the clamor. "I stand with you," he shouted emotionally. "I stand with you because you are the voices of the unheard, those who have rights but no one has listened." The crowd cheered. It seemed like a fine moment for Martinez, a strong moment, but in truth the defeat cost him dearly.

Later the Monday morning quarterbacks talked about Martinez's fatal blunder in being so quick to call a special session without being fully confident of support. His aggressive move, calculated to make him look strong and commanding, only emphasized his growing weakness.

Governor William P. Clements, Jr., of Texas, was no doubt watching Martinez's folly with more than academic interest.

Governor Clements had earlier promised that Texas "can bet on" a special session in the Texas legislature after the *Webster* ruling. Under Texas law, the governor sets the agendas for special sessions, and two were already planned—one regarding workers' compensation and one on school financing.

But after Florida, Clements's press secretary announced that there was no plan to consider abortion in either of those sessions, nor was there a plan to call a third session for that purpose. Governor Clements decided to wait and see how the other states acted.

Enthusiastically accepting the High Court's invitation to reconsider abortion on the state level, legislatures in many states started the wheels turning. Antiabortionist organizers formulated a two-part agenda. The first was to work for the passage of restrictions on a state-by-state level. But the deeper agenda was to find, within the myriad laws of individual states, the definitive case that could be carried to the Supreme Court. Experience had shown that even those justices who leaned toward limiting or overturning abortion rights would not do so unless a case touched directly on the issues raised in *Roe*—specifically the murky matter of fetal viability and the constitutional right to privacy.

BOISE, IDAHO, March 1990

Idaho is the kind of place people mean when they talk about returning to the land. Its beauty is great and rare, combining the best elements of the glorious Pacific Northwest.

The attitudes of the people are shaped by a rock-hard pride and independence. Folks don't put much store by government interference here but accept it as a necessary evil. Their chief concern is how to keep the hordes of new arrivals down. Many people grumble that Idaho has had more than its fair share of Vietnamese refugees spilling in from the West and urban-blighted would-be farmers spilling in from the East. Signs go up every once in a while: IDAHO: A NICE PLACE TO VISIT . . . BUT

PLEASE DON'T STAY. The influx of more liberal outsiders is distressing to residents, who fear that the moral climate might go the way of other states, usurped by people who have nothing to believe in.

National antiabortion activists who spotted Idaho as the ideal location from which to launch a "pure" Supreme Court test on abortion might have reconsidered had they realized how firmly entrenched this distaste for outsiders—indeed, for a national agenda—was. Idahoans may have leaned against abortion, but they were not the kind of people who aligned themselves with causes.

They might also have thought twice if they had taken time to study Governor Cecil D. Andrus and learned a little bit about the character of their antiabortion friend. Andrus was Idaho to the core, meaning that although the fifty-eight-year-old Democrat was solidly opposed to abortion, he was also an independent man who had traditionally tangled with people who thought they were his friends. In one especially revealing case Andrus, an avid fisherman and hunter, referred to the National Rifle Association as the "gun nuts of the world."

Andrus saw it as his mandate to promote and protect the image of the independent westerner. He held a fierce emotional attachment to his Northwest roots, and he aimed to see that it remained untouched.

But the outsiders didn't see it, and they set out for Idaho to make their point and to use a flawed system to build the law as they thought it should be. They carefully fashioned a bill that they believed could provide the test to overturn *Roe*. They thought they knew where the governor stood. After all, he had endorsed a law in the mid-seventies that would go into effect if *Roe* were overturned, a law that would carry a prison term for women who received abortions. And that's about as hard-line as they come.

Legislators in Idaho refashioned the old antiabortion bill, arriving at a contemporary version.
Abortion would be allowed only:

- In cases of rape if the victim reported the crime to authorities within seven days
- In cases of incest if the victim was under age eighteen and reported the incest before the abortion
- In cases of "profound" fetal deformity, based on the judgment of a doctor
- In cases in which a physician testified that the physical (not mental) health of a woman was in peril

Doctors performing abortions outside these parameters could be sentenced to ten years in prison at hard labor, be fined ten thousand dollars, and be subject to lawsuits by the father, the woman's parents, or anyone else with legitimate standing in the matter. A woman who tried to self-abort could be fined ten thousand dollars.

The bill was tailor-made for the Supreme Court since it purely addressed the central issue of right to life at conception. Conservative Idaho looked like the ideal setting. The legislators seemed to agree, and passed House Bill 625.

If the bill was signed into law, it was estimated that 95 percent of the approximately 1,650 abortions performed in Idaho each year would be outlawed.

The governor had three choices: He could sign the bill, he could veto the bill, or he could let it become law without his signature. Everyone thought he would sign it.

As Andrus grappled with the implications of the strictest abortion bill on record and consulted constitutional scholars on both sides of the issue, pro- and antichoice forces descended on the state, carving their battle lines across its lush landscape.

A key tactic of the pro-choice activists was to threaten repercussions—not just the traditional ballot box variety but economically as well. They dumped ten thousand pounds of potatoes on the Capitol steps, declaring that if Andrus signed the bill, they would stage a boycott that would cripple the state's $650 million potato industry.

Antichoice forces countered by promising that they would render the boycott ineffective by urging people who supported life to buy more potatoes. Signs appeared outside the Capitol: IF YOU LOVE LIFE, EAT IDAHO POTATOES and PRO LIFE, PRO SPUD!

Some of the legislators who had eagerly signed the bill admitted to being shocked by the promise of economic repercussions. It hadn't occurred to them that there might be a tangible price to pay for casting their votes.

Meanwhile, Andrus let it be known that he was struggling with the bill—from both a constitutional and a humane perspective. "I am concerned," he said, "that this bill may narrow it to the point where a woman who has suffered rape, incest or a threat to her life might be unable to receive an abortion. Basically, that's what I'm agonizing over."

On the day he was to announce his decision on House Bill 625, Governor Andrus received a transoceanic call from Calcutta. In a last-ditch effort to summon the biggest guns available, Right to Life field coordinator Scott Fischbach had arranged a linkup with Mother Teresa herself. The call came through. Mother Teresa was waiting on the other end. Andrus's personal secretary took the call and regretfully informed Fischbach that the governor would not be available that day for any calls or letters.

Even from Mother Teresa?

Yes, even from Mother Teresa.

Vetoing the bill later that day, Andrus acknowledged that he had trouble with the strictness required in reporting rape and incest. "The bill is drawn so narrowly that it would punitively and without compassion further harm an Idaho woman who may find herself in the horrible, unthinkable position of confronting a pregnancy that resulted from rape or incest," he said. "This law would force the woman to compound the tragedy of rape. On the eighth day, she ceases to be the victim and becomes a criminal."

Then, turning his attention to the slick national advocates who had designed the bill for Idaho, the governor spoke of his extreme distaste for the way the bill was railroaded through his state.

The bill, he said, "was conceived outside our state for the sole purpose of getting this issue back before the Supreme Court. I believe, and am confident the people of Idaho believe, that we can make our own judgments on this terribly important issue. Somebody thought Idaho looks like a patsy. I submit to you: Idaho is not a patsy."

In virtually every state across the country, right-to-lifers were organizing challenges to abortion rights.

In Illinois abortion clinic officials, with the support of the ACLU, challenged laws that required clinics to meet strict new licensing and performance standards, similar to those required in hospitals. The regulations would place a heavy burden on clinics, which would have to purchase expensive new equipment and hire additional staff in order to remain in operation. The regulations, which had been passed by the state legislature in 1978, were unenforceable prior to *Webster*. But with new permission to explore the limits of state control, the legislature dusted them off and attempted to enforce them. The immediate result was a court challenge by Richard Ragsdale, a Rockford physician. When the lower courts ruled in favor of Ragsdale, Attorney General Neil Hartigan vowed to take the case as high as it would go. He filed for, and was accepted for, a hearing by the Supreme Court, but only two weeks before the hearing (and in the midst of a gubernatorial run) Hartigan changed his mind and settled the case out of court. The settlement was a long way from the original law, stipulating only that clinics receive quarterly inspections from the Department of Public Health to assure that health regulations were being upheld.

The watered-down compromise distressed antiabortionists, who had seen the regulations as the ideal opportunity to encourage the Court to set up severe restrictions for abortion clinics. They felt betrayed by their former ally. James Bopp, Jr., the National Right to Life Committee counsel, complained: "In effect, Hartigan snatched defeat from the jaws of victory." But by now deeply involved in his campaign for governor, Hartigan was furiously wriggling away from his antichoice position. The politics of abortion had hit home, and for the first time it was beginning to dawn on candidates exactly how much was at stake.

But in state capitols across the nation legislators continued to push for statutes that would limit the accessibility of abortion.

In Wisconsin, where more Democratic legislators than Republicans were antichoice, a 1990 parental consent bill was passed by the state assembly and senate.

In Michigan Governor James Blanchard vetoed a measure that would require parental notification by teenagers seeking abortions, leading right-to-life organizers to stage a petition drive to put the matter on the ballot in the November election.

In Indiana the senate defeated legislation that would have banned most abortions in public hospitals.

In Maryland legislators rejected an effort by antiabortion members to introduce a bill that would restrict abortions in the state, while at the same time refusing to consider a bill that would guarantee access to abortion.

In New Hampshire the legislature passed a largely symbolic bill, the first of its kind, which ensured legal abortions until fetal viability. Republican Governor Judd Gregg vetoed the bill, saying, "The bill authorizes abortion for convenience, sex selection, as a form of birth control and with or without parental notification or consent in the case of a minor." Gregg said he vetoed the bill because it was his obligation to protect life.

GUAM, *March 1990*

Guam is a tiny island that most Americans would be hard pressed to find on a map, a tropical tag-on to United States territories. World War II veterans of the Pacific might remember it and perhaps weep again for the victory it symbolized, but others would puzzle at finding Guam in the news in such a big way. The 212-square-mile island, which was 6,000 miles from California, was legally bound by United States law, but it was an unexpected location for one of the most rigorous antiabortion efforts to follow *Webster*.

On March 19 Joseph F. Ada, the Catholic governor in this

predominantly Catholic territory, signed into law the most restrictive abortion legislation ever devised in the United States. "The question for me really boils down to one simple point," he said. "In my heart, I believe a fetus is a human being."

The law prohibited all abortions except when the mother's life was in danger. That danger would have to be established by two physicians, and their decision would be subjected to review by the Medical Licensure Board. The law made it a third-degree felony to perform an abortion or help in the procedure, a misdemeanor for a woman to solicit or have an abortion, and a misdemeanor for a person to solicit a woman to have an abortion.

Prior to the vote by the legislature, Archbishop Anthony Apuron said threateningly in a television interview that he was prepared to excommunicate any Roman Catholic legislator who voted against the bill. All but one legislator were Catholic.

One provision of the bill, regarding "solicitation"—an unfortunate choice of words—seemed to harken back to the days when Margaret Sanger was jailed for talking about birth control. Janet Benshoof could not let that provision stand without a challenge. The dedicated forty-two-year-old lawyer for the American Civil Liberties Union had flown to Guam to urge Ada not to sign the bill into law, but she was denied a hearing. So Benshoof waited around, anxiously killing time in what under other circumstances would seem a tropical paradise. The day after Governor Ada signed the bill, she spoke to the Guam Press Club, announcing, "Women who are pregnant, seeking an abortion, should leave the island. I encourage them to go to Honolulu." She then proceeded to read the phone number of an abortion clinic in Honolulu.

Was Benshoof's action solicitation or free speech that was protected by the First Amendment?

Solicitation, according to authorities, who arraigned Benshoof the following day. She faced a possible fine of one thousand dollars and a year in jail for speaking out in favor of a woman's right to seek abortion.

Suddenly there was a chill in the humid air. Although charges against Benshoof were later dropped, she and others vowed to fight the new law. A week later, on behalf of the American Civil

Liberties Union, Benshoof filed a lawsuit whose plaintiffs included "Mary Doe," who was eight weeks pregnant and wanted an abortion; the Guam Society of Obstetricians and Gynecologists; the Guam Nurses Association; an Episcopal priest; and three doctors. In the lawsuit she maintained that the new law violated constitutional guarantees of right to privacy, due process, free speech, equal protection, religious freedom, and freedom from slavery. The court placed a restraining order on enforcement of the abortion restrictions until the case could be appealed.

In August 1990 a federal district judge ruled that Guam's law was unconstitutional. In striking down the law, Judge Alex Munsun said, "After the emotionalism and stridency of the opposing views are stripped away, the strict legal issue before the court is not one difficult of resolution."

If appealed, the case could ultimately land in the Supreme Court, and it just might be the case that the Reagan-Bush Court was waiting for.

BATON ROUGE, LOUISIANA, June 1990

Robin Rothrock, president of the League of Women Voters in Louisiana, was disgusted. "Only in Louisiana," she said, "could a flag burning bill become a criminal abortion bill."

It was either a dramatically symbolic or a dramatically silly moment in legislative history. Maybe both. In any case, pro-choice advocates were deeply disturbed by the Louisiana trend. The ACLU's Janet Benshoof remarked sadly, "Rehnquist said in the *Webster* case he didn't think the states would lead us back to the Dark Ages, but he forgot about Louisiana."

Initially, Louisiana legislators figured, why bother writing a new bill when the old one, from 1885, was still on the books? But a panel of federal judges ruled that the state could not resume enforcement of the old law since it had been superseded by more recent laws.

The new bill, drawn up by State Representative Louis Jenkins, was, like the one vetoed in Idaho, designed to serve as a test for the Court. It was the most severely restrictive law written to date, leaving no exception for rape or incest and imposing penalties of up to ten years in prison at hard labor and fines of one hundred thousand dollars for those performing abortions. On June 26 the bill passed in the senate by a vote of 24 to 5 but was vetoed by Governor Buddy Roemer as being too restrictive. He indicated that he would not sign a bill that did not include provisions for rape and incest. "Women," he said, "cannot and should not be forced to bear the consequences of these traumatic, illegal acts."

What happened next was a sterling example of convoluted political maneuvering.

Within hours of the veto the Louisiana house of representatives voted 73 to 31 to override it—the first time in this century that either house had voted to override the veto of a Louisiana governor.

But the tally in the Senate was less optimistic. Antiabortion senators saw that they were three votes short of being able to override the veto, and they decided not to try.

Instead they attached a new abortion bill, which included provisions for rape and incest, to a separate piece of legislation. Thus a flag burning bill was amended to become an antiabortion bill. The original bill, calling for a twenty-five-dollar fine for people who assaulted flag burners, became a bill that called for sentences of up to ten years at "hard labor" and fines of up to a hundred thousand dollars for the physicians who performed abortions in the state. The gutted and repasted bill passed both houses of the legislature and was sent to Roemer for his signature.

The politics of abortion on the state level were growing less easy to track. Strongly antiabortion governors were making surprising choices when push came to shove, and Buddy Roemer proved to be yet another unpredictable voice in the abortion battle. A populist and Reagan Democrat, Roemer was one of the new breed of southern Democrats whose party loyalty was not conventionally liberal.

Even with the new provisions in the bill, Roemer was having

trouble with the language. The main sticking point was the rape provision. The governor had requested a thirty-day reporting period, but the new bill allowed only seven days for a woman to report rape in order to qualify for a legal abortion. During that same period the woman was required to have sought medical care from a licensed physician "to preclude pregnancy"—a stipulation whose meaning was unclear since pregnancy was impossible to detect within one week of conception.

Roemer, who frequently referred to himself as pro-life, was eager to restrict abortion, but after reviewing the flag burning-turned-abortion bill, he decided he could not sign it. Rape, he explained, "is treated unevenly and unsatisfactorily." But he added, "This veto should not end the debate." It wasn't likely that it would.

For the first time politicians were starting to feel the heat on abortion. So much so that some formerly outspoken anti-abortion legislators were privately admitting that the "victory" they had achieved on the *Webster* case might be backfiring.

The results of post-*Webster* state elections were telling the tale most vividly. From the most obscure small-town elections to those that were nationally tracked in the press, it was becoming increasingly clear that being staunchly antichoice might be a fatal liability.

In New Jersey, a heavily ethnic and Roman Catholic state, Republican gubernatorial candidate Jim Courter might have expected his antiabortion rhetoric to gain popular approval. But it was Democratic pro-choice candidate Jim Florio who seemed to be gaining from the issue. The New Jersey race was widely viewed as a test case for the national political stage. By the last weeks of the campaign Florio had Courter crying uncle on abortion. Courter, who had stressed his opposition to abortion in the Republican primary and had consistently voted to restrict abortion rights during his eleven years in Congress, began to backtrack in the last weeks of the campaign, when it was too late for him to present himself with credibility as a supporter of a woman's right to choose.

Ironically, Courter's flip-flop during the campaign effectively shielded Florio from criticism on the same count. Once a passionate right-to-lifer who was a volunteer with the Right to Life Speakers Bureau, Florio had switched positions in the 1970's. But pro-choicers did not consider Florio's change of heart to be pragmatically motivated, and he had maintained his revised position for so long that it had ceased being an issue—especially since his opponent was making all the headlines as he publicly debated his own conscience rather than his opponent. Florio's ultimate victory was hailed as a victory for the pro-choice side and a warning to elected officials that voters might be prepared to go down to the wire on this single issue in future elections.

In Virginia Democrat L. Douglas Wilder, who built his campaign around his support of abortion rights, won the election for governor against his antichoice Republican opponent, Marshall Coleman. In a flurry of advertising shortly before the election, Wilder made this single issue that crossed party lines the cornerstone of his appeal. "In the past, I have voted Republican," said a woman in one of his television commercials. "But this November I'm voting for Doug Wilder. Marshall Coleman wants to take away the right of a woman to choose, even for poor women who are the victim of rape and incest." It worked. Most postelection commentators credited abortion for providing the critical edge in Wilder's victory.

In the nationally watched 1989 New York City mayoral race, Democrat David Dinkins minced no words on his complete support of the prochoice position, while his Republican opponent, Rudolph Giuliani, stumbled through shifting positions in search of a popular view. In the past Giuliani had stressed his personal opposition to abortion and criticized *Roe* v. *Wade.* But it was not the kind of position that would fly well in the liberal stronghold of New York. He first tried to suggest that abortion was not a city concern, calling it a "silly, irrelevant" issue for a mayoral campaign. But embarrassed by the appalled reaction to this careless choice of words, he turned about-face and declared his new support for a woman's right to choose. Giuliani's revised stand was less than convincing. The issue dogged him throughout the campaign and could have been partially responsible for a Dinkins victory.

Little more than six months after the mayoral election, Pierre Rinfret, the New York Republican selected to run in the gubernatorial election against Mario Cuomo, the popular pro-choice governor, was quick to declare himself pro-choice, thus setting the stage for an unprecedented move by state Republicans to adopt a pro-choice platform—a significant break with George Bush and the national GOP.

Antiabortion politics had always played well in Iowa, where right-to-lifers had waged successful campaigns in the past. But as the state geared up for the 1990 gubernatorial and senate elections, officials who were formally outspoken against abortion were keeping their heads down as they scurried for a more middle-of-the-road position.

In Massachusetts a bitter gubernatorial race was shaping up in both parties on the basis of the abortion issue. Democrats planning for a runoff to secure Governor Michael Dukakis's job included Lieutenant Governor Evelyn Murphy, who was unwaveringly pro-choice, and former state Attorney General Francis Bellotti, the father of twelve children, whose wife was active in the right-to-life movement. Republican contender William F. Weld, who once worked for Attorney General Edwin Meese, was preparing to test the idea that what he called a modified pro-choice position could be adopted in a state where public opinion overwhelmingly favored choice. Weld believed there were compromises that could be made on the issue, but the public hardly seemed in a mood to compromise.

As the primary neared and the evidence of the polls became clear, Bellotti did an about-face, declaring that he was pro-choice, including being in favor of Medicaid funding for abortions. If political expediency precipitated this change of heart, it did not reach his wife, who continued her active involvement in right-to-life groups. Ultimately, his change of heart did no good. Democratic voters, disillusioned by the actions of the political establishment, nominated John R. Silber, president of Boston University, and a party outsider. During the campaign between

Silber and Weld, abortion faded as an issue, and the economic future of the state took center stage.

HARRISBURG, PENNSYLVANIA, October 1989

Pennsylvania has always been an anomaly in the liberal eastern bloc of states. Progressive and sophisticated in its urban areas, it is powerfully conservative elsewhere, its politics shaped by the Pennsylvania Dutch tradition. The concept of old-fashioned family values sells well here; Pennsylvania has long had one of the most restrictive sets of divorce laws in the country. And after the *Webster* decision legislators were eager to step to the front of the line on enacting stricter abortion legislation.

Pennsylvania legislators were activist on the subject of abortion, having passed eight antiabortion measures since *Roe* v. *Wade*. Although all but one (which banned Medicaid financing of abortions except in cases of rape, incest, or threat to a woman's life) had been overturned, the legislators were determined to reflect conservative public opinion on the issue. Unlike the case in most other states, in Pennsylvania the issue bled across party lines, with the most vehement antiabortion officials, including Governor Robert P. Casey, being Democrats.

The bill that was developed was called the Abortion Control Act of 1989 and was faithful to the model presented by the National Right to Life Committee. It proposed that abortion would be prohibited:

- For sex selection.
- After twenty-four weeks unless three physicians determined that a woman's life was in danger. In that case the physician performing the abortion was required to use a procedure that would provide the best chance for a live birth.
- At public hospitals except in the case of rape or incest or to save a mother's life.

Further regulations would limit the availability of abortions:

- A woman seeking an abortion would have to inform her husband except when the pregnancy resulted from spousal rape; when the woman's husband was not the father; when the husband could not be found; or when the disclosure would put the woman in danger of physical harm.
- Medical personnel would have to advise a woman seeking an abortion about the development of the fetus, risks of abortion, and alternatives. There would then be a twenty-four-hour waiting period before the abortion would be allowed.
- Nontherapeutic medical experiments on a fetus in the womb and the use of fetal tissues or organs would be barred.
- Medical personnel who violated the restrictions would be subject to criminal penalties. Women would not be held liable.

It was a particularly cynical bill, suggesting, among other things, that women were seeking abortions for reasons like sex selection and placing them in a position where they might have to prove spousal rape or paternity in court.

The state legislature's pro-choice strategist, Democrat Karen Ritter, scoffed at the sex selection provision. "I don't know of anybody who has an abortion on that basis in this country, unlike in India, where the aborting of female fetuses has been documented," she said, adding, "It's thought police." And Kathryn Kolbert, of the American Civil Liberties Union, raised one disturbing implication of the law. "Would any woman who knows the sex of her fetus be liable for questioning by authorities?" she wondered.

There was little room for optimism among pro-choice advocates. "Antiabortion bills move through the Pennsylvania legislature like hot knives through butter," one lobbyist observed wryly.

It would be about that easy. The bill slid through the house by a vote of 143 to 58 and through the senate by a vote of 33 to 17. In November Governor Casey signed it into law.

But it did not end there. In 1990, an election year, nearly all the 229 legislative races, plus the statewide races, would pit pro-choice and antiabortion candidates against each other in what promised to be a referendum on the most volatile single issue in Pennsylvania politics. Those who had so blithely raised the abortion restriction banner had reason to be unnerved as they checked the polls, which showed that nearly two thirds of Pennsylvanians were concerned that women might lose the right to have abortions. Even State Representative Stephen F. Freind, the fearless champion of the state's antiabortion policies and one of the sponsors of the restrictive legislation, was toning down his rhetoric in the face of the most serious challenge of his career, from pro-choice candidate Ellen Fisher. Freind was a favorite target of pro-choice activists who were eager to make an example of their most outspoken opponents.

In August 1990 a federal district judge struck down several of the new antiabortion law's provisions, declaring them unconstitutional. The portions of the law set aside included the requirements that a married woman inform her husband before seeking an abortion, that women listen to state-prepared talks from doctors about the relative risks and benefits of childbirth and abortion, and that women wait twenty-four hours after the talk before obtaining abortions. The judge also ruled unconstitutional the provision that a minor could only obtain an abortion with the consent of a parent twenty-four hours after the parent had heard the state-prepared lecture. Left intact was the provision that abortions were illegal for sex selection and that abortion was illegal after twenty-four weeks except to save the life of the mother.

It was a bittersweet victory for the pro-choice forces because immediately after the ruling Pennsylvania Attorney General Ernest Preate, Jr., announced that his office would appeal the decision, establishing the possibility that the Pennsylvania law would form the basis for a serious Supreme Court challenge. Many people believed that the law would provide the Court with a perfect opportunity to examine further the core issues of right to privacy and fetal rights, issues that could lead to an upset of *Roe* v. *Wade*.

In making his ruling, Judge Daniel H. Huyett wrote ominously: "What the future holds is uncertain. But one thing must be evident. Individuals can no longer feel as secure with the protections provided by the judiciary in this area. Instead, a woman's privacy rights and individual autonomy may soon be subjected to the vicissitudes of the legislative process."

For the time being the rights of women to have abortions in Pennsylvania were practically untouched (when one considered that no case of abortion for sex selection had ever been seen, and it was rare except in life-threatening circumstances for women to seek abortions after twenty-four weeks). But as the attorney general's office prepared its appeal, the wind was once again blowing in the direction of the Supreme Court, where the nine justices stood ready to consider the case that might allow them to reverse *Roe* v. *Wade*. The rights temporarily returned to the women of Pennsylvania might, as a result of Judge Huyett's decision, become the avenue for denying those same rights to every woman across the land.

EIGHT

Hellfire and Brimstone

What is a woman to think? That when life is in the hands of a woman, then to destroy it is always morally wrong, never to be condoned, always a grave and unusual evil? But when life is in the hands of men . . . then destruction can be theologized, and some people's needs and lives can be made more important than other people's needs and lives?

—SISTER JOAN CHITTISTER, speaking about the
arms race

The last place Mario Cuomo wanted to find himself was at odds with the church he loved so dearly. Unlike many public figures who flaunted their religious convictions but rarely appeared inside a church, the New York governor was a deeply devout, practicing Catholic whose struggle with theology in the modern world seemed authentic.

Cuomo was born in 1932 in Jamaica, Queens, a working-class neighborhood in New York City that boasted a United Nations flavor. His Italian immigrant family lived side by side with Irish, Jewish, and Polish families, many of them first- and second-generation immigrants. The American dream may have seemed a simpler concept then—more tangible. Cuomo's parents owned a small store where they put their children to work after school. They worked hard and lived frugally; their goal was to provide their children with the education and opportunities that they had never had themselves. Many years later Mario Cuomo paid tribute to their dream; standing in front of the 1984 Democratic Convention, he marveled that he, the son of working-class Italian immigrants, could grow up to become governor of the great state of New York.

As a young boy Cuomo was intellectually precocious and fascinated by the world of the mind. He was also very religious, and like many young Catholic boys of that era, he served as an altar boy. The Catholic mass was dazzling then—full of ritual and ceremony and cloaked in mystery with the use of a language that everyone knew by heart but few understood. At one point, Cuomo considered entering the priesthood; instead he chose the secular commitment of the law and government. He later compared the two, saying, "Politics is the highest calling after the religious vocation, because the business of politics and government is to distribute the goods of the world in such a way as to improve the condition of people's lives."

In many ways it is easy to see how Mario Cuomo could become the pivotal figure in the debate between church and state over abortion. To be sure, other practicing Catholic politicians, such as Edward Kennedy and Daniel Patrick Moynihan, were also publicly pro-choice, and Geraldine Ferraro had had a skirmish with the church over this issue when she was a candidate for Vice President in 1984. But only Mario Cuomo was theologically outspoken. He not only supported choice but sought to couch his arguments with the church's own theological premises. His ideological role model was the French Jesuit Pierre Teilhard de Chardin, whose efforts to reconcile science with faith— claiming matter and spirituality were part of the same dynamic— led to his being denounced by the church.

What fascinated Cuomo about Teilhard de Chardin was precisely this notion that humans could live fully and successfully in the world and in doing so fulfill their divine promise. It was a secular viewpoint that matched Cuomo's own desire to immerse himself fully in the political world.

By the 1960's, as the papacy of John XXIII began the process of transforming a stale and often irrelevant church into a vital twentieth-century institution, Teilhard's viewpoint had gained greater acceptance when a punitive morality was replaced by a more humanistic ideology.

But although many of the changes initiated by John XXIII took root, by the mid-1970's the church had begun a slow slide back to a more legalistic posture, which was solidified during the conservative papacy of John Paul II.

Catholics referred to their church as Mother Church, but it was more accurately Father Church, a classic patriarchy whose dictates were delivered by a handpicked cadre of aging clerics.

This was the church that Mario Cuomo ran up against in the 1980's.

Cuomo formed his position about abortion after much agonizing. As a Catholic he was personally opposed to abortion, but as a government representative he believed he could not impose his private morality on others. How could he, the Democratic governor of a politically liberal and economically suffering state, accurately represent the wishes of the population by being anti-choice?

The first hand grenade was lobbed at him in 1984 by New York Archbishop John J. O'Connor. O'Connor was well known as an outspoken prelate and something of a loose cannon, whose eagerness to speak his mind was viewed in turns with dismay and delight back in Rome. He was a stunningly conservative, pious man, who some speculated must have slept through Vatican II, and he represented the church's swing back to authoritarian law.

As Robert S. McElvaine tells the story in his biography of Mario Cuomo, Cuomo, his wife, Matilda, and their fourteen-year-old son, Christopher, were watching a television interview with O'Connor in which he said, "I do not see how a Catholic in good conscience could vote for a candidate who explicitly supported abortion." The interviewer then asked O'Connor, "Don't you think we should excommunicate the governor?" The archbishop didn't directly reject the idea. Matilda Cuomo recalled that Christopher became very upset, jumping up and crying.

"What are you saying—excommunicate my father?" And she said, "Mario got so white, so pale, and he stands up and leaves the room. They hit us like a hammer in the head."

Cuomo, being Cuomo, couldn't ignore the incident. It hurt him deeply. So he fought back using his most powerful weapons— logic and words. In a *New York Times* interview two months later, he challenged the church's right to interfere with the political process and suggested that the archbishop was out of line to threaten Catholic politicians who voted in opposition to its teachings.

Cuomo won the first round. O'Connor backed down, saying that he had been misunderstood and never intended to tell people for whom they should or should not vote.

Cuomo didn't leave it at that because once it was on the table, he believed the issue deserved a full examination. In this respect Cuomo was a curiosity as a modern politician, forsaking the sound bite for the carefully structured philosophical debate.

In September 1984 he made his now-famous speech about abortion on no less Catholic ground than the campus of Notre Dame University. It was a masterful speech. "I accept the church's teaching on abortion," he said. "Must I insist you do?" In a word, "No." He went on to say that it was dangerous to write moral positions into law unless they represented "a consensus view of right and wrong . . . shared by the pluralistic community at large." Since such a consensus about outlawing abortion clearly did not exist, Cuomo pointed out, any law passed would only have a "prohibition" effect; it would be unenforceable.

Further challenging the church, Cuomo said, "The hard truth is that abortion isn't a failure of the government. No agency or department of government forces women to have abortions. . . . Are we asking government to make criminal what we believe to be sinful because we ourselves can't stop committing the sin?"

BOSTON, MASSACHUSETTS, March 1990

Father Greg R. sat behind the desk of his cluttered office, which looked out over one of the worst ghettos in America.

Father Greg had been a priest in this Boston neighborhood for nearly fifteen years. He was only forty-five, but his lined face and drooped shoulders belied his youth. The ugliness of the neighborhood swept everyone into its crushing embrace; the despair settled like dust in every corner. Father Greg fought that despair every day. The presence of a benevolent God was not often evident in the Jobian circumstances of the Boston poor.

"I support my church's stand on abortion," he told his interviewer, then smiled. "I could not be a Catholic priest and do otherwise. But I also believe that it is the church's place to lend compassion to the people who are fighting so hard to stay alive both physically and morally—especially in communities like this one. How do we listen to their needs and legitimately minister to them?" He gazed thoughtfully out the window onto a playground where noisy children fought over a basketball. "That is the question, I, as a pastor, am most concerned with.

"Oh, I've seen some cases," he said. "I think I've seen it all. People here are poor. The men don't stay around. This is a community run by women. It's sad. Sometimes they beg me. 'Father, I can't have another child.' And I have little comfort to offer but the promise of a future glory that is at best vague and at worst something they don't even believe in anymore. Too often I can't save them, and their children are already lost to the streets."

The interviewer asked, "Can morality exist in a vacuum, Father? Doesn't it have to address people where they are?"

"Most definitely." He nodded. "But it is our task—the church's task—to communicate the message of salvation to people in every circumstance, not to bend the message to fit them, although I do think you could say that we are experiencing a very legalistic period. The hierarchy feels the need to bring people back to some center."

"There seems to be less focus on personal conscience and more on law," observed the interviewer. "I get the feeling that the Catholic Church doesn't have much confidence that its members can make distinctions between right and wrong."

"Well, we have lived through difficult times." Father Greg

laughed. "A great questioning of faith, a decline in moral values. The church is bound by its mission in the world to offer guidance, and sometimes that guidance is more an iron fist than a velvet glove. But perhaps it's necessary."

"All right. But let's talk specifically about birth control and abortion. What do you say to your parishioners about birth control? Polls suggest that Catholics in this country are ignoring the papal dictates against birth control."

"Yes, well, sometimes you have to make individual judgments. And until this current pope the church seemed to be moving away from such an extreme view about birth control. Many of us are dismayed by the return to such an unwavering position."

"Doesn't the church have to take some responsibility for the human community at large, beyond just the individual souls? Issues like survival of human life on this planet seem pretty close to home now with overpopulation and the poverty and despair. What about the quality of life of people in your neighborhood?"

Father Greg laughed and lighted a cigarette. "There's quite a difference of opinion about that," he said, blowing a puff of smoke in the air. "If you want my personal view, I'll tell you. It's a view that would not be too popular with my superiors. I'm sure you realize that the quality of life on earth is not held in any great esteem by Mother Church. But I do think sometimes about how different it must be to be a pastor in a middle-class white community. It's perhaps easier for people to be moral, in the ways we define morality. If the young daughter of a parishioner gets pregnant, abortion doesn't need to seem like the only choice. The pregnancy may be traumatic, but it's not tragic. There are good homes to send the girl to; there are wonderful couples lined up to adopt her baby. But in this community . . ." The sentence lingered. He stubbed out his cigarette, stood up, and went to the window. There were more boys tossing the basketball now, and a couple of men. "See that kid in the yellow T-shirt." He pointed. "His mother has six kids, and the youngest is less than a year old. The father doesn't work or come around much. The mother works five days a week in a Laundromat, and the older girls take care of the younger ones. The oldest son is already in trouble with the law. And I look at their life and I think, *My God, what despair.* How could you be human and not be touched by it?" He turned back from the window. "I am haunted by that woman's tears," he said sadly. "I am haunted by her pleas. Who am I to stand in judgment over her and tell her these children are a gift from God, that she must do what's right?" He sat heavily in his chair.

"The Christian family ideal, as our fathers spoke of it, does not exist for this woman. The procreative act is not one of love; it's closer to rape. This is a good woman, but she doesn't come to church anymore. You know what she said to me? She said words to this effect: 'Father, your God isn't sticking up for me, so I guess I've got to do it for myself.' Can you imagine such isolation? No Christian person should feel so abandoned. That's the entire point of our having this entity we call the Christian community. It binds us together in loving, caring responsibility for one another. But we have abandoned her."

"So you do what you can."

"Yes." He nodded. "I do what I can. When I give permission for them to use birth control, when I absolve them, I take full responsibility. It may be wrong, but I square it with my conscience as well as I can. And most priests do. It's not something you ever talk about, even among yourselves, much less to your bishop. But everyone knows about it."

"Whose law are you following then?"

"I believe God's law."

"But not the church's?"

He shrugged and did not answer.

In a sense, Father Greg, sitting in his twentieth-century ghetto parish, was doing battle with ancient demons. He viewed the battle through the embedded tradition of his church. But more than that, he viewed it, as all people must, from his place in the chain of human history. For him, it was a heavy weight.

At the 1989 annual meeting of the National Conference of Catholic Bishops, John Cardinal O'Connor was elected to lead the church's fight against abortion. The 308 bishops present also released a statement calling for a constitutional amendment to ban abortion, increased public information, and a greater commitment to the care of pregnant women.

Many church leaders privately believed that O'Connor was trouble—a shoot-from-the-hip zealot who would not further the goals of contemporary Catholicism. One prominent priest said uncharitably (and not for attribution), "He is one of the great assholes of the Western world." Father Andrew Greeley called him "an embarrassment to the church," adding this colorful description: "In his world view, there's no room for nuance, for sensitivity. . . . He's a rear admiral on the quarterdeck shouting, 'Damn the torpedoes, full speed ahead.' "

Religious leaders working for interfaith cooperation to heal the massive problems of society found O'Connor's doctrinaire Catholicism disturbing. "This guy's marching backwards into the fifteenth century, and if he had it his way, that's where he'd take the rest of us," complained Rabbi Balfour Brickner, a leader in interfaith affairs. "All he does is blather; he's the religious equivalent of Ronald Reagan."

Who was this man who dined with presidents and kings, held weekly press conferences after Sunday mass, and openly voiced controversial positions on everything from Israel to race relations to rock music? O'Connor liked to speak of himself as being a simple priest whose "flock" included more than two million Catholics in the New York Archdiocese. He was considered a power broker who was influential in the secular inner circles, and whose consultations included regular communications with President Bush.

For some, he was just another New York character, in the same vein as Donald Trump and George Steinbrenner—a tabloid's dream come true, with his sound-bitable quotes and flair for the dramatic.

Like Randall Terry, O'Connor believed an analogy could comfortably be drawn between abortion and the civil rights battle in the 1960's. "We have hostile laws and we must get rid of them," he said. "I am convinced if young women realized abortion was illegal and unnatural, the number of abortions would decline dramatically."

One of O'Connor's first announcements in his new position as vicar of the war on abortion was to propose the establishment of a religious order of nuns tentatively called the Servants of Life, devoted exclusively to fighting euthanasia and abortion.

Women to fight women.

Lucy Killea, sixty-seven, a California assemblywoman running for the state senate on a pro-choice platform, arrived at her office one morning to find a letter from the bishop in her fax machine. "I regret to inform you that by your media advertisements advocating the 'pro-choice' abortion position in the public forum, you are placing yourself in complete contradiction to the moral teachings of the Catholic Church," Bishop Leo T. Maher wrote. And with that he barred Killea, a practicing Catholic, from receiving communion—a step short of excommunication.

The bishop's letter arrived only three weeks before the election—an election Lucy Killea was struggling against great odds to win. His action made abortion the central issue of the campaign, and the voters, many of them angered by the bishop's attempt to intervene in government, handed Killea a 51 percent to 49 percent upset victory over her antiabortion opponent, state legislator Carol Bentley.

In New York, Mario Cuomo observed the sanctions against Killea with dismay and wondered aloud if the bishop's position would apply also to a Catholic official who supported the death penalty.

But as Cuomo soon learned, hellfire and damnation were back in vogue in his state as well.

Bishop B. Austin Vaughan, of Newburgh, New York, was born in Greenwich Village, the center of radical political thought, but if anything, his upbringing had influenced him to be more doctrinaire. A former teacher at the archdiocese seminary in Yonkers, Vaughan had been a pastor in Newburgh for ten years when he decided to get aggressive on the abortion issue. Joining the shock troops of Operation Rescue, Vaughan began making appearances at abortion clinic actions. He was arrested on three different occasions and spent time in jail when he refused to pay a $250 fine.

Vaughan was not shy about phrasing his antiabortion position in the most controversial manner possible. He had, for example, sent the Jewish community into an uproar by likening the pro-choice Cuomo to Adolf Hitler—in his support of the slaughter of innocent life. Henry Siegman, executive director of the American Jewish Congress, was furious. Vaughan's comment was "so outrageous and so outside the bounds of legitimate expression as to demand special condemnation," he said. Later Vaughan went even further. In an ambiguous but racist-sounding remark, he warned Catholics that abortion would result in America's being "mostly brown and yellow in forty years."

O'Connor admired Vaughan's courage and outspokenness and said of Vaughan's jailing that he had acted in the tradition of John the Baptist and St. Thomas More (ironically, one of Cuomo's favorite theological figures), who took stands against sinful public officials.

Encouraged by the positive reactions his involvement was generating from church hierarchy, Vaughan chose to go after the big fish. Cuomo, he said, was "in serious risk of going to hell" over his support of a woman's right to choose abortion.

Cuomo might have been surprised that the damnation talk had reached New York and that the first stone tossed had not come from his regular nemesis, O'Connor, but from Vaughan, who had never before tangled directly with the governor.

Once again Cuomo defended his position, attempting to draw a distinction between his private morality and his role as a public official. In a letter of explanation Cuomo wrote, "Here in America, where the law permits women to have abortions and preserves their right not to have abortions, the terrible, hard judgment which that freedom permits must be a matter of the woman's conscience."

Vaughan refused to consider the church-state issue, responding piously to Cuomo's argument, "All I was saying is what he learned, and I learned, and all of you learned in the first grade: If you commit a serious sin and die without repenting, you go to hell."

It didn't take long for O'Connor to join the fray. In an interview with *Catholic New York*, the weekly newspaper of the Archdiocese of New York, O'Connor defended Vaughan, saying:

Would anyone deny that the Bishop has the right and even the obligation to warn any Catholic that his soul is at risk if he should die while deliberately pursuing any gravely evil course of actions?

Where Catholics are perceived not only as treating church teaching on abortion with contempt, but helping to multiply abortions, by advocating legislation supporting abortion, or by making public funds available for abortion, bishops must decide that for the common good, such Catholics must be warned that they are at risk of excommunication. If such actions persist, bishops may consider excommunication the only option.

Cuomo didn't take the threat lightly. "No Roman Catholic I know could feel good about having a great cardinal of the great church suggest that your soul was in peril," he said in an interview. But O'Connor later denied that he was planning to excommunicate anyone.

In a *New York Times* editorial, Abe Rosenthal wrote that the suggestion that Catholic voters not vote for pro-choice candidates could have a deep influence on future elections, and that the church had perhaps crossed a line into dangerous territory. Noting that several prominent political leaders were at risk, Rosenthal wrote that "if they lose the votes of Catholics because of how they meld their religious and political obligations, it would be so dangerously retrogressive that we all have a stake in fighting it."

Catholic New Yorkers seemed to agree. In a poll conducted by the *Daily News*, 63 percent of New York City Catholics polled believed that women had the right to abortion "on demand." Noted Jeff Alderman, director of polling for ABC News, which assisted with the poll: "Catholics aren't any different than anybody else when it comes to abortion." Furthermore, 63 percent said they would like O'Connor to stay out of politics.

But O'Connor reminded reporters that the church wasn't running a popularity contest. His attitude toward Catholics who might disagree was essentially "Love it or leave it." How, he wondered, can one be a Catholic and ignore church teachings? "To me it would be a contradiction in terms to say, 'I'm a Catholic but don't believe what the Catholic Church teaches,' " O'Connor told reporters in his weekly press conference. "It's a free country, so people can pick and choose whatever they want to believe. . . . No one puts a gun behind our backs and says we must be Americans, and no one puts a gun behind our backs and says we must be Catholic."

New York's Catholic hierarchy was determined to present a united front on the issue. "I believe Governor Cuomo has been given a warning—that his views could land him in hell," opined Brooklyn Bishop Thomas V. Daily. "If anyone supports either directly or indirectly the practice of killing babies in the womb, that is terrible."

Countered Cuomo: "I think the person who knows best what's going to happen to your soul is you. If you do something that violates your own conscience, then probably your soul is in peril. If you do something that is in accord with a well-formed conscience, sincerely formed, it seems to me any God of good judgment would understand that."

What did excommunication mean for a Catholic? It was the most severe punishment that could be given, barring one from all sacraments (except for penance), and was as good as a condemnation to hell. Public excommunication was not common historically. It was reserved for the most severe crimes against the church, such as schism, heresy, apostasy, and persecution of Christians. To place devout Catholic politicians in that category was a phenomenal dare. Indeed, it was even questionable whether or not, according to church law, politicians could be excommunicated for supporting individual choice in abortion. More commonly, excommunication occurred privately. A Catholic who obtained an abortion was automatically excommunicated. Public excommunication was more dramatic, consisting of a document that referred to the "sinner" by name.

According to Father Richard McBrien, chairman of the theology department at the University of Notre Dame, Thomas Aquinas himself recognized that there was a distinction between moral and civil law. "Even if an individual Catholic politician were actively supporting state laws that made it easier to have an abortion without legal penalty, the code of moral law would still not call for excommunication. In fact, the only person excommunicated in the case of abortion is a person who procures an abortion. It's really stretching the law to say it applies to some politician in Albany who's nowhere near an abortion clinic and is not encouraging people to get an abortion and is not paying for abortions out of his own pocket."

In fact, as authoritatively as O'Connor and his colleagues in New York were declaring the right to excommunicate politicians, many priests and scholars in the church were cringing at the threats. And pro-choice public officials who were Catholic warned that the church's threats of excommunication would not make a difference. Times had changed, and the threat of hell was no longer enough to keep the faithful in line. Disputing the use of sanctions, Joseph Cardinal Bernardin of Chicago, said, "The church can be most effective in the public debate on abortion through moral persuasion, not punitive measures." And Jesuit scholar Thomas Reese of Washington, D.C., worried that "We could have the church looking very disunited if a state politician is excommunicated in one diocese while the bishop in another diocese thinks he's a fine Catholic."

Church leaders were on shaky ground when they attempted to intervene in the politics of Catholic voters. Could Catholics who supported pro-choice candidates eventually be charged with moral error? Cuomo was certainly not the first politician to tangle with the church in this way. More than sixty years earlier

New York Governor Alfred E. Smith had argued the same point. In his case the issue was his support of a child labor law that the Catholic Church warned would violate the sanctity of the family. "I'm bound to obey the Holy Father," said the Catholic governor. "But there's nothing in the law of the church that says I have to obey the church in matters that are economic, social or political. . . . This belongs to me. This is the Governor of the State of New York's duty, and it belongs to me. It doesn't belong to anybody else."

In spite of his strong stand for separation of church and state, Smith later encountered bigotry when he ran for President. Many people believed that if a Catholic were elected President, the United States would be governed by Rome, not by the people of this country. It wasn't until John Kennedy ran for President in 1960 that he put those fears to rest by saying:

> I believe in an America where the separation of church and state is absolute—where no Catholic prelate would tell the president (should he be Catholic) how to act . . . where no public official either requests or accepts instruction on public policy from the pope, the National Council of Churches or any other ecclesiastical source—where no religious body seeks to impose its will directly or indirectly upon the general populace or the public acts of its officials.

Certainly it seemed that in regard to abortion Rome was trying to govern the world and influence the political process. But good Catholic government officials like Mario Cuomo and many others were sending a message back that the operations of the state were sacred in their own right. George Bush, who had allowed the "evangelical papacy" to control his conscience on the abortion issue, might well have taken a lesson from some of his Catholic colleagues.

But now, it seemed, the country had come full circle. The first public excommunication in this new round of attacks occurred not in New York but in Corpus Christi, Texas. In July 1990 Rachel Vargas, an abortion clinic director, and Eduardo Aquino, a doctor at the clinic, disclosed that they had received notices of excommunication from Bishop Rene Gracida, who wrote, "Your cooperation in producing abortions is a sin against God and humanity and against the law of the Roman Catholic Church."

MILWAUKEE, WISCONSIN, March 1990

While the prelates in New York were becoming overnight media stars, a low-key concerned archbishop in the Midwest was eschewing hellfire and damnation in favor of lending a listening ear to the debate.

"The polarization about this issue has become so great that I had to admit we needed dialogue about it within the Catholic community as well as with others," sixty-two-year-old Archbishop Rembert G. Weakland said, explaining why he was organizing six "listening sessions" with groups of women on the issue. "A good teacher, if he senses that his teaching is not being effective, will step back, listen and ask some questions. I had to ask why there are so many Catholic women I respect who are not being reached by the church."

After the sessions a subdued Weakland said that his ears were ringing from the passion with which so many women disagreed with and felt abandoned by the church's intractability on birth control and abortion. He was the only U.S. bishop to listen to women in this way, and he admitted that he had made many rash assumptions about the relationship women have to conception and motherhood. "I would never [again] be so glib in talking about the 'moment of conception,' " he said, describing a new awareness that "conception is a long process, not a moment." He added that in his conversations with Catholic women, "I did not sense that there was much support" for the church's condemnation of birth control.

In some respects Cardinal O'Connor was very much a man of his times, so his decision to hire a public relations firm to sway Catholics back to the church's position on abortion was not a surprise. Failing appeals from the pulpit, he chose to place his efforts in the capable hands of the advertising and public relations industries. O'Connor didn't call it PR; he called it education. But the nature of public relations is to sway, more than it is to communicate, so the cardinal could not disguise his intentions. In the winter of 1990, he chose Hill & Knowlton, a public relations firm that employed two thousand people in its worldwide operations, to handle the account of the U.S. Catholic bishops. It was to be a five-million-dollar campaign. The Knights of Columbus, the conservative all-male organization that supports Catholic Church action, offered to provide at least three of the five million dollars needed to wage an effective campaign.

O'Connor's decision to spend massive funds on public relations drew mixed reviews. Even those who opposed abortion wondered if it was the most compassionate use of money—especially at a time when parishes and church schools were closing for lack of funds and when the demand for charitable services in the cities and rural areas of the country was reaching a crisis point. Many people questioned O'Connor's priorities. Was the campaign to save the unborn more urgent to him than the desperate circumstances of those already living?

There was a revolt inside the sophisticated public relations firm, too, with 136 staff members who opposed the company's taking on an antiabortion account signing a petition that read, "We should not be representing any group in its advocacy of a position which would restrict the fundamental rights of all of us as Americans. It would be the equivalent of supporting a group in its effort to repeal the Voting Rights Act."

For many people the idea that the greatest moral and pastoral force in the world would "go PR" was anathema. And at least some observers found the cardinal's choice of Hill & Knowlton highly ironic. Eugene Kennedy, a former Catholic priest and professor of psychology at Loyola University, wondered that "The bishops apparently don't see the incongruity of placing the pro-life issue—which they define as their deepest present moral concern—in the hands of Hill & Knowlton, which also represents Playboy Enterprises." Furthermore, Kennedy pointed out, "Hill & Knowlton . . . numbers among its clients the Warner-

Lambert Company, which makes oral contraceptives and condoms, and Baxter International, which makes intrauterine
devices. It has shaped the images of defense industries, whose
contracts do not read like the Gospels."

While American Catholics were loudly challenging the
church's edicts, Pope John Paul II was serenely traveling the
globe, preaching about birth control. In Chihuahua, Mexico,
the site of brutal poverty and overpopulation, the pope declared, "If the possibility of conceiving a child is artificially
eliminated in the conjugal act, couples shut themselves off from
God and oppose his will."

As he traveled to country after country, the pope saw no irony
as he raised his hands in blessing to the people of the starving and
suffering third world and exhorted them to "be fruitful and multiply."

The Catholic Church was making all the headlines, but among
Protestants the struggle was equally fierce, if less public. Mainline Protestant denominations had traditionally been in favor of
liberalized abortion laws, even before *Roe* v. *Wade.* Only the
fundamentalists, including Southern Baptists, were actually opposed to abortion. But in recent years several mainline denominations, including Eastern Orthodox churches, Mormons, and
the Lutheran Church, Missouri Synod had taken strong antiabortion stands. Even the Episcopal Church modified its formerly
liberal posture to support only abortions that were sought in
extreme situations. The Northern Baptists followed suit. The
United Methodist Church and the Presbyterian churches, officially pro-choice, watered down their positions to speak out
against the use of abortion as birth control or for purposes of sex
selection. Only the United Church of Christ remained vigorously pro-choice.

For Protestants, who were not bound by the heavy hierarchi-
cal hand of papal infallibility, there was more room for maneuvering within the complexities of the issue. But the trend toward
reduced support for abortion disturbed many who saw it as a

reversal of the progressive spirit of Protestantism in the United States.

NEW YORK CITY, May 1990

Fundamentalist Christians and Roman Catholic bishops make strange bedfellows, but they are of one mind on this: Abortion is a sin. Brooklyn's new bishop, Thomas V. Daily, no sooner had his bags unpacked than he announced that he would be participating in abortion clinic actions alongside Operation Rescue participants. However, unlike his colleague Bishop Vaughan in Albany, he wasn't planning to get dust on his clerical robes; there would be no blocking entrances, no sit-downs, no shouting. "No gimmicks, no signs, no microphones," Daily announced cheerfully. "Simply taking rosary beads and praying." He reminded Catholics who would prefer more aggressive tactics that "One Hail Mary can turn the world around."

Daily, the spiritual leader of a million and a half Catholics in Brooklyn and Queens, planned to lead a prayer service outside Choices Women's Medical Center in Queens. On a Saturday morning in spring he led one thousand of the faithful in prayer, as women streamed into the clinic, heads bent against the verbal and visual assault. The sounds of the rosary mingled eerily with the pleas of the "rescuers."

"Don't kill your baby! . . . Blessed are you among women and blessed is the fruit of your womb, Jesus. . . . Don't kill your baby!"

Police barriers held back a group of about fifty pro-choice demonstrators who shouted, as each bead slipped through the fingers of the bishop, "Keep your rosaries off our ovaries!"

"The repressive attitude toward married sex that affects the Vatican is a perversion of the genius of the Sacramental Imagination," wrote Father Andrew Greeley, noting that Augustine's repressive influence was still heavily felt in the modern Catholic Church. "The Vatican following Augustine, still thinks that what a man and woman feel when they lie side by side in bed at night is somehow perverse and cannot be enjoyed unless they intend to make the act in which they are engaging procreative. While this position is propounded as the 'teachings of Jesus' it is difficult to find any basis in Scripture for such an assertion."

The biblical support for Christian dogma against abortion was at best vague and subject to interpretation. In evaluating what constitutes moral truth, David Maguire, professor of moral theology at the Jesuit Marquette University, pointed out that historically church leaders were more inclined to define morality in the context of the greater good of society and community, leaving the individual to his or her conscience. For example, he noted, both Augustine and Thomas Aquinas found prostitution morally wrong but thought it should be legalized for the greater good of society. These theologians argued that a privately held moral view should not be imposed if imposing it would do more harm than good.

For a Catholic theologian, Maguire had a unique perspective, partially informed by several visits he made to an abortion clinic in 1984. He spoke with the counselors, sat in on interviews with women who sought abortions, watched the "scary" demonstrators outside the clinic, and held in his hands a cup containing the product of a six- to nine-week-old fetus. The experience gave Maguire an appreciation of reality beyond the absolutes. One of the women he met was five to six weeks pregnant. He later learned that she was being treated for manic depression and was receiving high doses of lithium—a drug that was known to be injurious to the formation of a fetus—to keep her mood swings under control.

Reflecting on the dilemma the woman faced, Maguire wrote:

As I watched this woman I thought of one of my colleagues who had recently made a confident assertion that there could be no plausible reason for abortion except to save the physical life of the woman or if the fetus was anencephalic. This woman's physical life was not at risk and the embryo would develop a brain. But saving *life* involves more than cardiopulmonary continuity. How is it that in speaking of women we so easily reduce human life to physical life? What certitudes persuade theologians that there are only two marginal reasons to justify abortion? Why is the Vatican comparably sure that while there may be *just* wars with incredible slaughter, there can be no *just* abortions? Both need to listen to the woman on lithium as she testifies that life does not always confine itself within the ridges of our theories.

Can abortion be a responsible act for a Christian woman? In *Unwanted Pregnancy*, Robert Bluford, Jr., and Robert E. Petres argue that it could, citing pragmatic examples from the Bible of human ingenuity and corresponding responsibility. They define "responsibility" to mean a person's appropriate response to a given circumstance. Bluford and Petres also point out that the context for rapid procreation cited in the Bible was related more to the times than to a universal edict. Then it was linked with the survival of the human race; today, when we are faced with overpopulation, the mandate might be the opposite.

But the question remains, What is the role of the church in the human community? What responsibility does it have to help direct public policy? Ed Sullivan, a thoughtful New York City assemblyman, reflected: "Practically speaking, the American church is in schism—dissenting from the teachings of the pope without renouncing its claim to Catholicism. Something like this has happened before, many times over the centuries, but the current situation is very unusual because the schism is being exacerbated—even orchestrated—by a hierarchy that is consciously distancing itself from the church militant."

Jesus was not a legalist; he was a revolutionary. In his teachings we hear an emphasis on the spirit and very little about the law. But once institutionalized, his teachings, like those of many great spiritual and social leaders of the ages, have been redefined to match a more practical piety.

The "community of God" has always stood apart in a "sinful world," bearing witness to the brokenness of humanity and the potential for redemption. Organized religion, whose purpose is to guide and transform the material experience, is tempted by a love of absolutes. But no religion invented by humans has ever managed to tame the mystery of life or to solve the moral dilemmas that are a daily part of the human experience. We search for a moral code that releases us from the ambiguities of our choices, but none can be found. Life does not always present itself neatly as a choice between right and wrong. Sometimes the choice that grabs at our hearts is between two wrongs, and in those cases we long to hear the legal and moral voice that tells us absolutely how to choose. But ultimately that voice rests in our own consciences, and we struggle on.

NINE

Truly the Youngest
Victims

When pregnancy is confirmed, one can no longer
discuss morality in the framework of rape or incest
(or whether birth control was or was not used, or
whether the child is "wanted" or whatever). The
unwanted pregnancy flows biologically from the
sexual act, but not morally from it . . . even deg-
radation, shame and emotional disruption are not
the moral equivalent of life. Only life is.

BERNARD NATHANSON

MINNEAPOLIS, MINNESOTA, October 1989

Fran Beekman was a thirty-six-year-old Christian woman, a
wife and the mother of four. She was a person of boundless
energy and spirit, who served on several church committees,
taught Sunday school to elementary school children, and always had a listening ear and a word of encouragement for
friends in trouble. She was one of the "new Christians,"
grounded in a contemporary experience that included antiwar
protests in the sixties and marches for the Equal Rights
Amendment in the seventies. Faith was very simple for Fran:
It meant following the teachings of Jesus and believing that he
would provide. "The most hopeless situation can be resolved

through prayer," she said. She had witnessed this miracle in her own life and had seen it happen in the lives of others.

But Fran had also seen how faith could be tested, and she was feeling the burden of that test now, as she contemplated the plight of her sixteen-year-old daughter, Julie.

Julie was the apple of Fran's eye—a beautiful, intelligent, and thoughtful girl, serious about her involvement in church and school and at the same time playful. Fran loved the way her daughter's eyes sparkled when she told a funny story or the blush on her cheeks when she mentioned a boy she liked. It had been easy to slip into a feeling of confidence where her daughter was concerned, for Julie had always seemed like one of those children who wore invisible shields of protection against the more hurtful realities of life.

But now this terrible event had shattered the calm and stolen the sparkle from Julie's eyes. She was pregnant. Fran hadn't noticed anything amiss until her daughter asked her and David if they could talk privately, away from the other kids. She had told them then, simply and directly, her long blond hair covering her face as she hung her head down in shame and misery. Fran and David sat out a heartbeat in silence before responding. Then Fran broke into tears. David rubbed the rims of his glasses in a nervous gesture, and his lips trembled.

"Oh, darling," Fran said finally, her voice thick with heartbreak.

Julie lifted her head; her face was solemn. "I told Pastor Ward," she said. "I wanted to do that before I told you. He's said if I wanted, he'd help me find a home for unwed mothers."

Home for unwed mothers. How archaic that sounded! How gloomy and shameful.

"You don't have to go away," Fran told her daughter. "We'll help you."

"Whose is it?" David asked quietly.

Julie shook her head. "Just . . . it doesn't matter. Nobody. It was a mistake."

"It matters. He should—"

"Dad!"

Fran wiped her eyes. "It's okay, honey."

"I haven't decided what to do yet," Julie said. "But maybe abortion . . ."

Fran and David recoiled at the mention of the word. "You're thinking of abortion?" Fran asked.

"I don't want to murder my baby," Julie said miserably, wrapping her arms around her stomach as if to protect it from the suggestion. "But see, I'm not sure if it is murder; maybe it's just a bunch of cells."

"Who have you been talking to?" her father demanded.

"Stop shouting, David," Fran said.

Julie looked trapped. She stood up and moved toward the door. "Look, I have to work this out by myself. I just wanted you to know. That's all."

As her daughter walked from the room, Fran reached out a helpless hand. "Darling! Anything . . . anything."

Fran had been praying her heart out, looking for a way to see through to the light. But the darkness was thick and all-encompassing. Prayer gave no comfort. No answer. David had been by turns brooding and angry, and she couldn't console him. She saw that he was hurting, and she wanted to comfort him, to find a way to bring them both back into the circle of faith, but she couldn't find the words; they'd left her along with the joy and warmth she felt only days before.

Faith is what remains when reason fails, she reminded herself. But her mind cried out in protest. She didn't want the dubious comfort of faith. She wanted a solution. She wanted to *do* something. God help her, she wanted to save their daughter.

Julie told her that she hadn't yet decided what to do but that she hated the idea of adoption. "I can't stand to think of my little baby going up for adoption," she said. "I might never be able to forgive myself. Nothing seems right."

"Let's talk about options."

Julie's face closed. "I appreciate your help, Mom, but I really have to figure this out for myself."

"At least see a counselor—I'll go with you."

"I told you, I've already talked to Pastor Ward."

"No, a different kind of counselor—at a clinic."

"You mean Planned Parenthood?"

"No, the church has . . . they might tell you."

Julie stared at her silently.

Communication seemed impossible. Words got swallowed before they reached the tongue. The threat of abortion hung in the air. "She needs our consent for that," David said the night before. "How could we ever give it?" But Fran had already looked into it. "She doesn't need our consent. Just to notify us. The decision is up to her."

"But she's only a child," David said in awe. "I don't understand how this could be her decision."

"We'll raise the baby," Fran blurted out now, willing her daughter to seek solace from her.

"Oh, Mom."

Children having children. It's a heartbreaking specter. Each year in America at least 1 million teenagers are faced with this premature plunge into adulthood. Half of them get abortions; in fact, teenagers account for almost one quarter of all abortions performed in America. Only about 20,000 of these teens give their babies up for adoption, leaving some 480,000 young girls raising babies, often in conditions of poverty, inadequate health care, and poor prospects for future stability. They are truly the youngest victims of the abortion conflict.

Emotional and economic factors aside, carrying a pregnancy to term can be a life-threatening choice for young girls, who are not physically equipped for the rigors of childbirth. Infants born to teenagers have high mortality rates; they are more than twice as likely to die at birth as infants born to mature women. Infants who survive are more likely to have low birth weights, leading to health complications and mental retardation.

Ignoring these factors, as well as the results of a study funded by the Department of Health and Human Services (HHS), his own agency, George Bush urged adoption rather than abortion for young girls. "We must change from abortion to adoption," he said. His philosophy was grounded in the loving ideal of society as a place where babies were lovingly conceived, where caring childless couples were standing in line to fill every motherless child's life with love. The romantic ideal was so far removed from the practical reality that the trade-off of adoption for abortion seemed ludicrous. But Bush was convinced that he could successfully make such an appeal to the American people, and shortly after he made that statement, his wife, Barbara, accepted an invitation to become the honorary chairwoman of the National Committee for Adoption. He wasn't aware of—or didn't care about—the statistics that came from prisons or from the streets, about the adopted children who were rejected because they didn't turn out to be the perfect, unflawed bundles of joy that were the fantasy of most parents. Bush's views were colored by his own upper-middle-class upbringing by millionaire parents who could well afford to give their children everything they needed to grow and be successful. He could not hear the cries of despair from the ghettos of America.

"Don't kill your baby! Have your baby. I'll raise it!" a woman screamed at a teenage girl who arrived at a clinic to obtain an abortion. But it was only rhetoric. What if it happened this way? What if the half million teenage girls who had abortions each year all chose to have their babies and give them up for adoption? Who would care for them? For while antiabortionists clamored for the rights of fetuses and embryos, George Bush's society was one in which one fifth of all children, one fourth of black children, and one third of all poor children had no health coverage. It was a society that often seemed more attentive to the rights of the unborn than to the rights of the born, a society in which "family values" were heralded even as the President refused to support family and medical leave and other practical pro-family legislation.

Moreover, those who resisted the idea of abortion for teenagers were often the same voices raised against sex education in schools, contraceptive education, and the distribution of contraceptives to teenagers. It was a real Catch-22.

The HHS-financed study released in 1990 indicated that teen-

age girls who obtained abortions fared better than those who
bore their children. The four-year study conducted by the Johns
Hopkins School of Hygiene and Public Health studied 334 pregnant girls age seventeen and younger and found that those who
had abortions did better educationally, economically, and emotionally and had fewer subsequent pregnancies. Dr. Laurie
Schwab Zabin, the principal author of the study, said, "Clearly
the abortion experience is not setting these kids back. If anything, it's probably giving them some sense of control over their
lives so that they can move on and do things that are important."

Further studies concluded that the teenagers who chose to
have and keep their babies came from the poorest environments
and had the fewest opportunities to improve their circumstances
in life.

But the antiabortionists turned a deaf ear to the tragedy of teen
pregnancy. Seeking ways to limit all abortions, they found teenagers, whose rights were already limited in other arenas, to be
the ideal targets.

Two cases reviewed by the Supreme Court in the fall of 1989
created a troubling new escalation in the abortion debate and
started fresh speculation about the inclinations of the Supreme
Court. The cases, *Hodgson* v. *Minnesota* and *Ohio* v. *Akron Center
for Reproductive Health*, addressed the question of parental notification for minors seeking abortions. It was the fifth time since
Roe v. *Wade* that the Court considered the issue of parents' rights
on this issue.

At first glance, parental notification legislation might have
seemed a cut-and-dried matter—and not a bad idea. Public opinion polls recorded overwhelming agreement that parental notification statutes were legitimate, even among those who supported
abortion rights. It was hard for the public to grasp the conflict
between the very adult circumstances of pregnancy and the still-
vulnerable status of minors. Laurie Anne Ramsey, director of
education for Americans United for Life, put it so simply, and it
seemed so reasonable: "Schools need permission from parents
before they can give a child an aspirin. When it comes to an
abortion that can affect a girl for the rest of her life, parents do

believe they should have the opportunity to talk about it." The agenda of organizations like Ramsey's was clearly directed toward placing limitations on abortions among teens, using parental notification as a wedge. Others simply believed it was a good idea as a guarantee that a minor who went ahead with abortion would have appropriate care and support.

Those who disputed the wisdom of parental notification statutes pointed out that most pregnant teenagers *did* notify their parents. It was the exceptions that caused legitimate concern. These exceptions highlighted some of the more unpleasant realities of family life in the cities and towns of America. Ian Morrison, president emeritus of Greer-Woodycrest Children's Services in Florida, pointed out that those in the field of children and family services recognized that mandatory parental notification statutes would do more harm than good; teens either would flee the state to obtain abortions elsewhere or would undergo dangerous illegal abortions. "The decision by a young woman to seek an abortion is rarely one made lightly," Morrison said. "It is almost always a decision made in fear, terror and extreme emotional trauma. To share that fear and shame is almost impossible, even in the most loving and understanding families. At times, incest or sexual abuse by a relative or neighbor is involved, at other times judgmental parental anger totally alienates the teenager and she finds herself even more alone and distraught. The simple fact is that early pregnancy is often indicative of lack of proper familial communication at an early time."

It was not the medical or social services professions that were initiating parental notification or consent laws. Those who were closest to the day-to-day health and well-being of families understood that it was not possible to legislate familial support. Rather, the efforts came from antiabortion groups that sought to mask their goal of eliminating abortions behind an emotional appeal to parents.

At the time the Supreme Court was preparing to hear the Minnesota and Ohio cases, thirty-two states already had some form of parental involvement laws on the books, although only eleven of these were in force, pending the Court ruling. Only the law in Utah did not provide the alternative of a judicial hearing.

But the issue was complicated by the factors of broken homes and abusive parents—realities most Americans stubbornly resist facing in an effort to maintain rosy pictures of family life in this country. Pro-choice activists pointed out that teenage girls who did not confide their pregnancies to parents often had good reasons for not doing so and said the law had no place within the complex tensions of American homes. Even in cases where parents might be supportive, teenagers ashamed of letting them down were known to procure illegal abortions with disastrous results that were eerily reminiscent of the dark ages of abortion law. In a study of teenage girls published by the National Organization for Women, a full 25 percent said they would not tell their parents about a pregnancy, regardless of any law.

Becky Bell was a case in point. Becky was a seventeen-year-old Indianapolis girl who panicked when she discovered she was pregnant. Indiana law required that minors either notify their parents of their intention to obtain an abortion or go before a judge. Becky did neither. Instead, ashamed and fearful, she had an illegal abortion that resulted in her death. Later, consumed by their grief, Becky's parents made tearful appeals to the Supreme Court to consider the complexities pregnant teenagers face. "She wouldn't go to the judge because the kids here all know his views," said Becky's mother. "She couldn't tell me because she was ashamed. When she told the boy, he'd told her to get lost, so she wrote us a letter we found after she died, saying, 'Mom and Dad, I don't want to lose you, too. Forgive me.' Becky told us she was going to a party, and I'll never know exactly what they did to her, but she got sicker than a dog. She went to school for two days and we thought she had the flu. When she started hemorrhaging, we took her to the hospital. After she died, they told us she'd been butchered."

The assumption that the judicial hearing provided a reasonable alternative ignored some basic realities. Teenagers (and for that matter, most Americans) were intimidated by the courts; they found them inaccessible. It was assuming a lot to think a teenager, feeling confused, isolated, and frightened, would find it anything but daunting to bypass her parents and go before a judge, where she would be required to supply intimate details about her sexual activity and family life. In cases where rape or incest was a factor, such a hearing might require a public admission of a shameful secret the young girl would feel too traumatized to reveal. It could be argued that in many cases the requirement of a judicial hearing would constitute an undue burden for the already fragile psyche of a pregnant teen. Furthermore, getting to see a judge in an overloaded court system was no small feat. The necessity of a court hearing often delayed abortions for three to four weeks, increasing both the medical risks and the emotional trauma. (Statistics showed that the adoption of the parental notification law in Minnesota caused the percentage of minors obtaining second-trimester abortions to increase by 26 percent.) Evidence presented to the Supreme Court in the Minnesota case showed that some pregnant minors "were so afraid of the proceeding that they turned mute in court, were 'wringing wet with perspiration,' and frequently required a sedative. Some vomited and one began to abort spontaneously during the court process." Judicial hearings seemed closer to state-sponsored child abuse than they did to a compassionate alternative.

Also at issue with parental notification was the question of rights. Although a minor had the right, once she had notified her parents, to proceed with an abortion, parents could exert considerable pressure. According to Rachael Pine, a lawyer with the ACLU, "Teenagers are emotionally and economically dependent on their parents. Once you require them to tell their parents, you are in effect giving parents the opportunity for a veto."

SEATTLE, WASHINGTON, August 1989

Barbara Allen had strong views about parental notification laws. She was convinced that they would save young girls from the trauma of abortion. She knew personally and could never delete from her memory her own feelings of sheer terror the day she went all alone to have her abortion. She remembered, too, her shame.

"Of course, a girl is going to be ashamed to tell her parents she's pregnant," she told an interviewer, smiling warmly. "But the point is that once the embarrassment is over, most parents are going to be supportive. They have the maturity to think about options that a panic-stricken young girl might not consider."

"Options that don't include abortion," the interviewer suggested.

Barbara leaned forward, emphasizing her point with an urgent tone. "It has been my experience that the young girls who find themselves to be pregnant don't really want abortions. But they're scared. They just don't think they have a choice. When we leave it to them to make the decision in fear and shame, we are really encouraging abortions to take place. Given the loving support of adults who can help them in practical ways, many, if not most, of these girls would choose not to have abortions. I could almost guarantee it."

"But what about the cases where the parents cannot offer that support? As you well know, not every household in America fits that ideal."

Barbara grimaced. "Of course, I know that. But we have to start someplace, and I believe this is the most logical place to start. You see, by encouraging young girls to believe that abortions are easy to obtain and that they carry no consequences, we are communicating a terrible and destructive message. I ask you, Should it be easy to kill a child? That's what's at stake here. And my heart aches for these young girls, but it doesn't mean I condone this murder. As much as I feel their hurt, I know that their suffering would be much greater in the long run if they were to have the abortions."

"You're referring to postabortion syndrome?" the interviewer asked.

"Yes," Barbara said. "People think we don't care about the mothers, just the babies. But they're wrong. Abortion is the worst kind of exploitation of women. I spoke with a young woman the other day. She was only twenty-five, but looking into her eyes, you'd think she was a thousand years old. She had an abortion when she was seventeen, and she still hasn't recovered emotionally. She sat in my office and sobbed. She said, 'When I had an abortion, I didn't know that it had a heart and arms and legs and that it was a real person. Now I can't get over it, the feeling of being a murderer.' She asked me how she could live with the guilt, and I honestly didn't know what to tell her. I have experienced it myself."

"I have read that statistical evidence shows very little indication that there is widespread psychological trauma from abortion," the interviewer said. "Many people say postabortion syndrome is just an invention of antiabortionists to recast women as victims rather than as murderers."

Barbara shook her head in disgust. "I've heard that claim, and it makes me angry, coming from people who supposedly care so much about women. Our research shows that postabortion syndrome affects vast numbers of women who have undergone abortions. Their symptoms include deep depression, flashbacks of the abortion, crying jags, sleeplessness, nightmares, and trauma when they are around pregnant women. In severe cases postabortion syndrome can lead to substance abuse, severe repression of all emotional expression, and even suicide. It doesn't necessarily happen right away, but it happens eventually. There are a lot of walking time bombs out there—women who had abortions and will not experience their grief for many years to come." Barbara smiled and laid a hand on the interviewer's arm. "So you see, we are not just saving one life. We are saving two lives."

The mood was tense on the November day that the Supreme Court gathered to consider the arguments in the parental notification cases. Beyond the immediate impact of the specific laws lingered the broader questions of abortion rights. Inside the courtroom observers were intense, trying to read the Court's overall predisposition on the abortion question—from its tone, its questions, and every tiny nuance. Although few believed that the parental notification cases provided even the shakiest basis for reversing *Roe* v. *Wade*, the Bush administration, leaving no stone, not even a pebble, unturned, intervened with a brief, asking the Court to use the cases as an opportunity to outlaw abortion entirely.

In his arguments Minnesota's chief deputy attorney general, John R. Tunheim, tenaciously clung to the contention that parental notification was in the best interest of everyone: the child, the parent, and ultimately the state. Furthermore, he argued, considering the responsible role parents take in the matters involving their children, there was no legitimate reason to provide the alternative of a judicial hearing. The state, he said, with middle-class certitude, could properly presume that a parent would have the best interests of a child at heart.

Even Sandra Day O'Connor, who seemed to favor the idea of parental notification, blinked at that sweeping generalization. "That may be true in general," she said to Tunheim. "But probably you would concede there might be circumstances where it is not in the best interests of the child to tell both parents of her problem and her intention." Tunheim did not respond, and the question was left hanging; but it seemed to get to the heart of the matter. Janet Benshoof, arguing for the American Civil Liberties Union, took the opening to note that more than half the Minnesota teenagers seeking abortions lived in single-parent families, making the necessity of obtaining both parents' permission a matter of forcing a parental role where none may exist. The requirement, concluded Benshoof, "tramples the integrity of families."

Arguing for the state of Ohio, Rita S. Eppler, an assistant attorney general, denied that parental notification was an infringement on a teenager's rights, and in doing so, she trivialized the matter. "At issue is only a minor's right to an abortion without parental notification," she told the Court, "not a minor's right to choose."

Countered Linda R. Sogg, appearing on behalf of the Planned Parenthood Federation of America: "We agree that loving parents can be helpful. But not all parents are loving." It was, of course, the heart of the matter.

The day's arguments carefully skirted discussion of the right to an abortion, fetal rights, or any of the other more explosive undercurrents of the abortion debate. And never was it suggested, as the Bush brief recommended, that *Roe* should be overturned as part of the decision. But at the end of the day a sense of frustration lingered, and even the justices seemed disturbed by the loose ends and by the lack of legal precedent.

It took nearly seven months for the Court to publish its decision. On June 25, 1990, in an opinion written by conservative Justice John Paul Stevens, the Court determined that the Minnesota requirement of notification of both parents was constitutional as long as an alternative judicial hearing was provided. The Court also upheld the Ohio law requiring notification of one parent as long as the alternative of a judicial hearing was provided.

O'Connor concurred in part but expressed concern about the potential unreasonability of Minnesota's two-parent provision. Agreeing with Benshoof, she wrote that the requirement "is all the more unreasonable when one considers that only half of the minors in the state of Minnesota reside with both biological parents."

In his dissent with the opinion, Justice Thurgood Marshall pointed out that no compelling state interest was served by the law and that it created a substantial burden on young women. "I strongly disagree with the Court's conclusion that the State may constitutionally force a minor woman either to notify both parents (or in some cases only one parent) and then wait 48 hours before proceeding with an abortion, or disclose her intimate affairs to a judge and ask that he grant her permission to have an abortion," Marshall wrote, adding, "I base my conclusion not on my intuition about the needs and attitudes of young women, but on a sizable and impressive collection of empirical data documenting the effects of parental notification statutes and of delaying an abortion."

Justice Marshall's dissent was a cry in the wilderness. With the Supreme Court's affirmation of the advisability of parental notification, many states immediately began taking action to impose their own versions.

Whose Life?

ROCKFORD, ILLINOIS, March 1990

Julie Beekman was seven months into her pregnancy, and she had only the faintest memory of the carefree young girl she used to be. She was living with her grandmother in a suburban community north of Chicago. Her grandmother was a kind and loving woman. Like Julie's parents, she did the best she could. Still, Julie felt isolated and burdened by her expanding waistline and aching muscles. Her parents had urged her to stay home during her pregnancy, but she was ashamed to be seen in their community, where people who knew her would try not to stare and would talk about her behind her back.

She had already made arrangements to give her baby up for adoption when it was born, and she was resigned to this decision, although she felt that she would never stop being haunted about the whereabouts of her child. Life would never again be as she had known it before, and sometimes, when she was feeling teary and vulnerable, she resented this. What she had done was not so bad. Maybe it was a mistake. But she felt that the consequences far outweighed the act.

She knew she could have had an abortion. By law, it was her choice, whether her parents liked it or not. But finally she was too afraid to confront a lifetime of religious belief. She grew weary of the arguments, and she could find no words to explain to her parents why their offer to raise the child as their own as an alternative to abortion was something she could not accept. Finally, she agreed to carry the child to term and give it up to a couple she would never know.

Now she was living out this prison sentence—yes, that was the way she viewed it—and waiting for the end so she could return to her normal life. She didn't know if she had chosen the right path. There was no way she'd ever know. What do you do when all the paths seem wrong to you, but everyone you love is so sure? During the nights, when the discomfort of her body forbade sleep, she wondered about that.

TEN

Ethics on an

Overflowing Planet

There is no right to life in any society on Earth
today, nor has there been at any former time . . .
what is (allegedly) protected is not life, but *Human*
life . . . even with that protection, casual murder is
an urban commonplace, and we wage "convention-
al" wars with tolls so terrible that we are, most of
us, afraid to consider them very deeply. . . . That
protection, that right to life, eluded the 40,000 children under 5 who died on our planet today—every
day—from preventable starvation, disease and neglect.
                    —CARL SAGAN AND ANN DRUYAN

Imagine: 3 billion people in China; 20 million people in New
York City; 2 billion people in India. It seemed an impossible
prediction, but it was what the world faced during the coming
decades if the population continued to grow at existing rates.
The stark reality of a population crisis—actually an explosion—
lent a pocket of objectivity to the emotional abortion debate.
According to the United Nations Population Fund, the world's
population was headed toward a calamitous rise, potentially tri-
pling in the next one hundred years—from 5.3 billion to 14

billion—unless there was a dedicated effort to increase family planning education and services around the globe.

The awareness of the problem didn't begin creeping into public consciousness until the 1950's, when we first began to hear about a threat that was potentially more devastating than any war that we could then imagine. It was termed the population explosion. Suddenly the earth itself seemed more fragile, and experts were warning that without a committed effort to rein in its human numbers, the planet might not survive the strain.

In 1968 Stanford University professor Paul R. Ehrlich brought the issue dramatically into focus with his shocking book *The Population Bomb*. In his vision of the future, Ehrlich imagined a world nine hundred years away that would, at 1968 population growth rates, reach an unimaginable 60,000,000,000,000,000 people. He wrote:

> Sixty billion million people. That is about 100 persons for each square yard of the Earth's surface, land and sea. A British physicist, J. H. Fremlin, guessed that such a multitude might be housed in a continuous 2,000-story building covering our entire planet. The upper 1,000 stories would contain only the apparatus for running this gigantic warren. Ducts, pipes, wires, elevator shafts, etc., would occupy about half the space in the bottom 1,000 stories. This would leave three or four yards of floor space for each person. I will leave to your imagination the physical details of existing in this ant heap. . . .

The consensus of virtually all population experts was ignored by the United States government, closeted in its own romantic images of a world that was "beautiful for spacious skies, for amber waves of grain." In 1974 the U.S. government decided that it would give no aid to any foreign health clinics that also provided abortions or abortion information—even if the aid money was used for other purposes, specifically for critically needed contraceptive services. In a country like Turkey, where abortion had been legalized at the peak of a population crisis,

U.S. funding regulations prevented counselors from even mentioning abortion. Meanwhile, ninety million people were being added to the planet every year.

During the Reagan administration and even in the "kinder, gentler" Bush era, millions of desperately poor women in developing countries continued to be held hostage by moralistic antiabortion policies here in the United States.

In 1985 the U.S. government suspended financial aid to the UN Population Fund, an organization devoted to family planning. In 1989 George Bush vetoed a $14.6 billion foreign aid bill because it included $15 million for the UN Population Fund, which operates in China, where a one child per family policy is enforced.

In the summer of 1989 thirty-seven U.S. senators (eight of them Republicans) wrote a letter to Bush pleading that he take a stand for the sake of the globe and allow funding to be resumed. The letter was never answered, and some people speculated that it never even got past John Sununu's desk. In any case George Bush had long ago left in the dust the impassioned plea he had made in 1973 as the U.S. ambassador to the United Nations. "Success in the population field, under United Nations leadership," he said, "may determine whether we can resolve successfully the other great questions of peace, prosperity and individual rights that face the world."

A second letter was sent to Bush in March 1990, signed by Senators Patrick Leahy (D., Vermont), Mark Hatfield (R., Oregon), Nancy Kassebaum (R., Kansas), and Barbara Mikulski (D., Maryland), begging for his attention to the critical matter. This letter, too, was unanswered.

Some senators argued that rather than an outright veto, there should have been some attempt at compromise, the obvious being to assure that none of the government funds were sent directly to China. Others grumbled that it was ironic that Bush was suddenly taking such a pious stand toward Chinese policies. He had not even reacted with his normal hyperbole against the slaughter of students that occurred in the summer of 1989.

As world health and population organizations scrambled for

funds, they continued to be dealt legal blows. In a decision that distressed family planning organizations in the United States and abroad, a federal appeals court ruled in October 1989 that the government's Agency for International Development was within its rights to deny financial aid to private groups (such as Planned Parenthood) that supported abortion in foreign countries. The decision set the stage for further tightening of restrictions against any agency that supported the right to abortion anywhere in the world.

Family Planning International Assistance, the international arm of Planned Parenthood, was feared to be the next target of the Bush Administration's stubborn stance. FPIA supported some 140 family planning programs in thirty-five third-world countries, providing contraceptive services to about 1.4 million people. Tragically the cutoff of family services led only to an increase in abortions. According to a 1987 study by Charles Hammerslough of the University of Michigan School of Public Health, if the United States government cut off funding to FPIA, it would result in 69,000 more abortions, 1,200 additional pregnancy-related maternal deaths, and an increase of 311,000 births in a three-year period.

Right-to-lifers pointed to population growth policies in China as an example of the kind of oppression that could occur if population control were given high priority. These policies, which pitted individual choice against the potential survival of the community, might have been acceptable thousands of years ago, but the twentieth century was a different time. People were screaming about "forced abortion," which they said would be the next logical step. Truly logical minds might suggest that China, whose policies were generally oppressive on every front, not just in matters related to population, served as a poor case study. But the human stories emerging from China were hard to ignore.

Take Wang Sai Zhen, a woman who had been forced to undergo four abortions by the time she and her husband, Li Jin Lin, were smuggled out of China to Washington, D.C. The couple decided to take desperate measures when Mrs. Li became pregnant. They feared that China's one-child policy would force a fifth abortion.

The Lis were caught by Immigration Department officials in Albany, and Li was deported. His wife was allowed to remain because of her advanced pregnancy, and the couple's second daughter was born in New York.

Li managed to be smuggled a second time into the United States but was caught once again and jailed. The Lis then hired an attorney to represent their plea for asylum. Their appeal was based on President Bush's earlier promise of safe haven to persons showing "a well-founded fear of persecution from forced sterilizations or abortions in their native land."

In China 1.1 billion people burst at the seams of the land—the largest population concentration on the globe. The pace of population growth has been alarming: In thirty years the population has grown by 800 million.

Traditionally, large families held a high value in China—a favorite saying goes "More sons, more joy"—but this changed as the government struggled to contain population growth. The policy of one child per family, except for approved exceptions, was hard to enforce, but officials believed it necessary. They rigorously denied that forced abortion, such as the Lis described, ever existed—only that women who became accidentally pregnant were "encouraged" to have abortions.

In the more sparsely populated Chinese-occupied country of Tibet, an American physician documented a brutal policy of birth control carried to its most devastating extreme. In his report, "Tibetan Women under China's Birth Control Policy: Tibetan Refugee Accounts of Forced Abortion, Sterilization and Infanticide," Blake Kerr wrote of the severe consequences women faced when they defied the edict against bearing a second child. "Three women I interviewed," Kerr wrote in a *Washington Post* article, "described how a relative or acquaintance of theirs had delivered a healthy baby, only to have a nurse kill it with a lethal injection in the soft spot on the forehead." Kerr added that the trend was toward sterilization, and sometimes incidences of forced abortion and infanticide were not limited to the second or third child.

The stories from China seemed to give credence to Bush's concerns and fueled the antiabortion hysteria. Abortion on demand, activists said, was only a step away from abortion on *command*. Refusing to be drawn into such a draconian scenario, those opposed to the Bush policies repeated the point that the issue was *choice*, including the right to bear children freely.

This debate was about freedom, not force, and the incidences of oppression across the globe appalled everyone. Even while China was clamping down on population growth, an eerie scenario was being played out to the west in Nicolae Ceausescu's Romania. Under Ceausescu's regime, pregnancy became a state policy. "Anyone who avoids having children is a deserter who abandons the laws of national continuity," declared the dictator who sought to bolster his nation's global status by increasing its population to thirty million by the year 2000. Before the regime was overthrown and the policy rescinded, the women of the nation, in spite of their desperate poverty, were forced at gunpoint to have children.

In Muslim India and Pakistan, where women were devalued to the point of subhuman status, their primary role was viewed as bearing children—preferably *male* children. It was feared that the availability of birth control and abortion services would give women an unthinkable status—that of sexual beings in their own right. Muslim traditions argued vigorously against population control, but at the same time it was not unheard of for female infants to be murdered at birth by force or neglect. And with technology available for determining the sex of a fetus prior to birth, it was also not unthinkable that female feticide might become rampant in India.

More extreme examples aside, there was virtually no place on earth that wasn't grappling in some way with the question of abortion. The reasonable route of providing wide access to contraceptive education and supplies to societies plunged in poverty was often ignored, although the outcome of anticontraception policies was a greater incidence of abortion and higher mortality for women.

In the Soviet Union, where it was estimated that the highest rate of abortions occurred—between five and eight for every birth—critics complained that absurd national health policies that opposed birth control education and services had led to rampant abortion. The absence of birth control education was so severe in the Soviet Union that even among educated women, archaic folk remedies, such as douching with lemon juice, were considered viable birth control methods in the 1980's. A 1987 report published by the UN Population Fund stated that the Soviet Union provided the second-lowest amount of birth control information in the world—surpassed only by Romania.

In Japan abortion had been a widely accepted method of family planning for centuries. While the Buddhist and Shinto religions viewed life as sacred, they imposed no policy against abortion. A 1983 government attempt to limit abortion failed.

In Africa, where large families had traditionally been viewed as a sign of relative prosperity, the trend was shifting out of necessity toward regulating procreation—especially in more sophisticated regions, where concern about overpopulation and the rampant spread of sexually transmitted diseases such as AIDS was intensifying the drive for birth control.

Generally, abortion laws in Latin America and the Caribbean were quite restrictive since both regions were under the influence of the Catholic Church. In some countries, such as Brazil, where government birth control policies were less rigid, a full-scale effort to reduce the population growth rate was being initiated. Nevertheless, abortion remained illegal, and although widespread birth control was partially effective, statistics showed that about three million Brazilian women resorted each year to illegal abortions.

In Western nations, birth control and abortion policies were often dominated by Christian sensibilities. For example, in Brussels, Belgium, the Christian Democratic party fought the liberalization of abortion law for almost twenty years before, in 1990, the Belgium Parliament at last reversed an 1867 law banning all abortions in the country. With a population that was 90 percent Roman Catholic, the wrangle was fierce, and even the liberalized law imposed limits, allowing abortion only in the first twelve weeks of pregnancy to a woman who demonstrated a "state of distress."

In France, where Catholicism dominated public policy, a woman who obtained an abortion was subject to a six-month prison sentence prior to legalization in 1974. President Valéry Giscard d'Estaing was far from liberal and was Roman Catholic, but he could not avoid the facts of life in modern France. "Civil law had to be made compatible with real social conditions," he later wrote in his memoirs. "It was not a question, as it had been said, of 'approving' abortion, but to transfer to personal responsibility a part of what until now was in the domain of collective law."

Ironically, the prospect of a reunited Germany presented problems for East German women, who had been unrestricted in their ability to obtain abortions. West German laws were more rigid, requiring the approval of two doctors before an abortion could be performed. Government officials trying to reach a middle ground for compromise were repeatedly bogged down in debate and remained unresolved, even as the two states reached agreement on other issues. Abortion was the explosive cause that divided them.

But the overall global trend since the 1970's has been toward liberalization of abortion laws. In the last two decades at least sixty-five nations have loosened existing restrictions.

Population control has never been an easy concept to build a movement around because it is by nature abstract. It is hard to relate emotionally to five billion people; their sheer numbers swarm across the consciousness and deaden the effect. Empathy rises closer to the surface when one is faced with the desperate plight of the individual poor—the woman burdened with too many children or the poverty-inflicted ghettos teeming with the sad faces of their lost youth. But even here the Reagan and Bush administrations managed to avoid a spark of feeling, most clearly illustrated on the abortion issue. It was the poor who suffered most dramatically from restrictions on contraception and abortion, but in the long run everyone suffered.

While individual states were slugging it out in the autumn of 1989, back in Washington the House and Senate were engaged in a slugfest of their own over a $157 million spending bill that included a Medicaid funding provision for abortions for poor women who were pregnant as a result of rape or incest.

The bill, which passed in both houses, was the first glimmer of hope that an eight-year ban on federal funding for abortions might be lifted. The decision was now in the hands of George Bush. California Democrat Barbara Boxer, who had been a leader in the drive to relax funding restrictions, warned that "the political momentum is so strong right now that if President Bush vetoed this he would be making a big mistake."

Alarmed by political trends that seemed to favor the pro-choice position on abortion, George Bush began easing his way back into the mainstream. Was his position so intractable, were his political debts so great that he could not find a compromise? Bush liked to appear as a reasonable man; his personal distaste for the dramatic was obvious, and he seemed uncomfortable mouthing hard-line words penned for him by his more assertive speech writers. Now he looked desperately for a way to return to the center on abortion. Medicaid funding for victims of rape and incest might prove to be an ideal opportunity since Bush had always left a small opening in his antiabortion ideology for these tragic exceptions. Prior to becoming Ronald Reagan's Vice President, he had even favored Medicaid funding in cases of rape and incest. Now, for the first time in almost ten years, the President hinted that he might be swinging back toward his original position. He let it be known that there could be room for "flexibility" regarding the bill.

Pro-choice legislators who may have experienced a brief moment of hope that the President was sincere about finding a common ground on the issue saw this hope dashed once John Sununu and his legislative assistant, Frederick McClure, began making their rounds on the Hill and describing exactly what kind of "compromise" the White House would be willing to consider. Sununu indicated that Bush might approve a modified rape and incest clause that required incidents to be reported within forty-eight hours (the logic being that this would prevent late-term abortions). He also said that the President wanted to limit the bill to victims of criminal rape, not statutory rape.

The so-called compromises seemed impossible to support. Detractors pointed out that a forty-eight-hour reporting time was completely unreasonable. Remarked Oregon Democrat Les AuCoin: "All a person needs to do is read 'Dear Abby' to realize the lag time in reporting such heinous crimes is measured in longer than hours." Women's groups protested the distinction being made between criminal and statutory rape. In effect, Bush's compromise seemed like no compromise at all.

In the end there was no room for flexibility. An entrenched White House indicated that the bill would likely be vetoed, and it was. Writing to Congress, the President sounded more deeply secure in his extremist position than ever: "That such a child may have been conceived through an unconscionable act of violence makes the question difficult and indeed agonizing. It does not, however, alter the basic fact that federal funding is being sought that would compound a violent act with the taking of an unborn life."

That was hogwash, countered his critics. What Bush was really saying was that poor women were being held to different (higher) standards. Protested Constance A. Morella, a Maryland Republican: "It's discriminatory because the President would support affluent women terminating their pregnancies in case of rape or incest but not allow poor women to get Medicaid funding."

AuCoin agreed, and said bitterly of the President, "Boy, can he show the poor women of America who's boss."

Only a month before, Bush had vetoed a budget measure for Washington, D.C., that included the use of federal and local funds to pay for abortions. Both vetoes seemed to ignore statistics showing that women with family incomes below eleven thousand dollars accounted for 33.1 percent of all those receiving abortions.

Warned John Deardourf, a Republican consultant: "Vetoing the bill is a tragic decision that will haunt him politically for the rest of his public life. It will be a very heavy load on the backs of Republican candidates in the 1990 elections because, in effect, it's saying, 'If you're a poor teenage girl and your father commits incest, you've got to find some other place to go because the government will not help.' "

Kate Michelman of NARAL was distressed by the veto, stating angrily that it showed "George Bush to be meanspirited, without compassion and dramatically out of touch with the public. With one stroke of his pen, President Bush condemned impoverished women to continue crisis pregnancies that can destroy their lives."

But the antiabortion minority in Congress was pleased with the President's veto. "We should thank God that George Bush is in the White House and standing firmly in defense of unborn children," proclaimed Chris Smith, of New Jersey. "Now prolifers have to redouble their grassroots political organizing efforts, so that the Congress elected in 1990 will work with the President in advancing the pro-life cause, rather than undermining it."

ELEVEN

Fetal Rights and Wrongs

Extending full personhood to an individual cell that
is barely visible makes no more sense than declaring acorns to be oak trees and selling them at oak
tree prices.

—CLIFFORD GROBSTEIN, professor emeritus of
biological science and public policy at the
University of California

The medical community has always had an uneasy relationship with the subject of abortion. From the fifth century B.C. the
Hippocratic oath pronounced a doctor's bargain with life, not
death. It is, in fact, one of the rare historical documents to mention abortion at all. The oath states: "I will not give a pessary to
a woman to cause an abortion," a ringing declaration that might
leave little doubt about where the medical community stands.

But more than two thousand years later doctors were not so
sure.

ROCKLAND COUNTY, NEW YORK, March 1990

"Doctors are not all-knowing," said Dr. Elizabeth Hanley
wryly, "much as we would have the population believe that we
are." She sat with her legs crossed in the comfortable study of
her home in upstate New York, as she explained her life and her
dilemma to the interviewer. Dr. Hanley, who was in her thirties

during the 1960's when she performed illegal abortions, was graying now. She had never married or borne children, although she had delivered, she said, by conservative estimate, nearly six thousand babies.

"I stood up and cheered when abortion was legalized in the state of New York," she said. "When the announcement was made, I felt the tension leave my body. It was the first time I had relaxed in eight years. I felt it as vindication, and the legalization also released me from having to perform abortions myself. I could lay down that burden. I have rarely performed an abortion since then; it's been twenty years now. But as an issue abortion has become very prominent in the medical community, and it's growing more so."

"What types of dilemmas are faced in the medical community?" the interviewer wondered.

She considered for a moment before answering. "Some people think it's simple for doctors, that our only concern is with objective issues of medicine and technology. But the doctor's role is quite complex. I think we in the medical community stand at the center of the storm and are pulled by every side. There is our moral responsibility as defined in the Hippocratic oath; there is our social responsibility to the poor, the sick, the needy; our responsibility for global issues of population and sustaining human life in spite of famine and disease; and, of course, our utterly personal responsibility for the best interests of each patient." She raised her hands in a hopeless motion. "All these must be juggled in our approach to abortion. And even if we can manage to form a stand in the midst of the existing technology, new technology continues to expand the nature of our dilemma."

"Such as the abortion pill?"

"Exactly. That's a perfect example. Here's a real dilemma! Of course, the AMA has promoted the testing of this pill in the United States. How could it not? It's a pill that causes fetuses to abort, and some people might immediately throw up the red flag and say, 'No, this is murder.' But wait! The pill also has the potential for saving lives. It is believed to be helpful in treating brain tumors, breast cancer, and other ailments. So how do you decide? Do you bargain one life for another?" She lifted her eyebrows and shrugged.

"Fetal tissue research is another issue with which the medical community has grappled."

"Yes, same dilemma. Naturally some people are going to argue that it's a tacit acceptance of abortion. And a few extremists insist that it could lead to what they so charmingly call wholesale abortion. But here we have this potentially life-giving resource that is tied up in political and legal tangles. In my opinion, it's a crime. The most exciting breakthroughs possible in treating diabetes, Parkinson's disease, and possibly Alzheimer's may be lost to us. And mind you, we're talking about fetuses that are already available. No doctor would ever support the termination of pregnancy for the sole purpose of having more fetal tissue available for research. That's maudlin and ridiculous. Personally, I would go so far as to suggest that fetal tissue research is pro-life, in the most tangible sense of the term."

"Does the answer to this dilemma rest in science rather than in the courts?" her interviewer asked, and Dr. Hanley waved a dismissive hand.

"The medical community presents itself as objective in that its premises are assumed to be scientifically based. But too often these so-called scientific pronouncements are heavily weighted by the personal prejudices of individual doctors. What people don't always appreciate is that every scientist and every medical professional is first and foremost a human being."

More than any other group, doctors and scientists are directly faced with the question of the real status of the fetus. Is the fetus biologically human? Is there any way to know for sure? Surely in the domain of science, answers could be found that are not available in the ideologically driven corridors of religion and politics. But the scientific community is not party to the answers that would make the most difference in a resolution of the debate. Here, too, opinions differ and passions flare.

On one side are doctors like A. W. Liley, a professor of fetal physiology at the National Women's Hospital in New Zealand. Dr. Liley has been called the father of fetology by right-to-lifers, who find him to be a powerful ally. Liley has written extensively, tracing the journey of the fetus, describing it in colorfully emotional and human terms. His work has added weight to the argument that the fetus is a person at every stage of its development. Writes Dr. Liley:

> . . . Biologically, at no stage can we subscribe to the view that the foetus is a mere appendage of the mother. Genetically, mother and baby are separate individuals from conception. . . .
>
> On reaching the uterus, this young individual implants in the spongy lining and with a display of physiological power, suppresses his mother's menstrual period. This is his home for the next 270 days and to make it habitable the embryo develops a placenta and a protective capsule of fluid for himself.

Liley goes on to trace the growth of the fetus during its earliest days. "By 63 days," he concludes, "he will grasp an object placed in the palm and can make a fist." He continues:

> We know that he moves with a delightful easy grace in his buoyant world, that foetal comfort determines foetal position. He is responsive to pain and touch and cold and sound and light. He drinks his amniotic fluid, more if it is artificially sweetened, less if it is given an unpleasant taste. He gets hiccups [*sic*] and sucks his thumb. He wakes and sleeps. He gets bored with repetitive signals but can be taught to be alerted by a first signal for a second different one. And finally he determines his birthday, for unquestionably the onset of labor is a unilateral decision of the foetus.

Dr. Liley's description might sound closer to poetry than science, yet it's hard to disagree that life—indeed, something that is potentially human life—is present from the moment of conception. But what kind of life is it? And what is its relationship to the unrefutably human life of its mother? The criteria for determining that are usually left to the theologians and ethicists.

But Charles A. Gardner, who is conducting his doctoral research on the genetic control of brain development at the University of Michigan Medical School's department of anatomy and cell biology, thinks the suggestion of personhood for an embryo contradicts all that scientists have learned in this century about the development of life. Gardner lends a fresh perspective to the argument when he notes, "The fertilized egg is clearly not a pre-packaged human being. There is no body plan, no blueprint, no tiny being pre-formed and waiting to unfold. It is not 'complete' or 'the totality' of a person. The fertilized egg may follow many different paths; the route will be penned in only as the paths are taken." So, is an embryo human? "It's of human origin," Gardner agrees, adding, "But so is every egg and every sperm cell. The problem is in the definition of the word 'human.' It may be either an adjective or a noun. As an adjective it carries no particular moral weight. We have human hair, human fingernails; the human cells in our saliva all have forty-six chromosomes, but they have no special significance." Gardner points out that the determining factor of humanity, as we understand it, lies in the brain function, which does not reach maturity until the sixth or seventh month. His premise is supported by other experts in embryology. Clifford Grobstein, who has dedicated much of his seventy-four years to the study of embryology, suggests that the assignment of human personality to the fetus is more an activity of our empathy than an actuality. At conception, he contends, only genetic individuality exists, "a set of hereditary properties that define an individual. . . . But there are five other essential aspects of individuality still to come: developmental, functional, behavioral, psychic and social—which means that full individuality emerges in stages over time."

WASHINGTON, D.C., November 1989

Dr. Louis Sullivan, the Bush choice for secretary of health and human services, told Congress during his confirmation hearing that "we have a number of medical advances that have occurred as a result of research with fetal tissue," a fact that Sullivan pointed to as a very positive development. He hinted that he might be in favor of discontinuing a ban on government-funded fetal tissue research imposed by the Reagan administration. Sullivan made this concession on the same day that, bowing to pressure from the Bush administration, he officially reversed his long-held view that women should be free to choose abortion. The tiny window of progressive medical policy left open by his potential support of fetal tissue research was somewhat encouraging.

But nearly a year later Sullivan was persuaded to close the window. In November 1989, ignoring the recommendations of two federal advisory panels that saw no conflict in the use of fetal tissue for research, his office issued a statement (most likely penned by Bill Wead, now Sullivan's speech writer) continuing the ban. "It's a matter of heart and mind," read James O. Mason, the assistant secretary who made the announcement. Mason, a Sununu-backed appointee, was said to have been placed in HHS by antiabortionists in order to keep a watchful eye on the none-too-solid Sullivan and assure that hard-line policies remained in force.

Exactly *how* the fetal tissue ban was a matter of heart and mind was deeply puzzling to many both within and outside the medical community. After all, the choice in this matter was not whether or not to perform an abortion. The choice was whether or not to use the tissue of already aborted fetuses for critical medical research or send it to the incinerator. Scientists believed the value of fetal tissue research was indisputable.

But according to Mason, fetal tissue research pitted the rights of fetuses against those patients who might be helped by it and therefore had questionable value as a research tool.

Mason's stated fear that women would begin selling their fetuses or, more absurdly, would choose abortions for altruistic, pro-research reasons was completely unsupported by evidence or common sense. In any case, such possibilities could be eliminated by the establishment of strict regulations—the same kinds of regulations that govern the sale of organs. In fact, the HHS panel that reviewed and recommended a lifting of the ban specifically suggested that there should be laws limiting the use of the tissue, including a prohibition on payment to donors.

It was unclear to scientists where Sullivan and Mason received the data upon which they based their decision to continue the ban. No statistics were given; no documents from medical experts. No formal studies had been conducted that showed women more likely to seek abortions if public health policy allowed the use of fetal tissue in clinical research. But Washington observers did notice that there were two powerful men involved behind the scenes in making the decision: the White House chief of staff John Sununu and Orrin Hatch, the right-wing Mormon senator from Utah. The involvement of these committed antiabortionists led some people to conclude that the issue really seemed to be about denying the legitimacy of anything that touched abortion.

More than an ethical dilemma, the issue appeared to be a simple regulatory matter. But policy continued to be clouded by the administration's intractability on the subject of abortion—in spite of pleas from the scientific community. Thirty-two medical research and education organizations, including the American Medical Association, the Association of American Medical Colleges, and the American Academy of Pediatrics, sent a letter to Sullivan, urging that the ban be lifted. "It is clear to us that the potential for good to result from this research outweighs the concerns about the impact on the abortion rate in this country, concerns that are at best speculative," the letter stated.

What one observer referred to as abortion gridlock was taking hold of the Capitol, making any related issue a hotbed of dissension and stalling. "I know of no precedents of repression of federal science like this one," complained Dr. John C. Fletcher of the University of Virginia, formerly the chief ethics officer of the Clinical Center of the National Institutes of Health. Added Dr.

Birt Harvey, president of the American Academy of Pediatrics: "It's like the Middle Ages. This ban interferes with research, with new knowledge that is going to save the lives of fetuses, babies and adults as well."

VANCOUVER, Canada, April 1990

As a nurse Nan Patton Harrison had seen abortion from every angle. But today the issue was more urgent because Nan Patton Harrison had Parkinson's disease. For years she had struggled with her inner turmoil—especially over abortions performed after four months. She had experienced the greatest trauma when women who aborted or miscarried asked to have their fetuses baptized. "It has happened to me more than once," she recalled. "Perhaps it was because of my empathy that they always asked me to do the baptism. It is difficult to describe what it feels like to take a bedpan and two sets of forceps and search for a fetus in this slough of incomplete placenta. I have done it, and literally it is a search for a blob of mucus. It is hard to find. Once a doctor came in while I was searching and watched and suddenly said, 'There it is.' I said, 'No, it's not.' He said, 'What difference does it make? Are you going to say a Hail Mary over it?' After I baptized the fetus, I flushed it down the hopper." Nan closed her eyes and shook her head. The memory was sobering and painful. After a moment she sighed.

"But today I have different thoughts about the significance of the fetus because of the diagnosis that I have Parkinson's disease. One of the newest medical discoveries is the fetal tissue transplant that replaces the dopamine lost in Parkinson's. It has proved successful in cases done so far, but because of the heated debate on abortion, vital research that can save the life and give quality of life to myself and tens of thousands of people on this continent is being lost."

She stared thoughtfully out the window at the tree-lined, prettily manicured street. "It's interesting, when you become involved in a discussion of the pros and cons of abortion, to find how strong people's positions are to save a fetus. My neighbor, who is a very dear friend and a devout Catholic, is adamantly opposed to abortion. One of the very few times we have had harsh words has been over abortion. She believes to take a life at any stage is wrong. When I suggested to her that if someone had an abortion, that fetal tissue could save my life, she looked at me in surprise and said, 'I never thought of it that way. I'll have to think about that.'

"It's different when you have to confront the issue on a personal level, and I think that people with very strong opinions against fetal tissue research should sit down and talk with someone who has Parkinson's disease and ask themselves, Is it more important to save a life or to bring an unwanted baby into the world?" A spark of anger glimmered from Nan's eyes. "It is easy to make decisions if they have nothing to do with you or walk with a sign on your back thinking you're righteous. But what if it was the choice of a fetal tissue transplant for your mother or father or sister or brother? What if it would save your own life?"

Medical technology was adding layers of complexity to the abortion issue.

Arguments over the status of the embryo came to a head in the summer of 1989 in a dramatic confrontation between an estranged couple in the sleepy southern town of Maryville, Tennessee. Mary Sue and Junior Davis's decision to dissolve their marriage had left one major issue unresolved: what to do with the seven frozen embryos Junior Davis had fertilized to enable his wife to become pregnant.

Mary Sue Davis believed the embryos belonged to her and were hers to have implanted if she chose. Her estranged husband disagreed, claiming that she had no right to have an embryo implanted without his permission. His argument, in a bizarre twist, was that he had the right to control his own reproduction.

The question facing the court was this: What were the frozen embryos? Marital property to be divided in a divorce settlement? The entitlement of the mother? Potentially impregnating matter to be taken from the couple and implanted anonymously? Prefetuses?

Fertility experts insisted that it was inaccurate to confuse the embryos with fetuses or to assign them rights to life. According to Joyce Zeitz of the American Fertility Society, the four to eight cells contained in each preembryo or blastocyst did not necessarily constitute matter that would take hold. In the ordinary fertilization process, two thirds of embryos at this early stage would not lead to fertilization.

The conflict was another example of how unprepared the courts and ethical scholars are to meet the unprecedented outcomes of new technology. More than four thousand frozen embryos, governed by state laws, are lodged in the United States. Some laws seem absurd. In Louisiana, for example, a 1986 statute defines a frozen embryo as a juridical person, giving it full legal status and the right to be represented by a lawyer in court. That's quite a stretch for four to eight cells! But in Tennessee, where the Davises lived, no precedent existed at all, including provisions for the disposal of the embryos in case of divorce or death.

Mary Sue Davis's appeal for "custody" was based not so much in her belief that the embryos were her property as in her belief that the embryos were the "beginning of life" and she was their "mother."

Of course, this was Tennessee, in the South, where preborn life was fondly treated. Judge W. Dale Young was therefore not content to rule on the appropriate disposal of the frozen embryos created by science with the help of Mary Sue and Junior Davis. Instead he chose to make his September 1989 ruling a grand pronouncement about human life. According to Judge Young, the frozen cells were "human beings existing as embryos." Despite scientific testimony that the four to eight cells in each embryo had not yet begun to exhibit unique characteristics, the judge wrote, "From fertilization, the cells of a human embryo are differentiated, unique and specialized to the highest degree of distinction. The court finds that human life begins at the moment of conception. Mr. and Mrs. Davis have accomplished their original intent to produce a human being to be known as their child."

Having thus ruled, Judge Young turned over temporary custody of the embryos to Mary Sue Davis, so that she might have them implanted in her womb. If a birth should result, custody, support, visitation, and other parental rights issues could be reviewed.

The Davises' battle did not end with Judge Young's decision. It dragged on and on, the subject of repeated appeals. Mary Sue Davis remarried soon after the divorce became final, and she decided to donate the frozen embryos to a fertility clinic for use by another childless couple. Junior Davis said he would continue to appeal. "There is just no way I am going to donate them," he said. "I feel that's my right. If there was a child from them, then I would be a parent to it. And I don't want a child out there to be mine if I can't be a parent to it."

Many observers could only shake their heads at how far the arguments related to reproductive rights could go. In this ruling Judge Young seemed to miss the obvious predicament of declaring these cells human life. What if Mary Sue Davis became impregnated with the first injection? Would the six others then by law have to be implanted in other women? Were they seven orphaned babies looking for homes? Clearly, Mary Sue Davis could not herself conceive seven children within the two-year life-span of the embryos. With tongue in cheek, Barbara Ehrenreich, a commentator on social issues, asked, "When you find a used condom, say, in the backseat of your husband's car, do you stop to say a few kind words to the millions of unborn—and in this case, unconceived—or do you just get out the sponge and the Formula 409?" For this absurd speculation, Ehrenreich handed the credit to medical science, which "just keeps turning up tiny *persons* where you'd least expect them."

When women were not being ignored completely in the skirmishes over the protection of fetal life, they were being subjected to a sharper scrutiny. Once the value of fetal life took center stage, the questions then became: How far could society take its protections? Was it enough to outlaw abortion, or would the behavior and health habits of every pregnant woman be monitored to ensure a healthy fetus? What some referred to as the pregnancy police were popping up with alarming frequency. In Wyoming a pregnant woman was charged with child abuse after prosecutors accused her of excessive drinking. In Florida a woman was convicted of delivering cocaine to a minor—her fetus via the umbilical cord. In a Wisconsin factory women of child-bearing age were barred from jobs that involved high lead exposure, whether they were pregnant or not—allegedly as insurance against problems if they were someday to become pregnant. These and other cases highlighted a dreaded trend. If fetal rights were assumed, virtually any pregnant woman could be held liable for what she ate, drank, and did every minute of the day. In a *New York Times* op-ed piece expressing alarm over this trend, Jeanne Mager Stellman, of Columbia University, and Joan E. Bertin, of the ACLU, wrote: "For women, the result can be awesome. At best, they will suffer the anxiety that even moderate normal activity can damage their real or potential offspring. At worst, women will be treated as walking wombs, perpetually pregnant until proved otherwise, with pregnancy police peeping in at every door and restricting every activity . . ."

The status of the embryo at its earliest stages was relevant to the most significant scientific trend related to abortion. For years scientists in France had been successfully testing a method of abortion that promised to change the issue forever and to make surgical methods of abortion obsolete. It came in the form of a pill.

Was it chemical warfare against the unborn or the most advanced birth control technology ever devised? Étienne-Émile Baulieu, a French biochemist, found himself swept up in this swirl of controversy after he announced the development of RU 486, an abortion pill that had been tested and found to be effective and symptom-free.

Baulieu, a handsome man, with a rugged face and a boyish shock of dark hair, looked far younger than his sixty-two years. He was charismatic and appealing; prior to RU 486, he'd been best known for the long love affair he had once conducted with Sophia Loren. Now he was to be in the news again, on an even more provocative matter.

More than ten years of research by Baulieu and his colleagues at the French pharmaceutical company Groupe Roussel-Uclaf went into the development of RU 486. It was an antihormone, a synthetic chemical that, when taken within the first seven weeks of pregnancy, induced miscarriage by blocking the action of progesterone, a hormone that enabled the uterus to retain a fertilized egg.

One tablet taken on each of three consecutive days, followed by a dose of prostaglandin, a drug that causes the uterus to contract, produced a result similar to miscarriage. Clinical trials on four thousand women worldwide showed the pill to have a 96 to 98 percent success rate, with virtually no side effects.

In announcing the development of the pill, Baulieu pointed out that more than fifty million women worldwide had surgical abortions each year. And by World Health Organization statistics, some two hundred thousand of these surgical abortions ended in death for women—particularly in poor, developing countries. Baulieu saw the pill as a breakthrough in lifesaving technology that might prevent these deaths from occurring.

Baulieu was not a firebrand of the pro-choice movement. His position on abortion had always remained carefully moderate. For example, he supported the use of the pill only in the first trimester of pregnancy, believing that later abortions were less justifiable.

He was also conscious of the role semantics played in the debate. "Because of the right-to-life people, abortion means a little baby that one pulls out of the mother," he said. "That's horrible. We must get rid of the word 'abortion,' which I have tried to do with the word 'contra-gestation.' "

He scoffed at the term "pro-life," saying, "The people who are really working for life are scientists who are trying to save the lives of the 200,000 women who die from botched abortions."

RU 486 also carried potential for being a method of enhancing life. Tests showed that it might be used safely and effectively to treat other hormone-related diseases, such as tumors and breast cancer.

In 1988 the French government gave permission for the pill to be marketed nationally, but the permission was followed by a horrified outcry by the Catholic Church, a force of considerable influence in France. Antiabortion activists in the United States scurried to join the debate, notifying Roussel and its German parent company, Hoechst AG, that they would stage a massive worldwide boycott of the company's products. Bowing to pressure, Roussel announced its decision to suspend marketing of the pill.

The decision was short-lived because an even greater furor accompanied news of the suspension. Then the French government stepped in. Because it owned 36 percent of the pharmaceutical company and had the power to take away Roussel's patent for RU 486, it was able to order the pill back on the market. Explained Health Minister Claude Évin: "From the moment government approval of this drug was granted, RU 486 became the moral property of women, not just the property of the drug company."

Roussel-Uclaf complied, but Hoechst AG announced that the pill would not be distributed outside France in the foreseeable future, except in China, where it had also been approved.

American women would not have it so easy. With strong opposition from the White House, the promise of a sluggish FDA approval process, the inevitable product boycotts, and other headaches, pharmaceutical companies in the United States were not exactly welcoming the pill's arrival with open arms—even though there were an estimated four hundred thousand U.S. women who would use the pill each year.

The birth control pill had once been the subject of a similar debate, with Catholic bishops at the forefront of the effort to prevent its use in this country, claiming it was part of an effort to "coerce" women not to conceive. But by the 1970's the availability of the birth control pill had become a nonissue except for the most extreme antiabortion groups, such as the American Life League (ALL). ALL, an organization with about 250,000 members, was opposed not only to abortion but to certain methods of birth control—in particular, the "abortifacients," such as the pill and IUD. ALL's president, Judie Brown, once suggested that married people who wanted control of conception use "self-restraint" or "natural methods of spacing children." According to Brown, "Contraception means better killing through chemistry."

More than fifty-seven million American women of childbearing age struggled each year with the failings and side effects of traditional methods of birth control. As evidence, about six million unwanted pregnancies occurred in the United States each year. There were little data indicating that these pregnancies were in any significant way due to women using no birth control at all. The abortion-as-birth-control accusation was merely a smoke screen for a more disturbing fact: the inertia of the United States in testing and making available more effective forms of birth control.

A 1990 study published by the National Academy of Sciences reported that contraceptive research was nearly nonexistent in the United States, while other countries had aggressively tested safer and more convenient methods. Among those available elsewhere but not in the United States were an injection that provided two months' protection and a skin implant that released a contraceptive hormone into the bloodstream for up to five years. (At this writing, the implant, under the brand name Norplant, has been approved for use in the United States.)

In this country efforts to increase federal support for contraceptive research and testing continued to run up against effective opposition from conservative and antiabortion groups.

The irony was that the very absence of effective birth control measures had been largely responsible for the necessity of 1.5 million abortions every year. Population experts estimated that at least half these abortions would be prevented were there more effective means of birth control.

Even former Surgeon General C. Everett Koop admitted that "we are at a very strange place in history where the people most opposed to abortions are also most opposed to the one thing that would stop them, which is contraceptive information."

Much of the abortion furor has traditionally been over late-term abortions, with antiabortionists waving their photos of bloodied mature fetuses like flags of righteousness. Privately many leaders within the antiabortion movement admitted that the introduction of the abortion pill would diminish the visual appeal of their message. Molly Yard, president of the National Organization for Women, speculated that what terrified the antiabortion movement about RU 486 was that it might end the abortion debate once and for all, finally placing abortion where it belonged: in the hands of each individual woman.

Meanwhile, the FDA had not even scheduled the pill for consideration. And although FDA regulations allow Americans to carry into the United States for personal use prescription drugs that are not yet approved for sale, they made a sole exception for RU 486.

In June 1990 the American Medical Association voted overwhelmingly in favor of testing RU 486, a vote that brought a fevered response from antiabortionists. "I think it is outrageous for doctors to be thinking up better ways for killing their little patients," said John Wilke.

Only the California Medical Center placed itself on the line: To date it is only institution that has started testing the drug in the United States.

In the background of the debate one can almost hear the wheels of the black market grinding into action. Privately even the pill's most determined opponents wonder if technology can be kept from American women—even if they have to procure it illegally. As Sharon Camp, Ph.D., vice-president of the Population Crisis Committee, observed, "If tons of cocaine can be shipped across the nation's borders despite the best efforts of thousands of law enforcement agents, how can a small pill like RU 486 be kept out?"

Ironically, the more the government restricts the availability of surgical abortions, the more likely it is that RU 486 will become widely used in this country, legally or illegally. As a method it is easy, it is private; once available, it would be virtually impossible to stop its widespread use. Then, at last, there would be no sure method or action of antiabortion activists that could prevent women from making choices about their bodies in the privacy of their own homes.

In 1977, five years before he became Ronald Reagan's surgeon general, C. Everett Koop wrote an article for the *Human Life Review* titled "The Slide to Auschwitz." In it he postulated that abortion was just the first trembling of a deadly avalanche that would lead ultimately to infanticide and the most brutal forms of euthanasia.

Koop's words reflected a despair over man's inhumanity, but they were not well grounded in any historical or ethical premise. It must be noted that the only widespread practice of infanticide recorded preceded the technology that could provide safe, early abortions. For our ancestors, infanticide was the safest and most effective means of population control. It would seem that with today's technology, it would become less, rather than more, likely that such brutality would be repeated. The nightmare vision that Koop promoted seemed to exist only in the minds of those who would close the doors to development of effective contraceptives or refuse to make the abortion pill available in this country.

In 1990 abortion was legal without restraint in most parts of the United States. But a new question was emerging from the strife of the past twenty years: Who would remain to perform these abortions? Statistics were showing a new trend toward doctors' refusing to perform the procedure.

In North Dakota, where restrictive abortion laws and conservative peer pressure within rural communities formed a joint barrier, it was hard to get an abortion. In the entire state there was not one doctor who performed abortions; clinics were forced to fly doctors in from other states. Public sentiment against abortion was so strong that North Dakota was the only state without a Planned Parenthood affiliate.

But even in locations of less bedrock conservatism, doctors were balking at performing abortions. A survey of four thousand members of the American College of Obstetrics and Gynecology reported that while 84 percent said they thought abortion should be legal and available, only one third of the doctors said they performed them, and two thirds of that number performed very few.

Some doctors spoke of the stigma of being an abortionist. It was considered the dirty work of medicine, a counteraction to the altruistic spirit of the profession. Doctors did not win awards for being good abortionists, and many of them felt stigmatized by the label and isolated from their colleagues in the medical profession. Furthermore, the constant harassment from anti-abortion groups within the local communities—which included bomb threats and picketing doctors' homes—took its toll. "Every day I have to walk through picketers who call me a murderer, who shout obscenities, and who make references to my children," reported a Texas doctor who performed abortions. "We get harassing letters and telephone calls, and I have received numerous death threats."

Sometimes doctors, like Bernard Nathanson, claimed to have experienced a conversion after years of performing abortions. But these conversions could not be taken at scientific face value; they required evaluation in the context of the personal, emotional, and social pressures that existed within a doctor's community and home environment. The combined factors of burnout and stigma might understandably lead to a change of heart. And many doctors, like Elizabeth Hanley, admitted that their decisions not to perform abortions were relatively safe because they were no longer the last desperate chances in an illegal abortion underground.

What was ironic about the medical community's move away from providing abortion care was that it opened the door for the revival of midwifery, whose existence organized medicine was trying to eliminate when it lobbied for tighter abortion restrictions in the nineteenth century. The doctors wanted control, but now they were abdicating responsibility.

TWELVE

Truth and Consequences

Yes, Jesus is my Lord and Savior. . . . Yes, I have
been born again. . . . Yes, I am opposed to abortion.

—GEORGE BUSH

SEATTLE, WASHINGTON, March 1990

Barbara Allen answered the hot line phone and immediately
recognized the quiet, hesitant voice of Roberta, the young
woman to whom she had spoken a couple of weeks earlier.

"I promised I'd call," the young woman said. "I—I felt like
you really cared, and I want you to know I appreciated that. I
felt very alone."

Barbara's heart went out to Roberta. "I know, honey. Believe
me, I know. Listen, did you call the numbers I gave you?"

"Yes. People were very nice. But nobody could really help me
very much, and I understand that." Her laugh sounded more like
a gulp. "This is my responsibility, not theirs. I've really given a
lot of thought to my options, and I know you'll hate this, but I've
decided to have an abortion."

Barbara felt her skin tighten; a lump crawled up her chest. For
a moment she didn't know what to say. Then, keeping her voice
level, she said, "I understand how desperate you feel. I wonder
if you could do one more thing."

"I've really made up my mind."

"Please, this is important. Just take one more hour and come in here. Take a look at a film we've prepared. Learn some of the facts."

"Oh . . . I don't think—"

"Roberta, I want you to know that I respect the fact that this is your decision to make. But it's only being fair to yourself that you make it carefully and have all the information available. Please. Just one more hour. Then you'll be ready to do whatever you have to do. I promise I won't interfere."

Roberta sighed. "Well, okay, maybe before I go to work. But I really think I've decided to go ahead with this."

"Can you come in tomorrow?"

"Um . . . yes. Okay. Around four."

"Good. I'll look forward to seeing you then."

The pregnancy consultation center was located on the fifth floor of a modern steel and glass building. Roberta sat by herself in the front room, waiting for Barbara to come out. It was a lovely room, designed to soothe with its indirect lighting and pale peach carpeting. A stereo played soft music. Neatly arranged racks of pamphlets and magazines lined the walls.

Roberta picked up a color brochure called *When You Were Formed in Secret*. She flipped through the pages. In the section titled "Birth Day," she was drawn to the dramatic photo of the moment of birth. The text moved her:

As you quietly waited, "locked" in the position for birth, a time came when you heard a loving whisper from afar saying, "It is time." And with all the strength of your being you responded with a resounding, "Yes!" And then the sounds around you began to change as you felt the first squeezes from the uterine muscles which you triggered into action.

Within hours, the noble labor of birth transported you from your warm, watery world into an environment which was a chilly, twenty degrees colder. Not having the buoyancy of water around you it was harder for you to hold your head upright and five times as hard for you to breathe. You experienced pangs of hunger as you adjusted from a constant flow of nourishment to some six meals a day. . . .

You soon began communicating your discomforts and needs to your mom and you again found solace and peace in her shared warmth. If she held your head next to her beating heart you heard it and fell asleep.

As your mother looked down upon you, she spotted your fingernails which needed trimming and as she continued to study you in your sleep, her heart would often fill with joy, realizing you would now know grace in the light of life. Her hope had become a certain, living love. She was very, very glad.

Barbara came out from the back, smiling widely, and she grasped Roberta's hand as she rose from the couch. "It's so good to meet you," she said fervently. Roberta judged Barbara to be in her forties—a pretty, motherly woman who inspired immediate confidence. If she hadn't felt the same vibrations over the phone, she certainly wouldn't have been here today. Barbara definitely had a way about her.

"So, how are you feeling?" Barbara asked.

"Fine, most of the time." Roberta blushed. She was embarrassed to be having a conversation about her pregnancy. Usually she tried not to think of herself as a pregnant woman.

"Good." Barbara was still holding her hand. "Come with me. I want you to look at a film we show people who come to the center. It gives you some of the facts about abortion that you may not know." They walked down a hallway as Barbara continued talking. "You know, Roberta, the pro-abortion people say we don't care about women; we just care about fetuses. But that's not true. As you'll see in this film, we are very concerned about your health and safety. The story that never gets told is how dangerous abortion is." They entered a conference room, and Barbara motioned Roberta to take a seat while she readied the projector. "I'm going back to my office," she said when everything was ready. "I'll be back when the film is over."

True to Barbara's promise, the early part of the film focused on dangers to women. Many women, it said, become sterile as a result of abortion. It went on to say that 16.7 percent of women who have abortions need blood transfusions, 4.2 percent experience torn cervixes, and 27 percent develop fevers following abortions.

Roberta shifted uncomfortably in her seat as the film changed focus to show graphic depictions of abortions, including piles of bloodied fetuses in garbage cans. "The baby is not an extension of the mother. It is a separate human being," the announcer said.

Barbara returned within minutes of the end of the film. She sat down next to Roberta at the table. "Would you like to talk about what you saw?" she asked gently.

Roberta felt shaky and tearful. She didn't trust her voice. She shook her head no.

Barbara's voice remained steady and compassionate. "It's a hard film to watch," she acknowledged. "I know it always gives me a chill. But I care about you. I wanted you to know the facts before you made a final decision. Ultimately it's going to be your choice. But such a big choice deserves careful thought and education." She smiled warmly at Roberta. "Would you like to sit here a while or just talk?"

Roberta stood up. "No . . . I have to go or I'll be late for work."

"You'll call if you want to talk?"

"Yes."

At the door Barbara grasped Roberta's hand. "Do you pray?" she asked.

"No."

"Try it. Take some time alone and just pray. I really believe, Roberta, that God will help you get through this and show you the way."

Abortion counseling is highly recommended by many medical and psychiatric organizations, but the question remains whether what occurs in clinics like the one Barbara Allen works in constitutes true counseling or merely masks the hidden agenda of antiabortion activism.

The facts presented are often contradictory to those offered by such organizations as the Centers for Disease Control in Atlanta. According to Dr. Herschel Lawson of the Division for Reproductive Health at the CDC, there is no evidence that abortion leads to increased incidence of infertility, only 0.2 percent of women need blood transfusions, fewer than 1 percent experience cervical tearing, and only 0.2 percent get significant fevers. Research conducted in Eastern European countries where abortion is legal supports the evidence of the CDC that abortions are relatively safe—with only three deaths registered for every hundred thousand abortions performed in the first twelve weeks. The so-called statistics of the antiabortion movement are more often invention than fact. But they are so packed with emotion and righteousness that often the voices of truth find themselves crying out in the wilderness. Once the idea is planted in the public consciousness that abortion leads to infertility or is fraught with medical danger, it is hard to undo the damage. Ideas seem to gain veracity the more often they are stated, and the antiabortion movement is vocal.

Scare tactics are easiest of all to employ against those who are most vulnerable. Roberta had many confusing feelings, and Barbara Allen was gentle and soothing. Her voice was measured; her words were reasonable. "Learn the facts," she said, "that's all I ask." But she was not above manipulating the facts. She didn't think it was wrong. If it meant saving a life, the end justified the means.

By early 1990 abortion was making many Republicans miserable. They had been drifting along nicely for so long, building their antiabortion platforms in the shifting sands. Suddenly it was as though a tremendous storm had risen in the night, and now they felt in danger of being overcome by the issue. To be sure, there were the hard-liners—those whose moral position against abortion could withstand any assault. But like the population they represented, most politicians fell into the muddled middle. They were ambivalent about abortion rights and now grew wary as the evidence mounted that they might be on the wrong side of a popular issue.

The political climate around abortion had changed since the *Webster* decision delivered its mandate to the states. As political consultant Robert Squier observed, "People who favored abortions more or less on demand didn't pay much attention to the pro-lifers' sit-ins at clinics as long as the Court said 'don't touch' on abortion to the states. But now that they know they can't hide behind the Court's skirts, they're out there in the country making sure that politicians pay attention."

American politicians have always had to walk the fine line between ideology and pragmatism, and when push comes to shove, most political figures prefer to err on the side of pragmatism. More than anything, Washington is a city where compromises are made and deals are struck; the nation's representatives scurry to win a point here, concede a point there. They are fundamentally unaccustomed to dealing with issues as complex and resistant to compromise as abortion. And until *Webster*, there was little concern about abortion as a tangible issue that could make or break political careers. Suddenly it was the litmus issue of every election, and in the whirlpool of emotion Republicans were finding that their party's platform was a noose around their necks. Liberal political commentator Michael Kinsley described the abortion issue for politicians as a "nightmarish gauntlet that has to be run between two ravening mobs."

Abortion is the kind of issue that any politician has to hate because it is not framed by the traditional borders. It is an issue that is most cogently defined in the moral and religious arenas; there is something faintly comical about the idea of a group of mostly male government officials debating when human life begins. Furthermore, it is revealing that virtually all women members of Congress, be they Democrats or Republicans, support a woman's right to choose.

The other problem politicians were facing was the widespread public view that the leadership of both the pro-choice and antiabortion sides were out of sync with general opinion. A 1989

New York Times/CBS News poll found that 58 percent of the American population viewed the leadership of both sides as "extremist." Indeed, the greatest headache in the abortion debate, from a politician's standpoint, was this lack of an acceptable middle ground on the subject. Once *Webster* had removed the safety net of the courts, many politicians found themselves being forced to seriously address the issue for the first time and were battered from side to side by the rhetoric of pro and con. The wide middle road had been sucked away in the storm of passion. Waffling was no longer allowed.

In the year following *Webster*, there was a great shuffle to get to safe ground in the nation's capital—mostly among Republicans whose position had been right-to-life. It was very rare indeed to find a change of heart from pro-choice to antichoice, although the few lagging antichoice Democrats, such as potential presidential candidate Sam Nunn were falling into line with popular sentiment. Even GOP party chairman Lee Atwater, a single-minded ideologue, relaxed the litmus test somewhat in 1990 when he addressed the abortion issue by floating a new definition of the GOP as an "umbrella party," saying, "We welcome different and diverse positions." Atwater was enough of a political pragmatist to understand that the party could suffer if it was perceived as taking an unreasonably extreme position on abortion—especially in light of the strong showing pro-choice candidates were achieving in elections. Could the umbrella of the GOP encompass those who defied its own platform position on abortion? According to Atwater, it could. "There is no litmus test on any issue which would be grounds for repudiating a Republican who believes in our overall philosophy and who supports the President and supports this party. I would hope that voters support Republican candidates regardless of their position on abortion."

Michael McCurry, spokesman for the Democratic National Committee, scoffed at Atwater's new show of tolerance. "We stand by our party platform," he said, "and it sounds like Mr. Atwater is taking a walk on his."

Atwater was similarly criticized by members of his own party who believed it was a bad precedent to back down on significant platform issues. "If you go around saying our party is big enough for people no matter what their view on abortion, I think you signal that it's not an important issue," observed Gary Bauer, an antiabortion activist who had served as a domestic policy adviser under Reagan. "We would not go around saying that the party is big enough for people who want to raise Federal income taxes, and we would not go around saying the party is big enough for people who want to gut the defense budget. If the Republican Party cannot turn saving lives into a winning issue then it has no business aspiring to be the governing party of this nation."

Other Republicans were falling out of step with devastating speed. Awkward as it might be to announce an overnight conversion from "Abortion is murder" to "Women have the right to choose," many politicians were nevertheless biting the bullet out of expediency and ambition. Political ambition had long been the basis for many remarkable conversions, such as George Bush's own rebirth on abortion.

In the aftermath of the November 1989 elections Republicans gamely tried to put a brave face on the defeats suffered, in part, because of the President's and the party's stand on abortion. As they looked ahead to 1990 and beyond, hope that the issue would simply go away was dimming. A new stance was needed, and that meant a revision of strategy. "If we go into 1990 and abortion is the issue . . . we will lose on that issue," predicted Senator Bob Packwood of Oregon, adding that "we deserve to lose on that issue if we have the position that we've had in the past."

What the politicians sweating bullets over abortion hoped for most desperately was that there was some way to make a compromise. Many believed that beneath the loud cries of pro-choice and antiabortion advocates rested a "pro-compromise" majority that supported a woman's right to choose, with reasonable limitations. Few believed that abortion would ever again be outlawed entirely; even if *Roe* v. *Wade* were overturned, it was almost inconceivable by 1990 that individual states would successfully return the matter to the dark days of illegality. Why not compromise? It was a reasonable question, but the chances of compromise seemed unlikely. First, it was doubtful that those people opposed to abortion could accept any compromise whatsoever. If one truly believed that abortion was equivalent to murder, how was compromise possible? By the same token, those who supported a woman's right to choose abortion were unenthusiastic about so-called compromises that they feared would place an undue burden on individual women—in particular the young and the poor. Every proposed compromise that had ever been suggested reinforced the division of classes. In essence, compromise was a code word meaning the limitation of rights for those who did not have the power or resources to fight.

At the White House there was growing concern that abortion might be George Bush's "tar baby"; not knowing the degree to which public attitudes were moderating on this issue, he had locked himself into an extremist position. And the great fear was that he might suffer personally from this position and, beyond that, take the GOP down with him.

There were signs of strain even within the First Family. In early 1990 Barbara Bush was forced to deny publicly that there was a rift between her and the President on abortion after a *Newsweek* item reported a family debate on the issue. According to the newsmagazine, at a Bush family gathering "Some of the women, including Barbara Bush, said that abortion should not be without controls, but all said they believed in a woman's right to choose in certain circumstances." The report said that all the Bush men took opposing right-to-life positions.

Many who knew Barbara Bush speculated that it would be uncharacteristic for the First Lady to be as intransigent on an issue like abortion as her husband. But true to form, Barbara Bush refused to acknowledge that there was any validity to the *Newsweek* report. And she refused to state her views on the subject. "I've never told a living human being whether I'm pro-choice or pro-life," said Mrs. Bush. In public at least she was standing by her man.

In 1990 Bush clearly was finding himself between the proverbial rock and hard place, not only on abortion but on the whole spectrum of issues that led to his election support by the religious right. If pressed, the President paid lip service to "family life" issues, but he was far from the committed pro-life Christian Doug Wead's office had painted him during the 1988 campaign. In fact, one year after Bush's inauguration, some televangelists were publicly expressing feelings of betrayal. "He patronized the Christians to get their vote, he's in office, and now he's doing what a lot of politicians are doing—riding the fence," said one religious programmer in disgust. Evangelists who had expected a more outspoken Bush and who had counted on his filling the White House from their ranks were hard pressed to relate to their supposedly born-again brother. But televangelism expert David Harrell was not surprised. "Bush has never been any-where near the same place on his political spectrum as people in that field," Harrell said. "We knew there would be a disillusion-ment on the religious right real soon."

SEATTLE, WASHINGTON, April 1990

Politicians wrangled over the issue of abortion, and massaged it in rhetoric until it became as moldable as putty. They at-tempted to master the semantics and invented convoluted new linguistic gems of their own. Watching the debates, as if from a million miles away, Roberta felt lost in the process. She was not naive; she knew how politics worked. Still, it seemed as though they were forgetting about her. There was plenty of passion spent on "fetal rights" and plenty more on "moral decline," but when it came right down to it, the government kept forgetting about women.

Roberta had made her decision, and she was not swayed by the arguments that raged all around her, any more than she had been persuaded by the grotesque pictures Barbara Allen had used to try to influence her against abortion. She knew in her heart that none of the arguments so neatly set forth by either side could begin to articulate the nature of the issue as she knew it or as any woman who had to argue the pros and cons inside the forbidding courtroom of her own conscience knew it.

THIRTEEN

The Conscience of a

Court and a Nation

I'll grant you it's no smoking gun
But in some ways it's hotter:
Can we confirm a judge who's got
Sununu's imprimatur?

CALVIN TRILLIN

When George Bush nominated David Souter for the Supreme Court in July 1990, he insisted that John Sununu had not lobbied for his candidate, but that was unthinkable. Sununu's fingerprints could be found on every significant decision to face the White House, and this was surely in that category. Furthermore, Souter was a fellow New Hampshirite, and the two men knew each other well. It was an insult to common intelligence to suggest that there was not a strong Sununu connection, although it was understandable that Bush would try to deny it. Sununu's name instantly sent up the antiabortion red flag. And George Bush desperately wanted the abortion issue on the back burner, if not in the trash can. Were it not for the scent of Sununu in the air, Souter might have been the perfect candidate to do that. His views on abortion (and on virtually every other constitutional issue) were unknown.

Bush would have the public believe that Souter's résumé was

so compelling that it caught his eye of its own accord. Politics had nothing to do with it, he insisted. But of course, it did. It came out later that a high-level political meeting, during which conservative hard-liners were assured of Souter's credentials, preceded the announcement. Who was at that meeting? John Sununu and Dan Quayle, America's right-wing point men at the White House. Part of the meeting's agenda concerned how to deflect attention away from Sununu's involvement in the nomination. It was decided that the press would be told that Souter had been recommended by Senator Warren Rudman, a New Hampshire Republican who was considered a moderate on social issues.

After the nomination Sununu was less circumspect than the President in admitting his role. He spoke enthusiastically about Souter as the perfect candidate for the highest court, one whose ideology matched the current administration's. Reflecting on the search process, he acknowledged that he "was looking for someone who would be a strict constructionist, consistent with basic conservative attitudes, and that's what I got. I was able to tell the president that I was sure he would do the same thing when he encountered federal questions."

Bush must have congratulated himself on his selection of this so-called stealth candidate. Souter was about as blank a slate as one could find, lacking even the faintest igniting spark of personality or philosophy. His near-hermetic existence on a farm near Concord, New Hampshire, placed him above suspicion about the usual vices, and his bland career history kept him out of the line of fire on the political front. A small, dour man who wore rumpled suits and had a poker face etched with five o'clock shadow, the fifty-year-old nominee seemed beyond the reach of either praise or blame. When asked if he knew Souter's attitudes on *Roe* v. *Wade*, Bush piously claimed that he had no idea, that it would have been inappropriate to ask the nominee about potential decisions that might come before the Court. It was a considerable stretch of credibility to think that Bush really had no idea how Souter might vote on a matter of such fundamental importance to the nation. If it were true, Bush at the very least

could be accused of public irresponsibility for not seeking to
access his candidate's point of view and principles. Besides,
Bush's statement assumed that the nation had forgotten the President's oft-proclaimed commitment to overturn *Roe* v. *Wade.*

In presenting his candidate, the President had certainly covered his tracks. In the weeks following the announcement, the
press scurried in vain for even the hint of a Souter viewpoint on
abortion.

Bush was playing a political game at which he was remarkably
adept. His own career had taught him that it was much easier to
maneuver the shifting waters of American public opinion when
one left no paper trail and no history of passionate advocacy.

But at the heart of the matter was the question of whether a
man so far removed from the mainstream of life as we know it in
this nation could be trusted to grasp fully and empathize with the
experiences and plights of those who came before the Court.
Souter lived the life of a small-town bachelor recluse, surrounded
by books, scorning television. While serving as attorney general
of New Hampshire, he once declared, to the astonishment of
many, that he read newspapers only when they were writing
about him. "I look at the front page of the local paper when it
comes up here," he said, "and if somebody is saying, 'Attorney
General excoriated,' I read it. If not, I generally don't go beyond
that." If some were gazing askance at Souter's extreme removal
from the vibrant center of American life, it left his administration mentor, John Sununu, positively beaming. "The man loves
the law to the point of keeping himself completely out of the
public eye," Sununu bragged. "He loves being a judge, reading
and doing private things, not showing off by writing and talking
about being a judge."

This might have been a reference to the verbosity that characterized Robert Bork and had landed him in such a hornets'
nest. But it was also in support of President Bush's repeated
assertion that Souter's apolitical nature would assure that he
would not "legislate" from the bench. Kathleen M. Sullivan, a
professor of law at Harvard University and a frequent commentator on constitutional issues, would remind the President that

although once they reached the bench, Supreme Court justices were immune from the dictates of politics, they didn't arrive there without a constitutionally directed political process. "Supreme Court justices are expected to transcend politics, but only after they have run a political gamut to reach the bench," Sullivan pointed out. "The Framers committed Supreme Court appointments to the political branches—to nomination by the President and advice and consent by the Senate. . . . If the Framers had meant the process to be apolitical, they could have assigned Supreme Court appointments elsewhere—for example, to selection by the courts themselves."

Even in a government of the people, by the people, and for the people—a broad and inclusive democracy—individuals dominate, and there was concern in many quarters that Souter did not have the stature to fill the substantial shoes of retiring Justice William Brennan. "This is a man who has never been married, never had children," said one dubious legal observer. "This is a man who has spent only a minimum of time in the public sector, who lives in a village of 2,000 people, almost all of whom are white, far from the crises of crime and drugs, in a state that is notorious for its social and political quirkiness. Is he really equipped to deal with the great national questions?"

Should a potential justice be asked to state his opinion on matters that might come before him in the court? Perhaps—but what about commentary on cases already decided, such as *Roe* v. *Wade*? Common sense would dictate that an endless string of hypothetical questions begs the issue, but a candidate for one of the most powerful positions in the land should certainly be able to articulate some basic premises related to constitutional issues—especially if his background was as deplete of writings and public statements as Souter's. Robert Bork, who had been subjected to a harrowing grilling by a Senate committee, was a legal scholar of wide renown. His writings were extensive. Why should Souter sail smoothly by because his opinion file was so slim? But Souter was determined to keep an anonymous face on his future. When asked by reporters shortly after his nomination if he could be persuaded to talk about abortion, Souter replied,

"In a word, no." But some senators saw it another way. While Souter might be perfectly within his rights to refuse speculation on future cases, there was nothing stopping him from commenting on a case that was seventeen years old—specifically, *Roe* v. *Wade*. Complained Harvard law professor Alan Dershowitz: "We're being asked to buy a pig in a poke. He has no public record on important issues that are going to come before the Supreme Court."

If David Souter was innocuous, retiring justice William Brennan was larger than life, a legal genius and an outspoken advocate for those who had traditionally been left high and dry by the political process: women, children, blacks, the handicapped— the voiceless ones too often ignored by our society. While Souter's ties with the twentieth century were at best tenuous, Brennan was immersed in the soup of his times. The goal of a Supreme Court justice, he once said, was to read the Constitution "the only way we can: as twentieth century Americans. The genius of the Constitution rests not in any static meaning it might have had in a world that is dead and gone, but in the adaptability of its great principles to cope with current problems."

When the eighty-four-year-old Brennan submitted his resignation to George Bush, he had served on the Supreme Court for thirty-four years and was the last remaining member of the Warren Court, often referred to as an activist, liberal period in the Court's history. In that respect Brennan's resignation was the end of an era.

Brennan, the product of Irish Catholic immigrants who settled in Newark, New Jersey, at the turn of the century, was appointed to the Supreme Court by President Dwight Eisenhower in 1956 and became known during his tenure for his colorful language, his sharp mind, and his defiantly firm view that the Supreme Court had a grave responsibility to sit at the center of American life, rather than view it from the distant peak of the bench.

Brennan's legacy was long, but the opinions that most stood

out were those that dealt with the protection of individual freedoms and the right to privacy of each citizen. He viewed the Constitution as the vehicle that guaranteed "the protection of the dignity of the human being and the recognition that every individual has fundamental rights which government cannot deny him."

On reproductive rights, he was clear. "If the right to privacy means anything," he wrote, "it is the right of the individual, married or single, to be free from unwanted governmental intrusions into matters so fundamentally affecting a person as to whether to bear or beget a child."

Angered by Bush's tactics and suspicions of their archenemy John Sununu's behind-the-scenes role in the selection, feminist groups went to work digging into Souter's background in search of opinions that would provide clues to his attitudes toward women and reproductive rights. The first thing they unearthed was a rape case that, they believed, was indicative of a disturbing antiwoman attitude on the part of the bachelor judge. In 1988, while associate justice of the New Hampshire Supreme Court, Souter wrote an opinion overturning a rape conviction based on the fact that the judge had ignored testimony about the victim's own behavior prior to the rape. Souter wrote: ". . . evidence of public displays of general interest in sexual activity can be taken to indicate a contemporaneous receptiveness to sexual advances. . . . The sexual activities of a complainant immediately prior to an alleged rape may well be subject to the defendant's constitutional right to present evidence." In other words, *she led him on*. From the standpoint of women's groups that had fought hard to rid the courts of their blame-the-victim attitudes, this opinion provided a first and telling glimpse of the bias within Souter's mind.

Then, finally, the reference to abortion was located—the potential "smoking gun" in the confirmation process. In 1976, when Souter was New Hampshire's attorney general, his office submitted a brief to the federal appeals court arguing that the state should not provide Medicaid funds to pay for abortions. The brief referred to abortion as the "killing of the unborn"—very clearly the language of the antiabortion movement. Although Souter refused to comment on the brief, Richard V. Weibusch, then assistant attorney general and the man whose signature appeared on the brief, said that the language was his own and had never been run past Souter. But it was hard to imagine that this could have been the case. Public financing of abortions was a lightning-rod issue in 1976. It was difficult to comprehend how public officials could casually release statements using language that took so clear a stand. Furthermore, Meldrim Thomson, Jr., New Hampshire's governor at the time, was an outspoken opponent of abortion, and it would not be beyond reason to think that the views of his attorney general, David Souter, might have been consistent with those of his boss—especially since in New Hampshire the attorney general was appointed by the governor, not elected by the people.

In any case, the discovery of the brief was significant because it opened the door on the issue and gave the Senate a piece of Souter's background around which they could build questions about abortion.

Arguably the most important legacy a U.S. President can leave is the selection of a Supreme Court justice. And the abortion hang-ups of the Reagan and Bush power brokers were tearing down the essential character of the Court, which was established to deliver justice to all the people—not to impose public policy from a narrow viewpoint. Those within the evangelical community who predicted that Bush would further their goals through appointments to the Supreme Court were articulating the dangerous potential of the President to slant the judicial process for decades to come. In a country whose collective democracy gives power to the people, the Supreme Court can be manipulated politically if a President achieves the luck of the draw.

And what is the responsibility of the President who is asked to make such a critical and lasting decision? Is it to maintain a diversity in the Court? Or is it to push through candidates consistent with the administration's ideology? No doubt, the Bush administration believed the latter. Upon hearing of William Brennan's intention to resign, one top aide exulted, "It's great news for conservatives and a great political opportunity for the President." Later Coalitions for America, an umbrella organization for extremist right-wing groups, enthusiastically endorsed Souter, noting that his record "paints a consistent picture of a conservative jurist passionately devoted to the rule of law."

It was certainly Reagan's intention to leave a rebuilt conservative Supreme Court as his legacy, and he largely succeeded. For the most part, the liberal and moderate minority watched with understandable fear while the conservative majority set precedent and reversed long-held policy on critical social issues that have been the foundation of American justice in this century. Now it seemed the Court was being created for the sole purpose of diminishing individual rights—with abortion as the epicenter.

Bush might have figured he was playing it safe by nominating Souter, conservative without portfolio, but some of his Republican colleagues were unnerved by the prospect of an overwhelmingly right-wing Supreme Court. While the justices themselves were immune from a backlash at the polls, Republican officials were on the firing line for any conservative opinions that might come down from the Court. And they were especially afraid of abortion because they had witnessed in recent elections the wrath of the voters on this issue.

Ultimately the single-issue selection process that had plagued the White House throughout the Reagan years and now into Bush's administration was threatening to backfire. Even Americans who were not solidly pro-choice were beginning to tire of the antiabortion litmus test. Only a minority of the population held views on the issue that were as extreme as the White House's. And making abortion the only issue of significance in appointments— be they Cabinet or Court—ignored other issues of concern to the public welfare. Even antiabortionist "liberal" columnist Nat Hentoff agreed with that. "Were I on the Senate Judiciary Committee, I would vote against David Souter because he lacks the

passion to preserve and protect the individual against the state,"
he wrote in the *Village Voice*.

But the loudest voice of concern was still from the left, that
coalition of liberal organizations that had so powerfully and effectively joined hands to block the Bork nomination three years
earlier. The Alliance for Justice and the People for the American
Way Action Fund, groups that monitored judicial nominations,
issued reports on Souter's record and expressed their concerns
about Souter's suitability for the High Court. Nan Aron, sum-
marizing the Alliance for Justice's stance, minced no words.
"Our conclusion," she said, "is that Judge Souter's opinions and
legal briefs threaten to undo the advances made by women, minorities, dissenters and other disadvantaged groups."

These groups wanted Souter's assurance that he believed there
was a constitutional right to privacy—certainly a critical distinction in the abortion debate—and they wanted to know how much
he relied on the intent of the framers in interpreting the Constitution. Both groups disagreed with the notion that Souter should
not be asked hard questions on his attitudes toward important
decisions like *Roe* v. *Wade*, saying the judge had not revealed
enough of his fundamental sense of the judiciary to warrant an
uncontested confirmation.

It was certainly easier to fight a wolf than to identify and fight
a wolf in sheep's clothing, and liberals were struggling to find the
right way to get the assurances they needed about Bush's candidate. But if it was any comfort to the skeptics in the pro-choice
lobby, who thought the Court might be "lost" to their cause for
decades to come, history offered soothing evidence that judges,
once seated, could prove maddeningly independent—often to
the chagrin of the Presidents who appointed them. For example,
Warren Burger, who wrote the opinion that the Watergate tapes
must be released, was appointed by Nixon himself, and Eisenhower appointed Earl Warren and William Brennan, who became two of the most liberal judges to sit on the Court.
Eisenhower once grumbled that his appointments were "the two
worst decisions I ever made."

What alarmed moderates, liberals, and even some conservatives most about the Reagan-Bush Court was its activist leaning. Traditionally conservatives bent over backward to avoid changing existing laws or carving new legal territory. But this Court was eagerly rolling up the long sleeves of its black robes and going to work on every major decision that had been sent down during the past twenty years. Where once a "conservative" justice was one who was interested in conserving precedent, it now seemed to mean one who was intent upon pressing the conservative agenda forward.

The question on everyone's minds was whether a conservative fire—the kind of fire that would set flame to the rights of women and minorities—burned inside David Souter's heart. Would he interpret the Constitution broadly or narrowly? Was he a Bush-Sununu man, or was he his own man? Did he harbor preconceived opinions about abortion rights as granted in *Roe* v. *Wade*, or was he open-minded?

The Senate confirmation hearings to determine David Souter's suitability for the Supreme Court began early on September 13. Judiciary Committee Chairman Joseph Biden, senator from Delaware, smiled warmly across the room at Souter, who seemed small and frail at his little table. Biden was working hard to put everyone at ease, acting out the protocol of cordiality that always accompanied the first moments of such hearings.

Before the hearings had even begun, the press had been reporting that Souter's confirmation was a sure thing. Everyone knew that the liberals on the committee were poised to ask hard questions about abortion, but few believed that even the most skillful questioner would be able to crack Souter's shell.

The hearings were long and arduous, and Souter was not a riveting presence in the room. His answers to even the simplest questions were long and convoluted, and he spoke slowly and without emotion. Only occasionally, when a senator pressed for a more direct answer or challenged a point, did the veins in Souter's neck tighten. Otherwise he showed little feeling.

Biden labored in vain throughout the proceedings to persuade Souter to share his fundamental philosophy about women's right to choose abortion. Repeatedly, Souter declined to answer. Biden was plainly exasperated, but by the second day of the hearings even he was referring to Souter as the "soon-to-be-justice."

In the end all Souter would say was that "I have not got an agenda on what should be done with *Roe* v. *Wade*. . . . I would listen to both sides of that case. I have not made up my mind and I would not go on the Court saying I must go one way or I must go the other way."

George Bush, listening to the hearings, lavishly praised his candidate as "magnificent" and "masterful." And he had good reason to feel that way. Without giving a direct answer on the most volatile issue of the day, David Souter won nearly unanimous approval by the Senate committee. The only dissenter was Senator Edward Kennedy of Massachusetts. With the committee's recommendation, Souter went on to easily win approval by the full Senate.

Feminist groups, who had opposed the nomination, were frustrated. "For the first time in history," said Kate Michelman, "the Supreme Court is on the brink of taking away a fundamental right—the right to choose." How, she asked, could Souter be so easily confirmed without acknowledging that he recognized that right?

But even as they expressed their disappointment that yet another conservative had been added to the Court, pro-choice groups were already looking down the road with fear and trepidation. The body of their defenders on the Court was growing smaller, and the remaining liberal justices were aging. There was little doubt that there would be other appointments during Bush's term. And the prospect of a High Court designed by George Bush and John Sununu made them shudder.

BINGHAMTON, NEW YORK, Summer 1990

Randall Terry's vision was as clear and pure as the sharp point of a needle. He was not a man plagued by doubts or swayed by setbacks. Nevertheless, in the summer of 1990 Terry had to admit that Operation Rescue was struggling.

In May the Supreme Court had dealt a brutal blow to Operation Rescue when it let stand rulings in New York and Atlanta that forbade demonstrators to block access to abortion clinics. In a 5–4 decision the Court ruled that the militant tactics employed by Operation Rescue were not protected by the free speech provision and, in fact, were a violation of the civil rights of others.

Terry was livid when he heard of the decision. "No court can prohibit us from rescuing babies," he said. "These judges have joined the heritage of Nazi judges who sanctioned the murder of the innocent."

But in spite of his bold words, Terry had to be feeling that something was unraveling within his organization. In New York alone there was nearly half a million dollars in unpaid fines outstanding, and the organization's national debt was soaring into the millions. During the past year more than forty thousand people had been arrested in Operation Rescue actions, often filling local jails to overflowing as they declined to pay fines. Terry himself had spent four months in a Georgia prison when he refused to pay a five-hundred-dollar fine.

Now Terry had to admit grudgingly that Operation Rescue's troop count was declining. The solid middle-class Americans who composed its ranks had grown weary of repeated arrests. With the court so solidly in opposition, the fight was beginning to seem interminably long.

But if anything, the setbacks only renewed Terry's fervor. He vowed to map new strategy and fight on. "In thirty years, we're going to have forced abortion," Terry predicted. "I can already write the decision about how in a society with limited resources we can only accommodate the needs of the most by limiting each family to two babies. You say that's farfetched, but what would you have said thirty years ago if I'd told you we would be killing 1.5 million babies a year, and having Gay Pride Week and AIDS and no prayer in public schools? The feminists got what they wanted, but are women better off with pornography and no-fault divorce and irresponsible fathers who don't pay child support? I don't think so."

*   *   *

At the 1990 convention of the National Right to Life Committee, in Sacramento, California, the mood was one of forced optimism. Plagued by numerous setbacks in the courts and at the voting booths, the once-confident antiabortion organizers were facing an uphill battle toward their ultimate goal of seeing abortions banned nationwide.

The nine hundred delegates who gathered at the convention might have felt a moment of relief to be in this oasis—away from the conflicts of the outside world. Everyone present was of one mind and one heart. They were sobered by the predictions that this fight might go on for ten or twenty years before they were victorious. Many of those present might not see that victory in their own lifetimes. But the unborn were calling, and they were determined to fight on.

WASHINGTON, D.C., August 1990

Someone in the White House had it in for Doug Wead—or that was the way it seemed. He brooded about this as he packed the contents of his office into boxes. Wead knew that having the ear of the President made him a natural target for those who would dispute his agenda. There were plenty of people who resented Wead's influence, but until now they had mostly been kept at bay by Wead's tight relationship with John Sununu and the President's son. But someone had got to Sununu, and suddenly Wead was out. Sununu's deputy chief of staff, Andrew Card, had delivered the news. "They" wanted Wead to leave "sooner rather than later." That was the way he put it. Sununu didn't even have the guts to do the deed himself.

Nobody said directly what had precipitated the firing. The White House was like that. It could be "off with your head," and nobody would even stop to say why. When Wead reached the President at his vacation home in Kennebunkport, Bush would only say vaguely that he held "no personal animosity" toward Wead and wished him well.

Wead suspected that many of Bush's staff were simply uncomfortable at having the White House linked so closely with the evangelical community. It was a constituency that had elected their man, but now they were flinching at the relationship. Maybe they thought Bush was so powerful that he didn't need the Christians anymore, that they embarrassed him. During the past year Wead had watched the President moving away from his commitments on issues like abortion. He was using words like "compromise" and "flexibility," and when he nominated David Souter for the Supreme Court, he seemed to bend over backward to distance himself from the abortion debate. This was the man who had promised evangelicals during the campaign that he would be their most vocal advocate in getting *Roe* v. *Wade* overturned. It was, Wead now believed, a typical case of George Bush's brand of lip service. Promise them anything; then reverse yourself as soon as you feel a little heat.

Wead believed that insiders at the White House had been plotting ways to get rid of him for a long time and had finally found their opportunity. In the spring Bush had signed a "hate crimes" law, and some White House staff had decided to invite members of the homosexual community to the signing ceremony. Of course, Wead heard about it from the evangelicals. They weren't happy to see the President acknowledging gays as though they represented a legitimate constituency. It was Wead's job to soothe ruffled feathers, so he sent out a letter, assuring evangelicals that the presence of gays at the White House was an error on the part of Bush's staff. "Quite frankly, the President's staff did not serve him well" by inviting them, Wead wrote, adding, "In no way does the President endorse the lifestyle of all groups which attend such briefings. I can assure you that he is especially offended by the attacks against Cardinal O'Connor and the other manifestations of religious intolerance that some of the homosexual groups invited into the White House have espoused."

Most likely, some of Wead's enemies had intercepted the letter and taken it to Sununu, along with a laundry list of other complaints against Wead.

Wead was angry, but he knew that in the long run if the White House continued to turn its back on the religious right, Bush would suffer. The evangelicals and their millions of followers would remember at the next election how they had been used. Meanwhile, Doug Wead would leave quietly. He wasn't about to burn any bridges. He assumed that it wouldn't be long before they would be asking for his help again.

Doug Wead was only one man in the back rooms. Others who shared his vision remained in place and grew stronger every day. Doug's brother Bill had been promoted from Louis Sullivan's speech writer to White House liaison to the Department of Health and Human Services, giving him far greater influence to direct the agency's policies on abortion, contraceptive issues, and fetal tissue research. And John Sununu stood at the apex of all that occurred at the White House.

There would always be those in the back rooms and on the front lines of power who would carry the torch in the battle against women's rights. Doug Wead had been only one cog in a massive rolling wheel that continued to roll faster and faster into the heartland of America, gaining momentum as it went. It threatened to crush millions of women before it stopped.

EPILOGUE

Whose Life?

SEATTLE, WASHINGTON, June 1990

Roberta wasn't due at the hospital until 6:30 A.M., but she was up at 4:00, unable to sleep. She was edgy and unfocused. Her head felt as if it were wrapped in gauze; her body felt swollen—*was* swollen with the early signs of her pregnancy. Motherhood. How amazing that a brief act, a moment of pleasure and intimacy, could produce such a monumental result. Had her mother been alive, she would have admonished Roberta that she had no business being sexual if she was not ready to accept the consequences. But Roberta discarded that notion. The night that had produced this life within her was far removed from her idea of the circumstances under which she would embrace motherhood. Her mother was her model for that, for Roberta had often been told of how joyfully she had welcomed the news of her pregnancy. Perhaps there would come a time when Roberta might experience the fullness of that emotion. But this was not the time.

She felt lonely without her mother, and frightened. She wanted to cry for the mother she had lost and for the new life that was not to be. The weight of her isolation felt enormous.

* * *

At 6:30 A.M., when Roberta arrived at the hospital, the early-morning hum had begun. She was admitted immediately, blood tests and insurance forms having been completed the day before. The admissions clerk didn't even look at her twice, and Roberta felt relieved by that, and surprised. Everyone was very professional—not casual, really, but blank. She was a patient here, protected from derision by the cool objectivity of the medical environment. She began to relax. It would be over soon.

She was taken to a room that held three beds, handed a white hospital gown, and left alone. Outside her door she could hear the heavy groan of the hospital waking to a new day.

She had been lying in the bed for twenty minutes when Dr. Friedman walked in. She smiled cheerfully at Roberta. "They'll be taking you down in a few minutes," she said. "You okay?"

Roberta smiled weakly. "Nervous."

"That's normal." Dr. Friedman touched her forehead. "You'll be fine. By noon you'll be ready to go home. Do you have someone coming to pick you up?"

Roberta nodded. She had arranged for her best friend, Pat, to take her home.

Dr. Friedman left, and Roberta was alone again. She could hear the loud clatter of breakfast carts being rolled down the hallways. The smell of food nauseated her. *In a few hours, I won't be pregnant anymore*, she thought. *My life will return to the way it was before.*

Lights blazed in the operating room. Roberta was transferred from the gurney onto a long table. Behind her the anesthesiologist whistled as he busied himself with a tangle of equipment. Roberta shivered. "I'm cold," she moaned. The room felt like an icehouse.

"We're going to start an IV in your arm," a nurse said pleasantly. "This will prick a little bit." Roberta held out her arm and bit her lip as the needle traveled under the skin of her right hand. "There." The nurse smiled. "All set."

Dr. Friedman entered, holding her hands in the air. She teased one of the nurses, and there was laughing. "How are you doing, Roberta?" she asked.

"Cold," Roberta murmured. It was all she could think of— how cold the room was.

The doctor laughed again and said something to one of the nurses. There was more general laughter. Roberta couldn't see how many people were in the room. The anesthesiologist stroked her forehead.

"Let's go," said Dr. Friedman, and the room turned black.

They were shouting at her, "Roberta! Roberta!" and she was rising out of a tomb of mist. "Roberta!" She opened her eyes. A woman's round, smiling face was looking down at her. "Hey, sleepyhead," she said. "You're awake. We're going to take you to your room now."

Roberta was only half aware of being moved onto the gurney; she fell in and out of consciousness during the long roll down the hallway, up in the elevator, down another hallway. All around her voices were speaking, faces staring down at her. No one spoke directly to her. She was desperately trying to get her bearings and to focus on what had occurred—the fact that she wasn't pregnant anymore. She was conscious of heavy padding between her legs. But her mind wasn't working; she fell asleep again.

Only hours later she would be home in her own bed. In a day or two she would be back at work. Life would go on as before— with one difference: She would always and forever be the person who had made this choice.

And outside Roberta's quiet hospital room, the war rages on, populated by figures she will never know: the robed monks of the Court; the tense bureaucrats roaming the corridors of the Capitol; the pain-racked, hungry voices from the third world; the white-jacketed scientists bent over their microscopes; the priests lifting their arms on the perfumed altars of the nation's churches; the men and women who work the back rooms and fill the front lines of the movement.

The rhetoric of outrage rises from the steamy earth in a cacophony of voices. From a distance the voices become indistinguishable, forming a single message, the only message possible: "We stand for life!"

Ah, yes. But choose.

Whose life?

Appendix A

Supreme Court Abortion

Scorecard

Roe v. Wade and Beyond

January 22, 1973   In a 7–2 decision, the Court, ruling on *Roe* v. *Wade*, legalized abortion nationwide, on the basis of the precept of a woman's right to privacy. On the same day the court struck down *Roe* v. *Bolton*, refusing to consider restrictions against facilities performing abortions.

July 1, 1976   The Court ruled in *Planned Parenthood* v. *Danforth* that husbands had no veto power over their wives' freedom to choose abortion. Nor could parents be given an absolute veto over their minor daughters' right to abortion.

June 20, 1977   In *Maher* v. *Roe* the Court ruled that states have no constitutional obligation to pay for "nontherapeutic" abortions.

January 9, 1979   The justices gave doctors broad authority, in *Colautti* v. *Franklin*, to determine when a fetus was viable outside the womb and ruled that on the basis of doctors' recommendations, states could act to protect fetal life at viability.

July 2, 1979   In a further clarification of the parental consent decision of 1976, the Court ruled that states may be able to insist on parental consent for unmarried minors seeking abortions but must provide as well an alternate source of approval, such as a hearing before a judge.

June 30, 1980   In a 5–4 vote the Court ruled in *Harris* v. *McRae* that federal and state governments could not be required to pay for abortions for women on welfare, even when they were deemed medically necessary.

March 23, 1981   In *H. L.* v. *Matheson* the Court ruled that the states may require doctors of minors they judged to be too immature to choose abortions on their own to try to inform parents before performing the abortion.

June 15, 1983   In three cases—the *City of Akron* v. *Akron Center for Reproductive Health, Planned Parenthood of Kansas City* v. *Ashcroft,* and *Simopolous* v. *Virginia*— the Court ruled that states and local communities may not require abortions after the first trimester to be performed in hospitals and struck down twenty-four-hour waiting periods.

June 11, 1986   In a Pennsylvania case, *Thornburgh* v. *American College of Obstetricians and Gynecologists,* the Court overturned a law requiring doctors to inform women about potential risks and about pregnancy and child care options.

December 14, 1987   In *Hartigan* v. *Zbaraz* the Court invalidated an Illinois law that might have restricted access to abortions for some teenagers.

July 3, 1989   In *Webster* v. *Reproductive Health Services* the Court handed new authority to the states to limit women's right to abortion.

June 25, 1990   In two cases, *Hodgson* v. *Minnesota;* and *Ohio* v. *Akron Center for Reproductive Health,* parental notification regulations were strengthened. In the Minnesota case the Court ruled that a state could require a minor to inform both parents before having an abortion so long as she had the alternative of a judicial hearing. In the Ohio case the Court upheld a law requiring notification of one parent as long as the alternative of a judicial hearing existed.

Appendix B

Abortion Regulations on

the Books

Many states still have old laws on the books restricting abortion, and others have passed new laws. While these are generally unenforceable under *Roe* v. *Wade*, they indicate the direction individual states would move if the Court struck down *Roe* or allowed greater independence on the state level.

Alabama   The parents of minors must consent to an abortion.

Alaska   None.

Arizona   Pre-*Roe* statute makes performing an abortion a crime. Not enforceable.

Arkansas   A 1989 referendum making fetal protection a state policy.

California   None.

Colorado   No public funding for abortion.

Connecticut   Old laws protecting fetal life are still on the books, but no current restrictions apply.

Delaware	None.
Florida	Parental consent law.
Georgia	None.
Hawaii	None.
Idaho	Pre-*Roe* law mandates a prison term for women obtaining abortions.
Illinois	None, but leans against choice.
Indiana	None, but leans against choice.
Iowa	None.
Kansas	None.
Kentucky	State law provides for a ban on abortion if *Roe* is overturned.
Louisiana	None, but leans against choice.
Maine	Bans use of state Medicaid funds for abortion.
Maryland	None, but leans pro-choice and funds abortions for the poor.
Massachusetts	None.
Michigan	None.
Minnesota	Parental consent laws approved by the Supreme Court.
Mississippi	Pre-*Roe* law forbids nearly all abortions.
Missouri	Abortion limitations approved by the Supreme Court.

Montana	None.
Nebraska	None, but leans against choice.
Nevada	None, but leans against choice.
New Hampshire	None.
New Jersey	None.
New Mexico	None, but leans pro-choice.
New York	None, but leans pro-choice.
North Carolina	State funding reduced.
North Dakota	None.
Ohio	Parental notification laws.
Oklahoma	None.
Oregon	Increased state funding for abortions.
Pennsylvania	Abortion restrictions overturned by lower courts; currently in appeal.
Rhode Island	Restrictions on abortions on the books.
South Carolina	Reviewing legislation to ban abortions except when the mother's life is threatened.
South Dakota	Law of 1877 bans abortions.
Tennessee	Parental notification laws.
Texas	None, but leans against choice.
Utah	None, but leans against choice.

Vermont	None, but leans pro-choice.
Virginia	None.
Washington	None, but leans pro-choice.
West Virginia	Parental notification and limitations on use of public facilities.
Wisconsin	Antiabortion laws still on the books.
Wyoming	Parental notification laws.

Selected Bibliography

Andrusko, David, ed. *The Triumph of Hope: A Pro-Life Review of 1988 and a Look to the Future.* Washington, D.C.: The National Right to Life Committee, 1989.

——. *Window on the Future: The Pro-Life Year in Review.* Washington, D.C.: The National Right to Life Committee, 1986.

Augustine, Saint. *Confessions.* New York: Dorset Press, 1961.

Bader, Eleanor J. "Stranger in a Strange Land: Attending a Right to Life Conference." *On the Issues,* 1989.

Baehr, Ninia. *Abortion Without Apology: A Radical History for the 1990s.* Boston: South End Press, 1990.

Barnes, Deborah M. "Abortion Policy Curtails Biomedical Research." *Journal of NIH Research,* January-February 1990.

Barr, Samuel J., M.D. *A Woman's Choice.* New York: Rawson Associates Publishers, 1977.

Bay Area Coalition Against Operation Rescue. *Stop Operation Rescue Right Wing Attacks on Women's Clinics.* San Francisco: Bay Area Coalition Against Operation Rescue, 1989. Pamphlet.

Bayles, Martha. "Feminism and Abortion." *The Atlantic Monthly*, April 1990.

Bennett, Leslie. "God's Man in New York." *Vanity Fair*, August 1990.

Benshoof, Janet, Kathryn Kolbert, Lynn Patrow, and Rachael Pine. *Reproductive Rights Update*. New York: ACLU Reproductive Freedom Project, 1989.

Bergell, Gary. *When You Were Formed in Secret*. Washington, D.C.: The National Right to Life Committee, 1980, 1988. Pamphlet.

Bernstein, Stacey. "Tibet: The Darkness Behind the Veil—Forced Sterilization and Abortion in Tibet." *NOW-NYS Action Report*, May-June 1989.

Bourke, Vernon J., ed. *The Pocket Aquinas*. New York: Washington Square Press, 1960.

Bronner, Ethan. *Battle for Justice: How the Bork Nomination Shook America*. New York: W. W. Norton and Company, 1989.

Bush, George. "Remarks of V.P. George Bush at the Republican National Convention." New Orleans: August 18, 1988.

————, with Doug Wead. *Man of Integrity*. Eugene, Ore.: Harvest House Publishers, 1988.

Center for Constitutional Rights. *Docket: 1989–1990*. New York: Center for Constitutional Rights, 1989.

Cohen, Marcia. *The Sisterhood*. New York: Fawcett Columbine, 1988.

Condit, Celeste Michelle. *Decoding Abortion Rhetoric: Communicating Social Change*. Urbana/Chicago: University of Illinois Press, 1990.

Copelon, Rhonda, and Kathryn Kolbert. "Imperfect Justice." *Ms.*, July-August 1989.

Cramer, Jerome, Dan Goodgame, and Andrea Sachs. "A Blank Slate." *Time*, August 6, 1990.

Dellinger, Walter. "Considering Judge Souter and the Constitution." *Washington Post National Weekly Edition*, September 17–23, 1990.

———. "Should We Compromise on Abortion?" *The American Prospect*, Summer 1990.

Diamond, Sara., *Spiritual Warfare: The Politics of the Christian Right.* Boston: South End Press, 1989.

Dworkin, Ronald. "The Future of Abortion." *New York Review of Books*, September 28, 1989.

Dwyer, John C. *Foundations of Christian Ethics.* New York: Paulist Press, 1987.

Eagan, Andrea Boroff. "Who Decides for Women?" *American Health*, September 1990.

Ehrenreich, Barbara. "Saving My Zygotes." *Mother Jones*, December 1989.

———, and Deirdre English. *For Her Own Good.* New York: Anchor Press/Doubleday, 1978.

Eisley, Loren. *The Immense Journey.* New York: Random House, 1957.

Erens, Pamela. "Anti-Abortion, Pro-Feminism?" *Mother Jones*, May 1989.

Erlich, Dr. Paul. *The Population Bomb.* New York: Sierra Club/Ballantine Books, 1968.

Faluda, Susan. "Where Did Randy Go Wrong?" *Mother Jones*, November 1989.

Faux, Marian. *Roe v. Wade.* New York: New American Library, 1988.

Ferraro, Barbara, and Patricia Hussey, with Jane O'Reilly. *No Turning Back: Two Nuns Battle with the Vatican over Women's Right to Choose.* New York: Poseidon Press, 1990.

Frankfort, Ellen. *Vaginal Politics.* New York: Bantam, 1983.

Freeman, Jo, ed. *Women: A Feminist Perspective.* Mountain View, Calif.: Mayfield Publishing Co., 1989.

Fried, Marlene Gerber. *From Abortion to Reproductive Freedom: Transforming a Movement.* Boston: South End Press, 1990.

Gardner, Charles A. "Is an Embryo a Person?" *The Nation*, November 13, 1989.

Goldstein, Leslie Friedman. *The Constitutional Rights of Women.* Madison: The University of Wisconsin Press, 1979, 1988.

Goldstein, Robert D. *Mother-Love and Abortion: A Legal Interpretation.* Berkeley/Los Angeles: University of California Press, 1988.

Goodgame, Dan, and Andrea Sachs. "Right Turn Ahead." *Time*, August 6, 1990.

Goodman, Ellen. "The Body Politic." *Savvy Woman*, October 1989.

Gordon, Linda. *Woman's Body, Woman's Right.* New York: Penguin Books, 1977.

Gordon, Mary. "A Moral Choice." *The Atlantic Monthly*, April 1990.

Greeley, Andrew M. *The Catholic Myth: The Behavior and Beliefs of American Catholics.* New York: Charles Scribner's Sons, 1990.

————, and Mary Greeley Durkin. *How to Save the Catholic Church.* New York: Viking, 1984.

Greer, Germaine. *Sex and Destiny: The Politics of Human Fertility.* New York: Harper & Row, 1984.

Hall, Elizabeth. "When Does Life Begin?: A Conversation With Clifford Grobstein." *Psychology Today*, September 1989.

Hancock, Lynnell. "Censoring Abortion." *The Village Voice*, January 9, 1990.

Harrison, Beverly Wildung. *Our Right to Choose: Toward a New Ethic of Abortion*. Boston: Beacon Press, 1983.

Harvey, Brett. "The Morning After." *Mother Jones*, May 1989.

Hellman, Peter. "No Way Out." *Savvy Woman*, November 1989.

Hollyday, Joyce. "Abortion and the Law: How Do We Choose Life?" *Sojourner*, November 1989.

Holmes, Stephen, Naushad S. Mehta, and Elizabeth Taylor. "Whose Life Is It?" *Time*, May 1, 1989.

Holtzman, Elizabeth. "Testimony by Elizabeth Holtzman, Comptroller of the City of New York Before the Senate Judiciary Committee on the Nomination of David Souter to the United States Supreme Court, September 18, 1990."

Illick, Hilary Selden. "Pro Choice Movement." Z Magazine, January 1990.

Kaminer, Wendy. *A Fearful Freedom: Women's Flight from Equality*. Reading, Mass.: Addison-Wesley, 1990.

Kaplan, David A., and Bob Cohn. "Presumed Competent." *Newsweek*, September 17, 1990.

Kasindorf, Jeannie. "Abortion in New York." *New York* magazine, September 18, 1990.

Kennedy, David M. *Birth Control in America: The Career of Margaret Sanger*. New Haven: Yale University Press, 1970.

Klein, Hanny Lightfoot. *Prisoners of Ritual: An Odyssey into Female Genital Circumcision in Africa*. Binghamton, N.Y.: The Haworth Press, 1990.

Lacayo, Richard. "Abortion's Hardest Cases." *Time*, July 9, 1990.

———. "Pro-Choice? Get Lost." *Time*, December 4, 1989.

Lader, Lawrence. *Abortion*. Indianapolis: Bobbs-Merrill, 1966.

———. *Abortion II: Making the Revolution*. Boston: Beacon Press, 1973.

———. "Margaret Sanger: Militant, Pragmatist, Visionary." *On the Issues*, 1990.

———. *Politics, Power and the Church: The Catholic Crisis and Its Challenge to American Pluralism*. New York: Macmillan Publishing Company, 1987.

Lauersen, Niels, M.D., and Steven Whitney. *It's Your Body*. New York: Grosset and Dunlap, 1977.

Lazarre, Jane. *The Mother Knot*. New York: Dell Publishing Company, 1976.

Lippis, John. *The Challenge to Be Pro-Life*. Santa Barbara, Calif.: Pro-Life Education, Inc., 1978, 1982. Pamphlet.

McDonnell, Kathleen. *Not an Easy Choice: A Feminist Re-Examines Abortion*. Boston: South End Press, 1984.

McElvaine, Robert S. *Mario Cuomo*. New York: Charles Scribner's Sons, 1988.

McInerny, Ralph. *A First Glance at St. Thomas Aquinas*. Notre Dame, Ind.: University of Notre Dame, 1990.

Maguire, Daniel C. "A Catholic Theologian at an Abortion Clinic." *Ms.*, December 1984.

Marshall, Thomas R. *Public Opinion and the Supreme Court*. Boston: Unwin Hyman, Inc., 1989.

Maury, Marian. *Birth Rate and Birth Right*. New York: MacFadden, 1963.

Messer, Ellen, and Kathryn E. May, Psy.D. *Back Rooms: Voices from the Illegal Abortion Era.* New York: St. Martin's Press, 1988.

Mills, Sarah. "Abortion Under Siege." *Ms.*, July-August, 1989.

Morgan, Robin. *Going Too Far*. New York: Random House, 1968.

Nathanson, Sue. *Soul Crisis: One Woman's Journey Through Abortion to Renewal*. New York: New American Library, 1989.

The National Right to Life Committee. "U.S. House of Representatives Roll Call Votes on Abortion, 1983–1988." Washington, D.C., 1989.

———. "U.S. Senate Votes on Abortion, 1983–1988." Washington, D.C., 1989.

New York Pro-Choice Coalition. *The Battle to Defend Abortion Clinics: Organizing Against Operation Rescue*. New York: Pro-Choice Coalition, 1988. Pamphlet.

Nicholas, Susan Cary, Alice M. Price, and Rachel Rucbin. *Rights and Wrongs: Women's Struggle for Legal Equality*. New York: The Feminist Press, 1986.

O'Connor, John Cardinal, and Mayor Edward I. Koch. *His Eminence and Hizzoner: A Candid Exchange*. New York: William Morrow and Company, 1988.

Ranke-Heinemann, Uta. *Eunuchs for the Kingdom of Heaven—Women, Sexuality, and the Catholic Church*. New York: Doubleday, 1990.

Raymond, Janice. "The Chilling of Reproductive Choice." *On the Issues*, 1990.

Reagan, Ronald. *Abortion and the Conscience of a Nation.* Nashville: Thomas Nelson Publishers, 1984.

Reese, Michael, Daniel Glick, and Patricia King. "Pro-Choice Politicking." *Newsweek*, October 9, 1989.

Rothman, Barbara Katz. *Recreating Motherhood.* New York: W. W. Norton and Company, 1989.

Sagan, Carl, and Ann Druyan. "Is It Possible to Be Pro-Life and Pro-Choice?" *Parade*, April 22, 1990.

Salholz, Eloise et al. "The Battle over Abortion." *Time*, May 1, 1989.

———. "The Future of Abortion." *Newsweek*, July 17, 1989.

Schur, Edwin M. *Crimes Without Victims: Deviant Behavior and Public Policy.* Englewood Cliffs, N.J.: Prentice-Hall, 1965.

Scott, Anne Firor, and Andrew MacKay Scott. *One Half the People: The Fight for Woman Suffrage.* Urbana, Ill.: University of Illinois Press, 1975.

Selcraig, Bruce. "Reverend Wildmon's War on the Arts." *New York Times Magazine*, September 2, 1990.

Seligman, Jean, with Mary Hager, and Deborah Witherspoon. "Abortion in the Form of a Pill." *Newsweek*, April 17, 1989.

Shaw, David. "Abortion Bias Seeps into the News." *Los Angeles Times*, July 1990.

Simpson, Peggy. "Constitutional Crisis." *Ms.*, September 1989.

Sommer, Joseph, S. J., Ph. D. *Catholic Thought on Contraception Through the Centuries.* Liguori, Mo.: Liguorian Pamphlets and Books, 1970.

Sorrentino, Mary Ann, as told to Maureen Orth. "My Church Threw Me Out." *Redbook*, June 1986.

Steinem, Gloria. "A Basic Human Right." *Ms.*, July-August 1989.

Stokes, Geoffrey. "Go to Hell: John Cardinal O'Connor, Prince of a Crumbling Church, Takes On the 'Cuomo Catholics' over Abortion." *The Village Voice*, September 11, 1990.

Tauris, Carol, Ph.D. "The Politics of Pregnancy." *Vogue*, September 1989.

Tax, Meredith. "March to a Crossroads on Abortion." *The Nation*, May 8, 1989.

Tickle, Phyllis, ed. *Confessing Conscience: Churched Women on Abortion.* Nashville: Abingdon Press, 1990.

Totenberg, Nina. "Decoding the Court." *The Washington Post*, October 1989.

Traynor, Carol. "Teens, the Real Victims of Parental Court Consent Laws." *NOW-NYS Action Report*, Spring 1990.

Tribe, Laurence. *Abortion: The Clash of Absolutes.* New York: W. W. Norton and Company, 1990.

Verny, Thomas, M.D., with John Kelly. *The Secret Life of the Unborn Child.* New York: Dell Publishing Company, 1981.

Wilke, Dr. and Mrs. J. C. *Abortion: Questions and Answers.* Cincinnati: Hayes Publishing Company, 1985.

Wolfe, Alan. *Whose Keeper?: Social Sciences and Moral Obligation.* Berkeley, Calif.: University of California Press, 1990.

Yorkey, Mike. "Is George Bush the Answer?" *Focus on the Family-Citizen*, August 1988.

Index